DATE DUE

~~MAY 10 2002~~	
~~MAY 24 2013~~	
~~DEC 20 2003~~	

THE POWER OF GOD

Readings on Omnipotence and Evil

Edited by

LINWOOD URBAN

DOUGLAS N. WALTON

New York
OXFORD UNIVERSITY PRESS
1978

Copyright © 1978 by Oxford University Press, Inc.

Library of Congress Cataloging in Publication Data

Main entry under title:

The Power of God.

    Bibliography: p.
    Includes index.
    1. God—Omnipotence—Addresses, essays, lectures.
2. Theodicy—Addresses, essays, lectures.
3. Providence and government of God—Addresses, essays,
lectures.   4. Good and evil—Addresses, essays,
lectures.   I. Urban, Linwood.   II. Walton, Douglas.
BT133.P68   231'.4   78-6069
ISBN 0-19-502201-7
ISBN 0-19-502202-5 pbk.

Printed in the United States of America

In Memoriam

FRANK McGLYNN
and
LOUIS WERNER

*The souls of the righteous are in the hand
of God, and there shall no torment touch
them. In the sight of the unwise they
seemed to die: and their departure is
taken for misery, and their going from us
to be utter destruction: but they are in
peace.*

Wisdom of Solomon 3:1–3

Acknowledgments

We would like to thank Thomas N. Mitchell, Associate Professor of Classics at Swarthmore College, for his patient help with difficult passages in the Latin, and Professor M. J. Cresswell of Victoria University of Wellington, New Zealand, for discussions on the logical form of action sentences which have been influential in forming our views on the language of action and power. We would also like to express our gratitude to the Council for Philosophical Studies whose Conference in the Philosophy of Religion in the summer of 1973 sowed the seeds of our collaborative work. We would like to thank all the participants of that conference, and especially those scholars whose lectures contributed so much to our study of the concept of omnipotence in philosophical theology: Alvin Plantinga, Roderick Chisholm, Peter Geach, Anthony Kenny, George Mavrodes, Terence Penelhum, and Nelson Pike. Professor J. L. Mackie was most helpful in giving us some editorial guidance with his selections. Finally, we thank Ruth Boyle and Amy Phillips for their expert typing.

L.U.
D.N.W.

April 1978

THE POWER OF GOD

Contents

THE POWER OF GOD

Introduction

LINWOOD URBAN and DOUGLAS N. WALTON

An important component of most monotheistic religions is the belief that God is almighty or all-powerful. Certainly this conception is strongly fixed in Christianity. Occasionally Western religious philosophers or theologians have conceded that God may not be literally all-powerful, that he cannot do quite literally anything, yet even in this concession it is generally maintained that God is *very* powerful, or that the limits of his powers are beyond the human imagination and awesome in their scope.

The reasons for stress upon the extensive power of God are not difficult to discover. First, the Perfection, the Holiness, and the Majesty of God seem to demand that he transcend the world and everything which is in it. Hence he is said to be supremely wise and supremely powerful. Second, only such a being seems to be a fitting object of worship. If God has maximal power, then man's sense of awe and wonder is magnified. Stupendous power makes credible man's fear of the Lord.

Third, only a God who has supreme power is a fitting object of trust and can assure salvation. The best guarantee that God will be able to keep his promises and answer prayers is that no being is stronger than he. For while maximal power breeds fear of God, it also brings assurance that he can do what he wills to do.

So essential an attribute ought to have been thoroughly examined in philosophical theology, but this has not been the case. Traditionally, more attention has been paid to the divine attribute of omniscience insofar as it has been distinguished from omnipotence. The literature in philosophical theology specifically on omniscience is more voluminous, the lines of controversy more clearly drawn. Perhaps the notion of infinite power has seemed too obscure, too shrouded in mystery and ineffability for us to analyze our feelings of awe and bring them into the domain of pure concepts. Yet recently, skeptics have challenged theologians with arguments that center on omnipotence, pressing theologians to clarify the meaning of this enigmatic property. One such argument is the argument from evil.

1. Evil

The argument from evil claims that classical Western theism, based on a deity infinitely wise, powerful, and just, is hopelessly involved in logical contradiction. How is it possible to reconcile the death by cancer of a small child with the existence of a just and benevolent deity sufficiently powerful to have circumvented this tragedy? In the face of this challenge, several options are open to the theist. He may deny that there is evil. However, the endless catalogue of suffering, deprivation, and distress of human beings and nature's appalling waste seem sufficient to demonstrate vast evil in the world. He may deny that God is almighty or deny that God is omniscient. He may likewise deny that God is morally excellent. No one of these alternatives is particularly attractive; but if the argument from evil is sound, one of the traditional attributes will have to be sacrificed.

However, in controversy the lines of assault are often not chosen by the defender, but by the aggressor. The militant atheist wants to show either that God does not exist or that he is irrelevant to human concern. Hence he has not usually attacked the notion of God's moral excellence. A morally depraved but omnipotent God would be a source of much human anxiety. However, a God who lacks omnipotence might safely be forgotten. A morally excellent God who struggles against evil and yet who is not able to bring about his good designs is caught in the same tragic situation as are men. Hence he is more to be pitied than to be worshipped.

The arguer from evil thus attempts a *reductio ad absurdum* of classical theism. He questions whether God is literally omnipotent or whether there are some evils that, for whatever reason, he cannot prevent. The task faced by Christian theodicy is to explain or justify evil without eroding omnipotence to such a point that the deity thus described becomes irrelevant.

2. Flew's Challenge

The skeptic who argues from evil suggests that classical theism is meaningful, but false. Recently some challengers have attempted to demonstrate the stronger thesis that the basic tenets of classical theology are not merely false, but meaningless in the sense that they do not really assert anything about the world. The most notable protagonist of this view is Antony Flew. In the tradition of Logical Positivism, Flew laid it down that any cognitively meaningful statement, i.e., one that makes a genuine assertion about the world, must be such that some conceivable evidence could conclusively falsify it.[1] Many religious utterances were once meaningful in this sense, but are no longer so since they have been "killed by inches, the death by a thousand qualifications." Isaiah proclaimed that the righteous God ruled the world. He supported this claim by appealing to the fact that Assyria was about to overwhelm a sinful and unfaithful Israel. But today believers have so qualified the claim "God rules the world" that no conceivable evidence ever seems to hold good against it. Whoever wins in battle, God is still said to arrange everything. Since the claim is now consistent with every conceivable state of affairs, it cannot be falsified and thus cannot be taken to assert a fact about the world.

This challenge was particularly acute for the believer who refused to qualify the traditional conception of God: he insisted that God is all loving and all powerful and that no amount of evil in the world could falsify his claim. Attempts to buttress his position by saying "God works in mysterious ways" seemed an obvious evasion. Flew and others drew the conclusion that most religious utterances which seemed to make genuine assertions were actually without assertive force.

This skeptical attack of the verificationists seemed a temporary secular triumph. It actually had the effect of eliciting the concession of cogni-

tive emptiness of religious utterances from some theologians; an effect
that, as Alvin Plantinga remarked, seemed rather like a civil rights
worker welcoming the Ku Klux Klan.

Subsequent developments within the philosophy of science, however,
soon had the effect of eroding and neutralizing Flew's challenge.
Statements of the so-called Verification Principle were overwhelmed
by counter-examples and difficulties. It became increasingly clear that
a statement of the Verification Principle that would permit the claims
of natural science to count as meaningful and rule out the claims of
theology and metaphysics could not be produced. Flew assumed that
any meaningful statement must be capable of conclusive falsification,
i.e., we must be able to conceive of a state of affairs in which the
statement could be shown to be false. Unfortunately even some very
simple claims characteristically made by scientists fail to meet this
test. In an infinite universe, the claim "For every metal there is an
acid that will dissolve it" can neither be conclusively verified or falsified. The statement might be verified on the planet earth; but then on
another planet, a metal that could not be dissolved by any known acid
might be found. However, on another planet a new acid might be dis-
covered, and so on *ad infinitum*. As a result, it turns out that it is theo-
retically impossible to verify or to falsify the universal claims that
have an important place in the physical sciences. Although some philosophers of science have clung to the notion of empirical verifiability
as an article of faith, others have become increasingly reluctant to accept what seemed a kind of simplistic empiricism associated with early
statements of the Verification Principle. Most philosophers have rejected Flew's challenge and admit that a statement is factually meaningful as long as some empirical evidence counts for or against the
claim. Since the good and evil found in the world count for and
against the existence of God, theology is once again meaningful.

3. Power and Freedom

The skeptics' strongest line of attack is then to concentrate upon the
supposed incoherence of the traditional conception of God. In order to
bring his point home, he sometimes argues as follows. If God is om-

nipotent, then he can create any possible state of affairs. Why then did he not create a world in which people always freely do right? It is actually the case that people sometimes freely do right—it is therefore logically possible that people should *always* freely do right. It is possible that evil might not exist. Since an omnipotent God can actualize any possibility, it follows that he must have been able to prevent evil. Why then, did he not? Given the assumption that God is omnipotent and given the presence of actual moral evil in the world, it appears that God must have failed to create a world in which all men freely choose what is right through lack of moral excellence. How then can the attributes of benevolence, justice, and moral perfection be saved for a God who is able yet unwilling to prevent or even lessen the pain, misery, and injustice in the world?

The characteristic response of the theologian, perhaps the only rebuttal that has even partially succeeded in effectively meeting the thrust of this argument, is called the 'Free Will Defence.' This reply asserts first that God's decision to create men having the power to freely choose between good and evil is the best choice he could have made. Creatures who can freely choose between good and evil are better creatures than necessitated beings. Second, if men choose to do evil, that is up to them, not up to God. In other words, the Free Will defender concedes that it is possible that God could have created a world in which no evil exists if in fact it had turned out that, through their free choice, men had always done the right thing. That, however, the world has not turned out this way is not something that God could have remedied. Only the individual moral agents created by God could have rectified the existing sad state of affairs. For we presume that men are free to do good or evil as they alone choose. If God were to bring it about that a man does right, if he were to see to it that this man does not do the wrong thing, this individual would have lost his freedom to do either right or wrong. So it seems to the Free Will defender.

An important aspect of the Free Will Defence thus outlined is that it denies absolute omnipotence to God. Having created beings with the freedom to choose, God thereby lacks the power to exercise control over the decisions of these beings in any manner that would foreclose on their freedom. If Lee Harvey Oswald pulled the trigger freely, then he had the option of either pulling the trigger or not, and provided this is so, God could not have prevented Oswald's pulling the trigger.

Thus the Free Will Defence imposes an inherent limitation on divine omnipotence. If there is to be more than one center of power in the universe, no one being can be exclusively and totally omnipotent in the sense of being literally able to bring about or prevent anything. A plurality of free moral agents necessarily entails a sharing of power within certain limits that are not very well defined. The limitations on omnipotence inherent in the Free Will Defence has been clearly recognized by Alvin Plantinga, who writes, "What is really characteristic and central to the Free Will Defence is the claim that God, though omnipotent, could not have created just any possible world he pleased. . . ."[2]

4. Limits and Omnipotence

The initial problem faced by theologians is that it seems logically absurd to suggest that there can be any limits to omnipotence. For an omnipotent being can, by definition, have no limits to his power. Yet several considerations suggest the incoherence of the concept of omnipotence construed as the power to do quite literally anything. The literature concerning the definition of "omnipotence" is fairly extensive, and it is now time to set out the issues schematically.

(1) Although men from earliest times have called God omnipotent, it is not until the Middle Ages that one finds treatments of the possible limits to omnipotence. One of the earliest is found in the writings of St. Anselm, who was struck by the fact that men can do certain things that God cannot do. Men can change, but God who is immutable cannot. However, St. Anselm concluded that the ability to change is really a defect of power, an impotence, and not a power in a positive sense. Hence he concluded that God is omnipotent because he does nothing through impotence and nothing has power against him.

(2) But what does it mean to say that nothing has power against God? Does it mean that God is not bound by the law of non-contradiction?

Descartes argued that since God decreed or created this law, God could not be bound by it.

(3) However, views like Descartes' had seemed unreasonable to St. Thomas Aquinas, and in fact it has seemed unreasonable to the majority of theologians to require of an omnipotent being that he be able to bring about states of affairs that exemplify self-contradictions or other logical inconsistencies. A world in which God could bring it about that black is white, or in which Caesar on some historic occasion simultaneously crossed the Rubicon and did not cross that river, is a world that we would be hard pressed to imagine or understand. Of course if we regard the law of non-contradiction and similar binary principles of standard first-order logic as artificial contrivances, we might fail to see any good reason why God, in his infinite wisdom, should be bound to this two-valued conventional system. Yet the demand for logical consistency goes deep, and to jettison it without a clear alternative yields a total bereftness of orientation which seems tantamount to a Kierkegaardian irrationalism. Perhaps ultimately in the religious quest, consistency must be surrendered, but to do so will reduce our ability to attain even a dim and imperfect grasp of the divine nature, admittedly the best we can aspire to. To proceed further we must concede that an omnipotent being need not be required to be able to instantiate self-contradictions and the like. Nor do we normally require of finite beings that they ever have this power, so perhaps this limitation applies to all power generally and not uniquely or distinctively to an omnipotent agent.

(4) For parallel reasons, we need not require of an omnipotent agent, or any agent, that he be able to bring about states of affairs that are logically possible but nevertheless "unbringaboutable." For example, the following state of affairs is logically contingent: the door is open but I do not directly bring it about that the door is open. An instance would occur, say, where *you* open the door. Yet it is impossible that I myself should bring about this state of affairs. It is absurd that I should directly bring it about both that the door is open and that I do not directly bring it about that the door is open. Thus there are certain states of affairs that, while they do not admit of logical inconsistency in themselves, are *unbringaboutable* by a certain agent, for bringing them about is logically impossible for that agent to do.

(5) At this point a shift in terminology might seem appropriate. If an omnipotent being must be one who can bring about literally anything, even one of the peculiar states of affairs listed above, perhaps it is less misleading to say that God is *almighty* rather than absolutely omnipotent, meaning that he is all-powerful only within certain conceptual limits. Some have wanted to be even more restrictive. To many theologians, frightened by the possibility of logical entrapment, it has seemed expedient to say simply that "omnipotence" means only that God is the source of all power, or that he is "the power of Being in everything which exists" (Tillich). Whatever conceptual advantages this suggestion may have, it is too early in our discussion to adopt it. For one thing, it is not very helpful; for it does not tell us what creative powers God can be said to possess. Is an almighty Creator limited by the past? Can he lie, cheat, and steal? As to the first of these questions, St. Peter Damian, assuming Anselm's account of omnipotence, argued that since God does nothing through impotence and is not limited by anything outside himself, he must be able to change the past, because the past is something outside God. To the contrary, St. Thomas Aquinas argued the past is not in God's control, since changing the past is an incoherent notion. This is really an issue in the philosophy of time and is similar to the problem "Can God make time go backward?" If at *t,* God puts the universe in reverse, it does not appear that time goes backward, but that time continues to go forward. Only the causal sequence is reversed. Likewise at *t* God decreed that Rome should be founded, and at *t'* that it should be destroyed. But it does not seem possible for God to have decreed that at *t'* Rome should not have been; time has been continually moving ahead, and the past is lost to the control of any power. Although Peter Damian attempted to answer this challenge by an appeal to the atemporal character of God's will, it seems best to think of power as essentially furture-directed, and we ought not require that an omnipotent agent have the power to change the past.

(6) Certain theological constraints are introduced by the assumption of the moral perfection of God. It would appear to be inconsistent with much of the western theological tradition to allow that God could be tired, oblivious, or angry, that God could be deceived, circumvented, or frustrated, that God could break a promise or commit any kind of

moral indiscretion. The reason for these restrictions is that omnipotence is only one of God's perfections. If God is that being than which no greater or more perfect can be conceived, he must be morally perfect and he must be omnipotent because of his moral perfection. A God who could not carry out his good designs would not be as perfect as one who can. Thus some of God's perfections limit others. In particular, a Christian cannot believe in absolute, uncircumscribed omnipotence.

(7) If God is that being than which no greater or more perfect can be conceived, then it appears that there can be only one of him. For if there were two Gods, neither could be more perfect. Likewise Duns Scotus argued that if "omnipotence" means "unlimited by anything outside the self," then there could be only one omnipotent being. If there were two, each would limit the other; and hence neither would be omnipotent. However, suppose "omnipotence" is defined as "the ability to do anything which does not involve a contradiction." Then, as William of Ockham pointed out, there could be more than one omnipotent being if they are necessitated by nature to co-operate with each other. This subtle shift in the definition of "omnipotence" has enormous consequences and puts considerable strain upon our natural conceptual scheme.

(8) But does God necessarily will what he wills? Spinoza argued that the perfection of God demands that he wills what he wills necessarily. Only if God's will is necessitated can he be free from any external influence. The majority of theologians have rejected this suggestion, arguing instead that the freedom to choose between alternatives is a perfection, and that, therefore, God must have it.

(9) It might seem absurd to require that an omnipotent agent must be able to bring about states of affairs that are *self-limiting,* that is, states of affairs that might result in a loss of power by the agent. However, Bishop Charles Gore thought that God must be able to divest himself of some of his power. According to him, the omnipotent God must be able to lay aside his omnipotence if he were to become truly incarnate in Jesus of Nazareth. This *kenotic* theory of the incarnation seems to lead directly to the paradoxical assertion that an omnipotent agent is not omnipotent if he cannot divest himself of some of his power.

A similar problem can be put in the form of a dilemma: can God create a stone that is too heavy for him to lift? If not, he is not omnipotent. If so, he is not omnipotent either, since there is something he cannot lift. One way out of this dilemma, Bishop Gore to the contrary, is to relax the requirement that an omnipotent being can do just anything, ruling that such a being need not be required to bring about self-limiting states of affairs.

(10) However, to adopt the strategy just outlined may bring us into conflict with the Free Will Defence. We have already observed that a universe containing a plurality of free agents necessitates a different kind of limit on the sphere of the power of even an almighty agent. For if the actions of men are sometimes free, as seems required if they are to be held morally accountable, the control of a creator over these free actions will have to be sufficiently indirect and subtle not to negate that freedom. A totally omnipotent being, rigidly conceived, must, as such, usurp all power, leaving no room for human controllers or other free agencies such as Satan and his cohorts.

(11) But then could God create beings who always freely choose the good? Some have argued that only by necessitating the agents could God create a world in which men always choose the good. However, he has created a world in which men sometimes freely choose the good. Why, then, could he not create a world in which they always choose the good? The logic of this problem is not well understood; and because of this fact, it is fitting to refer the reader to the concluding selections.

(12) Finally, it might be argued that an omnipotent being should not be required to violate the lawlike regularities of nature. This observation raises the question whether miracles involve violations of physical laws, and is thus a wider and separate problem to some extent. As such it raises issues which are too extensive to be included in this volume. Suffice it to remark that it may be theologically preferable to countenance the notion of an almighty God whose agency is seen as operational only within certain limits of the causal nexus.

Notice that some of the limits listed above apply to finite agents as well as to an almighty agent, whereas some mark limits that are unique to divine power. Finite agents often and typically bring about self-limiting states of affairs; many of the things we do result in inabilities to do other things. And (6) shows that, somewhat paradoxically, there are many things that you or I can do that God cannot—for example, execute twenty-five pushups or cheat at backgammon.

If we reflect on the several kinds of limitations, it may well be that if we are to have a concept of omnipotence or almightiness that is minimally logically consistent, and consistent with the mainstream of the western theological tradition, we must accept certain conceptual limits on the divine power. That none of these limits are as clear or well-behaved as we might like indicates at once the difficulty of constructing a consistent and adequate theodicy and the problems inherent in giving a clear account of the deep skeptical worries and doubts about the problem of evil. Only through further attempts to define and clarify the scope and nature of the several limits can a definitive understanding of these classical problems be expedited. The necessity for these limits may ultimately be due to intrinsic conceptual limitations of the human understanding. There may still remain some sense not very well understood, in which it is correct to say that pure potency has no limits. Conceptual limits are not to be confused with deficiencies.

At any rate, we hope to have shown the need for the analysis of the attribute of omnipotence, both as a required item of vocabulary in the adjudication and rational understanding of the dialogue between the theologian and the secular skeptic, and as an essential element in systematic theology. Logic is no more a good substitute for faith than for creativity, vision, inspiration or beauty. Yet when inconsistency runs deep, to the very roots of belief, to the essential foundations of our commitments, dissonance dulls and clouds belief; and logical considerations play a role in the eventual readjustment to consistency. An awareness of the importance of the place of logic in theology is conveyed in the work of the great scholastics, in their judicious balance of faith and reason. Logic is neither the beginning nor the end of religious belief, but an illogical theology is unworthy of and cannot support a mature faith.

Notes

1. A. Flew and A. MacIntyre, *New Essays in Philosophical Theology,* London,
   S. C. M. Press, 1955, pp. 96ff.
2. Alvin Plantinga, *The Nature of Necessity,* Oxford, Oxford University Press, 1974, p.
   168.

A MODERN
STATEMENT

1

Evil and Omnipotence

J. L. MACKIE

The traditional arguments for the existence of God have been fairly thoroughly criticized by philosophers. But the theologian can, if he wishes, accept this criticism. He can admit that no rational proof of God's existence is possible. And he can still retain all that is essential to his position, by holding that God's existence is known in some other, nonrational way. I think, however, that a more telling criticism can be made by way of the traditional problem of evil. Here it can be shown, not that religious beliefs lack rational support, but that they are positively irrational, that the several parts of the essential theological doctrine are inconsistent with one another, so that the theologian can maintain his position as a whole only by a much more extreme rejection of reason than in the former case. He must now be prepared to believe, not merely what cannot be proved, but what can be *disproved* from other beliefs that he also holds.

The problem of evil, in the sense in which I shall be using the phrase, is a problem only for someone who believes that there is a God who is both omnipotent and wholly good. And it is a logical problem, the problem of clarifying and reconciling a number of beliefs: it is not a scientific problem that might be solved by further observations, or a practical problem that might be solved by a decision or an action. These points are obvious; I mention them only because they are sometimes ignored by theologians, who sometimes parry a statement of the problem with such remarks as "Well, can you solve the problem your-

From *Mind*, Vol. LXIV, No. 254 (1955). Reprinted by permission of the author and the editor of *Mind*.

self?'' or ''This is a mystery which may be revealed to us later'' or ''Evil is something to be faced and overcome, not to be merely discussed.''

In its simplest form the problem is this: God is omnipotent; God is wholly good; and yet evil exists. There seems to be some contradiction between these three propositions, so that if any two of them were true the third would be false. But at the same time all three are essential parts of most theological positions: the theologian, it seems, at once *must* adhere and *cannot consistently* adhere to all three. (The problem does not arise only for theists, but I shall discuss it in the form in which it presents itself for ordinary theism.)

However, the contradiction does not arise immediately; to show it we need some additional premises, or perhaps some quasi-logical rules connecting the terms ''good,'' ''evil,'' and ''omnipotent.'' These additional principles are that good is opposed to evil, in such a way that a good thing always eliminates evil as far as it can, and that there are no limits to what an omnipotent thing can do. From these it follows that a good omnipotent thing eliminates evil completely, and then the propositions that a good omnipotent thing exists, and that evil exists, are incompatible.

Adequate solutions

Now once the problem is fully stated it is clear that it can be solved, in the sense that the problem will not arise if one gives up at least one of the propositions that constitute it. If you are prepared to say that God is not wholly good, or not quite omnipotent, or that evil does not exist, or that good is not opposed to the kind of evil that exists, or that there are limits to what an omnipotent thing can do, then the problem of evil will not arise for you.

There are, then, quite a number of adequate solutions of the problem of evil, and some of these have been adopted, or almost adopted, by various thinkers. For example, a few have been prepared to deny God's omnipotence, and rather more have been prepared to keep the term ''omnipotence'' but severely to restrict its meaning, recording quite a number of things that an omnipotent being cannot do. Some have said that evil is an illusion, perhaps because they held that the whole world of temporal, changing things is an illusion, and that what we call evil belongs only to this world, or perhaps because they held that although temporal things *are* much as we see them, those that we call evil are not really evil. Some have said that what we call evil is merely the privation of good, that evil in a positive sense, evil that would really be opposed to good, does not exist. Many have agreed with Pope that disorder is harmony not understood, and that partial evil is universal good. Whether any of these views is *true* is, of course, another question. But each of them gives an adequate solution of the problems of evil in the sense that if you accept it this problem does not arise for you, though you may, of course, have *other* problems to face.

But often enough these adequate solutions are only *almost* adopted. The thinkers who restrict God's power, but keep the term "omnipotence," may reasonably be suspected of thinking, in other contexts, that his power is really unlimited. Those who say that evil is an illusion may also be thinking, inconsistently, that this illusion is itself an evil. Those who say that "evil" is merely privation of good may also be thinking, inconsistently, that privation of good is an evil. (The fallacy here is akin to some forms of the "naturalistic fallacy" in ethics, where some think, for example, that "good" is just what contributes to evolutionary progress, and that evolutionary progress is itself good.) If Pope meant what he said in the first line of his couplet, that "disorder" is only harmony not understood, the "partial evil" of the second line must, for consistency, mean "that which, taken in isolation, falsely appears to be evil," but it would more naturally mean "that which, in isolation, really is evil." The second line, in fact, hesitates between two views, that "partial evil" isn't really evil, since only the universal quality is real, and that "partial evil" is really an evil, but only a little one.

In addition, therefore, to adequate solutions, we must recognize unsatisfactory inconsistent solutions, in which there is only a half-hearted or temporary rejection of one of the propositions which together constitute the problem. In these, one of the constituent propositions is explicitly rejected, but it is covertly reasserted or assumed elsewhere in the system.

Fallacious Solutions

Besides these half-hearted solutions, which explicitly reject but implicitly assert one of the constituent propositions, there are definitely fallacious solutions which explicitly maintain all the constituent propositions, but implicitly reject at least one of them in the course of the argument that explains away the problem of evil.

There are, in fact, many so-called solutions which purport to remove the contradiction without abandoning any of its constituent propositions. These must be fallacious, as we can see from the very statement of the problem, but it is not so easy to see in each case precisely where the fallacy lies. I suggest that in all cases the fallacy has the general form suggested above: in order to solve the problem one (or perhaps more) of its constituent propositions is given up, but in such a way that it appears to have been retained, and can therefore be asserted without qualification in other contexts. Sometimes there is a further complication: the supposed solution moves to and fro between, say, two of the constituent propositions, at one point asserting the first of these but covertly abandoning the second, at another point asserting the second but covertly abandoning the first. These fallacious solutions often turn upon some equivocation with the words "good" and "evil," or upon some vagueness about the way in which good and evil are opposed to one another, or about how much is meant by "omnipotence." I propose to examine some of these so-called solutions, and to exhibit their fallacies in detail. Incidentally, I shall also be considering whether an adequate solution could be reached by a minor modification of one or more of the constituent propositions, which would, however, still satisfy all the essential requirements of ordinary theism.

1. "Good cannot exist without evil" or "Evil is necessary as a counterpart to good."

It is sometimes suggested that evil is necessary as a counterpart to good, that if there were no evil there could be no good either, and that this solves the problem of evil. It is true that it points to an answer to the question "Why should there be evil?" But it does so only by qualifying some of the propositions that constitute the problem.

First, it sets a limit to what God can do, saying that God *cannot* create good without simultaneously creating evil, and this means either that God is not omnipotent or that there are *some* limits to what an omnipotent thing can do. It may be replied that these limits are always presupposed, that omnipotence has never meant the power to do what is logically impossible, and on the present view the existence of good without evil would be a logical impossibility. This interpretation of omnipotence may, indeed, be accepted as a modification of our original account which does not reject anything that is essential to theism, and I shall in general assume it in the subsequent discussion. It is, perhaps, the most common theistic view, but I think that some theists at least have maintained that God can do what is logically impossible. Many theists, at any rate, have held that logic itself is created or laid down by God, that logic is the way in which God arbitrarily chooses to think. (This is, of course, parallel to the ethical view that morally right actions are those which God arbitrarily chooses to command, and the two views encounter similar difficulties.) And *this* account of logic is clearly inconsistent with the view that God is bound by logical necessities—unless it is possible for an omnipotent being to bind himself, an issue which we shall consider later, when we come to the Paradox of Omnipotence. This solution of the problem of evil cannot, therefore, be consistently adopted along with the view that logic is itself created by God.

But, secondly, this solution denies that evil is opposed to good in our original sense. If good and evil are counterparts, a good thing will not "eliminate evil as far as it can." Indeed, this view suggests that good and evil are not strictly qualities of things at all. Perhaps the suggestion is that good and evil are related in much the same way as great and small. Certainly, when the term "great" is used relatively as a condensation of "greater than so-and-so," and "small" is used correspondingly, greatness and smallness are counterparts and cannot exist without each other. But in this sense greatness is not a quality, not an intrinsic feature of anything; and it would be absurd to think of a movement in favor of greatness and against smallness in this sense. Such a movement would be self-defeating, since relative greatness can be promoted only by a simultaneous promotion of relative smallness. I feel sure that no theists would be content to regard God's goodness as analogous to this—as if what he supports were not the *good* but the *better,* and as if he had the paradoxical aim that all things should be better than other things.

This point is obscured by the fact that "great" and "small" seem to have an absolute as well as a relative sense. I cannot discuss here whether there is absolute magnitude or not, but if there is, there could be an absolute sense for "great," it could mean of at least a certain size, and it would make sense to speak of all things getting bigger, of a universe that was expanding all over, and therefore it would make sense to speak of promoting greatness. But in *this* sense great and small are not logically necessary counterparts: either quality could exist without the other. There would be no logical impossibility in everything's being small or in everything's being great.

Neither in the absolute nor in the relative sense, then, of "great" and "small" do these terms provide an analogy of the sort that would be needed to support this solution of the problem of evil. In neither case are greatness and smallness *both* necessary counterparts *and* mutually opposed forces or possible objects for support and attack.

It may be replied that good and evil are necessary counterparts in the same way as any quality and its logical opposite: redness can occur, it is suggested, only if nonredness also occurs. But unless evil is merely the privation of good, they are not logical opposites, and some further argument would be needed to show that they are counterparts in the same way as genuine logical opposites. Let us assume that this could be given. There is still doubt of the correctness of the metaphysical principle that a quality must have a real opposite: I suggest that it is not really impossible that everything should be, say, red, that the truth is merely that if everything were red we should not notice redness, and so we should have no word "red"; we observe and give names to qualities only if they have real opposites. If so, the principle that a term must have an opposite would belong only to our language or to our thought, and would not be an ontological principle, and, correspondingly, the rule that good cannot exist without evil would not state a logical necessity of a sort that God would just have to put up with. God might have made everything good, though *we* should not have noticed it if he had.

But, finally, even if we concede that this *is* an ontological principle, it will provide a solution for the problem of evil only if one is prepared to say, "Evil exists, but only just enough evil to serve as the counterpart of good." I doubt whether any theist will accept this. After all, the *ontological* requirement that nonredness should occur would be satisfied even if all the universe, except for a minute speck, were red, and, if there were a corresponding requirement for evil as a counterpart to good, a minute dose of evil would presumably do. But theists are not usually willing to say, in all contexts, that all the evil that occurs is a minute and necessary dose.

2. "Evil is necessary as a means to good."

It is sometimes suggested that evil is necessary for good not as a counterpart but as a means. In its simple form this has little plausibility as a solution of the problem of evil, since it obviously implies a severe restriction of God's power. It would be a *causal* law that you cannot have a certain end without a certain means, so that if God has to introduce evil as a means to good, he must be subject to at least some causal laws. This certainly conflicts with what a theist normally means by omnipotence. This view of God as limited by causal laws also conflicts with the view that causal laws are themselves made by God, which is more widely held than the corresponding view about the laws of logic. This conflict would, indeed, be resolved if it were possible for an omnipotent being to bind himself, and this possibility has still to be considered. Unless a favorable answer can be given to this question, the suggestion that evil is necessary as a means to good solves the problem of evil only by denying one of its constituent propositions, either that God is omnipotent or that "omnipotent" means what it says.

3. "The universe is better with some evil in it than it could be if there were no evil."

Much more important is a solution which at first seems to be a mere variant of the previous one, that evil may contribute to the goodness of a whole in which it is found, so that the universe as a whole is better

as it is, with some evil in it, than it would be if there were no evil.
This solution may be developed in either of two ways. It may be supported by an aesthetic analogy, by the fact that contrasts heighten
beauty, that in a musical work, for example, there may occur discords
which somehow add to the beauty of the work as a whole. Alternatively, it may be worked out in connection with the notion of progress,
that the best possible organization of the universe will not be static,
but progressive, that the gradual overcoming of evil by good is really a
finer thing than would be the eternal unchallenged supremacy of good.

David Hume

In either case, this solution usually starts from the assumption that the
evil whose existence gives rise to the problem of evil is primarily what
is called physical evil, that is to say, pain. In Hume's rather half-
hearted presentation of the problem of evil, the evils that he stresses
are pain and disease, and those who reply to him argue that the existence of pain and disease makes possible the existence of sympathy,
benevolence, heroism, and the gradually successful struggle of doctors
and reformers to overcome these evils. In fact, theists often seize the
opportunity to accuse those who stress the problem of evil of taking a
low, materialistic view of good and evil, equating these with pleasure
and pain, and of ignoring the more spiritual goods which can arise in
the struggle against evils.

But let us see exactly what is being done here. Let us call pain and
misery "first order evil" or "evil (1)." What contrasts with this,
namely, pleasure and happiness, will be called "first order good" or
"good (1)." Distinct from this is "second order good" or "good (2)"
which somehow emerges in a complex situation in which evil (1) is a
necessary component—logically, not merely causally, necessary. (Exactly *how* it emerges does not matter: in the crudest version of this
solution good [2] is simply the heightening of happiness by the contrast with misery, in other versions it includes sympathy with suffering, heroism in facing danger, and the gradual decrease of first order
evil and increase of first order good.) It is also being assumed that second order good is more important than first order good or evil, in particular that it more than outweighs the first order evil it involves.

Now this is a particularly subtle attempt to solve the problem of evil.
It defends God's goodness and omnipotence on the ground that (on a

sufficiently long view) this is the best of all logically possible worlds, because it includes the important second order goods, and yet it admits that real evils, namely first order evils, exist. But does it still hold that good and evil are opposed? Not, clearly, in the sense that we set out originally: good does not tend to eliminate evil in general. Instead, we have a modified, a more complex pattern. First order good (e.g., happiness) *contrasts with* first order evil (e.g., misery): these two are opposed in a fairly mechanical way; some second order goods (e.g., benevolence) try to maximize first order good and minimize first order evil; but God's goodness is not this, it is rather the will to maximize *second* order good. We might, therefore, call God's goodness an example of a third order goodness, or good (3). While this account is different from our original one, it might well be held to be an improvement on it, to give a more accurate description of the way in which good is opposed to evil, and to be consistent with the essential theist position.

There might, however, be several objections to this solution.

First, some might argue that such qualities as benevolence—and a fortiori the third order goodness which promotes benevolence—have a merely derivative value, that they are not higher sorts of good, but merely means to good (1), that is, to happiness, so that it would be absurd for God to keep misery in existence in order to make possible the virtues of benevolence, heroism, etc. The theist who adopts the present solution must, of course, deny this, but he can do so with some plausibility, so I should not press this objection.

Secondly, it follows from this solution that God is not in our sense benevolent or sympathetic: he is not concerned to minimize evil (1), but only to promote good (2); and this might be a disturbing conclusion for some theists.

But, thirdly, the fatal objection is this. Our analysis shows clearly the possibility of the existence of a *second* order evil, an evil (2) contrasting with good (2) as evil (1) contrasts with good (1). This would include malevolence, cruelty, callousness, cowardice, and states in which good (1) is decreasing and evil (1) increasing. And just as good (2) is held to be the important kind of good, the kind that God is concerned to promote, so evil (2) will, by analogy, be the important kind of evil, the kind which God, if he were wholly good and omnipotent, would eliminate. And yet evil (2) plainly exists, and indeed most theists (in other contexts) stress its existence more than that of evil (1). We should, therefore, state the problem of evil in terms of second order evil, and against this form of the problem the present solution is useless.

An attempt might be made to use this solution again, at a higher level, to explain the occurrence of evil (2): indeed the next main solution that we shall examine does just this, with the help of some new notions. Without any fresh notions, such a solution would have little plausibility: for example, we could hardly say that the really important good was a good (3), such as the increase of benevolence in proportion to cruelty, which logically required for its occurrence the occurrence of some second order evil. But even if evil (2) could be explained in this way, it is fairly clear that there would be third order evils contrasting with this third order good: and we should be well on the way to an infinite regress, where the solution of a problem of evil, stated in terms of evil (n), indicated the existence of an evil $(n + 1)$, and a further problem to be solved.

4. "Evil is due to human free will."

Perhaps the most important proposed solution of the problem of evil is that evil is not to be ascribed to God at all, but to the independent actions of human beings, supposed to have been endowed by God with freedom of the will. This solution may be combined with the preceding one: first order evil (e.g., pain) may be justified as a logically necessary component in second order good (e.g., sympathy) while second order evil (e.g, cruelty) is not *justified*, but is so ascribed to human beings that God cannot be held responsible for it. This combination evades my third criticism of the preceding solution.

The free-will solution also involves the preceding solution at a higher level. To explain why a wholly good God gave men free will although it would lead to some important evils, it must be argued that it is better on the whole that men should act freely, and sometimes err, than that they should be innocent automata, acting rightly in a wholly determined way. Freedom, that is to say, is now treated as a third order good, and as being more valuable than second order goods (such as sympathy and heroism) would be if they were deterministically produced, and it is being assumed that second order evils, such as cruelty, are logically necessary accompaniments of freedom, just as pain is a logically necessary precondition of sympathy.

I think that this solution is unsatisfactory primarily because of the incoherence of the notion of freedom of the will: but I cannot discuss this topic adequately here, although some of my criticisms will touch upon it.

First I should query the assumption that second order evils are logically necessary accompaniments of freedom. I should ask this: if God has made men such that in their free choices they sometimes prefer what is good and sometimes what is evil, why could he not have made men such that they always freely choose the good? If there is no logical impossibility in a man's freely choosing the good on one, or on several, occasions, there cannot be a logical impossibility in his freely choosing the good on every occasion. God was not, then, faced with a choice between making innocent automata and making beings who, in acting freely, would sometimes go wrong: there was open to him the obviously better possibility of making beings who would act freely but always go right. Clearly, his failure to avail himself of this possibility is inconsistent with his being both omnipotent and wholly good.

If it is replied that this objection is absurd, that the making of some wrong choices is logically necessary for freedom, it would seem that "freedom" must here mean complete randomness or indeterminacy, including randomness with regard to the alternatives good and evil, in other words that men's choices and consequent actions can be "free" only if they are not determined by their characters. Only on this assumption can God escape the responsibility for men's actions; for if he made them as they are, but did not determine their wrong choices, this can only be because the wrong choices are not determined by men as they are. But then if freedom is randomness, how can it be a characteristic of *will?* And, still more, how can it be the most important good? What value or merit would there be in free choices if these were random actions which were not determined by the nature of the agent?

I conclude that to make this solution plausible two different senses of "freedom" must be confused, one sense which will justify the view that freedom is a third order good, more valuable than other goods would be without it, and another sense, sheer randomness, to prevent us from ascribing to God a decision to make men such that they sometimes go wrong when he might have made them such that they would always freely go right.

This criticism is sufficient to dispose of this solution. But besides this there is a fundamental difficulty in the notion of an omnipotent God creating men with free will, for if men's wills are really free this must mean that even God cannot control them, that is, that God is no longer omnipotent. It may be objected that God's gift of freedom to men does not mean that he *cannot* control their wills, but that he always *refrains* from controlling their wills. But why, we may ask, should God refrain from controlling evil wills? Why should he not leave men free to will rightly, but intervene when he sees them beginning to will wrongly? If God could do this, but does not, and if he is wholly good, the only explanation could be that even a wrong free act of will is not really evil, that its freedom is a value which outweighs its wrongness, so that there would be a loss of value if God took away the wrongness and the freedom together. But this is utterly opposed to what theists say about sin in other contexts. The present solution of the problem of evil, then, can be maintained only in the form that God has made men so free that he *cannot* control their wills.

This leads us to what I call the "Paradox of Omnipotence": can an omnipotent being make things which he cannot subsequently control? Or, what is practically equivalent to this, can an omnipotent being make rules which then bind himself? (These are practically equivalent because any such rules could be regarded as setting certain things beyond his control, and vice versa.) The second of these formulations is relevant to the suggestions that we have already met, that an omnipotent God creates the rules of logic or causal laws, and is then bound by them.

It is clear that this is a paradox: the questions cannot be answered satisfactorily either in the affirmative or in the negative. If we answer "Yes," it follows that if God actually makes things which he cannot control, or makes rules which bind himself, he is not omnipotent once he had made them: there are *then* things which he cannot do. But if we answer "No," we are immediately asserting that there are things which he cannot do, that is to say that he is already not omnipotent.

It cannot be replied that the question which sets this paradox is not a proper question. It would make perfectly good sense to say that a human mechanic has made a machine which he cannot control: if there is any difficulty about the question it lies in the notion of omnipotence itself.

This, incidentally, shows that although we have approached this paradox from the free-will theory, it is equally a problem for a theological determinist. No one thinks that machines have free will, yet they may well be beyond the control of their makers. The determinist might reply that anyone who makes anything determines its ways of acting, and so determines its subsequent behavior: even the human mechanic does this by his *choice* of materials and structure for his machine, though he does not know all about either of these: the mechanic thus determines, though he may not foresee, his machine's actions. And since God is omniscient, and since his creation of things is total, he both determines and foresees the ways in which his creatures will act. We may grant this, but it is beside the point. The question is not whether God *originally* determined the future actions of his creatures, but whether he can *subsequently* control their actions, or whether he was able in his original creation to put things beyond his subsequent control. Even on determinist principles the answers "Yes" and "No" are equally irreconcilable with God's omnipotence.

Before suggesting a solution of this paradox, I would point out that there is a parallel Paradox of Sovereignty. Can a legal sovereign make a law restricting its own future legislative power? For example, could the British parliament make a law forbidding any future parliament to socialize banking, and also forbidding the future repeal of this law itself? Or could the British parliament, which was legally sovereign in Australia in, say, 1899, pass a valid law, or series of laws, which made it no longer sovereign in 1933? Again, neither the affirmative nor the negative answer is really satisfactory. If we were to answer "Yes," we should be admitting the validity of a law which, if it were

actually made, would mean that parliament was no longer sovereign.
If we were to answer "No," we should be admitting that there is a
law, not logically absurd, which parliament cannot validly make, that
is, that parliament is not now a legal sovereign. This paradox can be
solved in the following way. We should distinguish between first order
laws, that is laws governing the actions of individuls and bodies other
than the legislature, and second order laws, that is laws about laws,
laws governing the actions of the legislature itself. Correspondingly,
we should distinguish two orders of sovereignty, first order sovereignty (sovereignty [1]) which is unlimited authority to make first
order laws, and second order sovereignty (sovereignty [2]) which is
unlimited authority to make second order laws. If we say that parliament is sovereign we might mean that any parliament at any time has
sovereignty (1), or we might mean that parliament has both sovereignty (1) and sovereignty (2) at present, but we cannot without contradiction mean both that the present parliament has sovereignty (2)
and that every parliament at every time has sovereignty (1), for if the
present parliament has sovereignty (2) it may use it to take away the
sovereignty (1) of later parliaments. What the paradox shows is that
we cannot ascribe to any continuing institution legal sovereignty in an
inclusive sense.

The analogy between omnipotence and sovereignty shows that the
paradox of omnipotence can be solved in a similar way. We must distinguish between first order omnipotence (omnipotence [1]), that is unlimited power to act, and second order omnipotence (omnipotence
[2]), that is unlimited power to determine what powers to act things
shall have. Then we could consistently say that God all the time has
omnipotence (1), but if so no beings at any time have powers to act independently of God. Or we could say that God at one time had omnipotence (2), and used it to assign independent powers to act to certain
things, so that God thereafter did not have omnipotence (1). But what
the paradox shows is that we cannot consistently ascribe to any continuing being omnipotence in an inclusive sense.

An alternative solution of this paradox would be simply to deny that
God is a continuing being, that any times can be assigned to his actions at all. But on this assumption (which also has difficulties of its

own) no meaning can be given to the assertion that God made men with wills so free that he could not control them. The paradox of omnipotence can be avoided by putting God outside time, but the free-will solution of the problem of evil cannot be saved in this way, and equally it remains impossible to hold that an omnipotent God *binds himself* by causal or logical laws.

Conclusion

Of the proposed solutions of the problem of evil which we have examined, none has stood up to criticism. There may be other solutions which require examination, but this study strongly suggests that there is no valid solution of the problem which does not modify at least one of the constituent propositions in a way which would seriously affect the essential core of the theistic position.

Quite apart from the problem of evil, the paradox of omnipotence has shown that God's omnipotence must in any case be restricted in one way or another, that unqualified omnipotence cannot be ascribed to any being that continues through time. And if God and his actions are not in time, can omnipotence, or power of any sort, be meaningfully ascribed to him?

PROBLEMS OF
DEFINITION

2

God Does Nothing from Impotence, Nor Has Anything Power Against Him

ST. ANSELM

How he is omnipotent, although there are many things of which he is not capable.—To be capable of being corrupted, or of lying, is not power, but impotence. God can do nothing by virtue of impotence, and nothing has power against him.

But how art thou omnipotent, if thou art not capable of all things? Or, if thou canst not be corrupted, and canst not lie, nor make what is true, false—as, for example, if thou shouldst make what has been done not to have been done, and the like—how art thou capable of all things? Or else to be capable of these things is not power, but impotence. For, he who is capable of these things is capable of what is not for his good, and of what he ought not to do; and the more capable of them he is, the more power have adversity and perversity against him; and the less has he himself against these.

He, then, who is thus capable is so not by power, but by impotence. For, he is not said to be able because he is able of himself, but because his impotence gives something else power over him. Or, by a figure of speech, just as many words are improperly applied, as when we use "to be" for "not to be," and "to do" for what is really "not to do," or "to do nothing." For, often we say to a man who denies

From *Proslogium*, Chap. VII. Reprinted from *St. Anselm: Proslogium; Monologium; etc.*, translated by Sidney Norton Deane, Chicago, Open Court Publishing Co., 1903.

the existence of something: "It is as you say it to be," though it might seem more proper to say, "It is not, as you say it is not." In the same way, we say: "This man sits just as that man does," or, "This man rests just as that man does"; although to sit is not to do anything, and to rest is to do nothing.

So, then, when one is said to have the power of doing or experiencing what is not for his good, or what he ought not to do, impotence is understood in the word power. For, the more he possesses this power, the more powerful are adversity and perversity against him, and the more powerless is he against them.

Therefore, O Lord, our God, the more truly art thou omnipotent, since thou art capable of nothing through impotence, and nothing has power against thee.

3

God Can Do the
Logically Impossible

RENÉ DESCARTES

The mathematical truths which you call eternal have been laid down
by God and depend on Him entirely no less than the rest of his creatures. Indeed to say that these truths are independent of God is to talk
of Him as if He were Jupiter or Saturn and to subject Him to the Styx
and the Fates. Please do not hesitate to assert and proclaim everywhere
that it is God who has laid down these laws in nature just as a king
lays down laws in his kingdom. There is no single one that we cannot
understand if our mind turns to consider it. They are all *inborn in our
minds* [1] just as a king would imprint his laws on the hearts of all his
subjects if he had enough power to do so. The greatness of God, on
the other hand, is something which we cannot comprehend even
though we know it. But the very fact that we judge it incomprehensible makes us esteem it the more greatly; just as a king has more majesty when he is less familiarly known by his subjects, provided of
course that they do not get the idea that they have no king—they must
know him enough to be in no doubt about that.

It will be said that if God had established these truths He could change
them as a king changes his laws. To this the answer is: "Yes he can,
if his will can change." "But I understand them to be eternal and
unchangeable."—"I make the same judgement about God." "But

From letters to Mersenne, Mesland, and More. From *Descartes: Philosophical Letters,*
translated and edited by Anthony Kenny, © Oxford University Press, Inc., 1970, pp.
11f, 14f, 236f, 150f. Reprinted with the permission of the publisher.

His will is free."—"Yes, but his power is incomprehensible." In general we can assert that God can do everything that we can comprehend but not that he cannot do what we cannot comprehend. It would be rash to think that our imagination reaches as far as His power.

I hope to put this in writing, within the next fortnight, in my treatise on Physics; but I do not want you to keep it secret. On the contrary I beg you to tell people as often as the occasion demands, provided that you do not mention my name. I should be glad to know the objections which can be made against this view; and I want people to get used to speaking of God in a manner worthier, I think, than the common and almost universal way of imagining him as a finite being. . . .

You ask me *by what kind of causality God established the eternal truths*. I reply: *by the same kind of causality* as he created all things, that is to say, as their *efficient and total cause*. For it is certain that he is no less the author of creatures' essence than he is of their existence; and this essence is nothing other than the eternal truths. I do not conceive them as emanating from God like rays from the sun; but I know that God is the author of everything and that these truths are something and consequently that he is their author. I say that I know this, not that I can conceive it or comprehend it; because it is possible to know that God is infinite and all-powerful although our soul, being finite, cannot comprehend or conceive Him. In the same way we can touch a mountain with our hands but we cannot put our arms around it as we could put them around a tree or something else not too large for them. To comprehend something is to embrace it in one's thought; to know something it is sufficient to touch it with one's thought.

You ask also what necessitated God to create these truths; and I reply that just as He was free not to create the world, so He was no less free to make it untrue that all the lines drawn from the centre of a circle to its circumference are equal. And it is certain that these truths are no more necessarily attached to his essence than other creatures are. You ask what God did in order to produce them. I reply that *from all eternity he willed and understood them to be, and by that very fact he created them*. Or, if you reserve the word *created* for the existence of things, then he *established them and made them*. In God, willing, understanding, and creating are all the same thing without one being prior to the other even *conceptually*. . . .

But I do not think that we should ever say of anything that it cannot be brought about by God. For since everything involved in truth and goodness depends on His omnipotence, I would not dare to say that God cannot make a mountain without a valley, or that one and two should not be three. I merely say that He has given me such a mind that I cannot conceive a mountain without a valley, or an aggregate of one and two which is not three, and that such things involve a contradiction in my conception. . . .

I turn to the difficulty of conceiving how it was free and indifferent for God to make it not be true that the three angles of a triangle were equal to two right angles, or in general that contradictories could not be true together. It is easy to dispel this difficulty by considering that the power of God cannot have any limits, and that our mind is finite and so created as to be able to conceive as possible things which God has wished to be in fact possible, but not to be able to conceive as possible things which God could have made possible, but which he has in fact wished to make impossible. The first consideration shows us that God cannot have been determined to make it true that contradictories cannot be true together, and therefore that he could have done the opposite. The second consideration shows us that even if this be true, we should not try to comprehend it since our nature is incapable of doing so. And even if God has willed that some truths should be necessary, this does not mean that he willed them necessarily; for it is one thing to will that they be necessary, and quite another to will them necessarily, or to be necessitated to will them. I agree that there are contradictions which are so evident, that we cannot put them before our minds without judging them entirely impossible, like the one which you suggest: *that God might have made creatures independent of him*. But if we would know the immensity of his power we should not put these thoughts before our minds, nor should we conceive any precedence or priority between his understanding and his will; for the idea which we have of God teaches us that there is in him only a single activity, entirely simple and entirely pure. This is well expressed by the words of St. Augustine: *They are so because you see them to be so;* [2] because in God *seeing and willing* are one and the same thing. . . .

Notes

1. Italics represent Latin words in a French context (as also below).
2. *Confessions,* xiii. 30.

4

Are Those Things Which Are Impossible in Nature Possible for God?

ST. THOMAS AQUINAS

It must be asked whether those things which are impossible in nature are possible for God. And it appears that they are not. . . .

2. Just as everything necessary in nature is demonstrable, so every impossibility in nature is also demonstrable. But every conclusion of a demonstration is implied by the principles of that demonstration. However, the principle, "The affirmation and negation of a proposition cannot be true simultaneously," is included in every demonstration. Therefore, this principle is implied in whatever is impossible in nature. But God cannot bring it about that the affirmation and negation of a proposition be simultaneously true, as the respondent has admitted. Therefore, God can do nothing which is impossible in nature.

3. Under God are two principles, reason and nature. But God cannot do those things which are contrary to reason, e.g. that genus be not predicable of species. Therefore, neither can he do those things which are impossible in nature. . . .

6. It is written in *Timothy* 1:13: "Faithful is God who cannot deny himself." However, he would deny himself, as the interlineary gloss says, if he did not implement his promises. But just as a promise of

From *Quaestiones Disputatae, De Potentia Dei,* q. 1, a. 3, Parma, 1856, pp. 5–7. Translation and notes by Linwood Urban. Material in [ ] is added for clarification.

God is from God, so also every truth is from God, because according to Ambrose's gloss on I *Corinthians* 12:13, "No man can say Jesus Christ but by the Holy Spirit," every truth [is by the Holy Spirit] no matter by whom it is uttered. Therefore, God cannot do anything whatever contrary to the truth. However, he would do something against the truth if he did something impossible. Therefore, God is unable to do anything impossible in nature. . . .

1. On the contrary, it is said in *Luke* 1:37: "No word shall be impossible with God."

2. A power which can do this and not that is a limited power. Thus if God can do what is possible in nature and not what is impossible, or this impossibility and not that impossibility, it seems that the power of God would be limited, which is contrary to what was proved above.[1] Therefore, nothing is impossible for God.

3. Everything not limited by something in existence cannot be impeded by something in existence. Now God is not limited by anything in existence. Hence he can be impeded by nothing in existence. So the truth of the proposition, "The affirmation and negation of a proposition cannot be simultaneously true," cannot limit what God can bring about. By like reasoning, the same is true for everything else. . . .

6. Just as blindness is opposed to vision, and virginity to parturition, and God can bring it about that a virgin remain a virgin after having given birth, so by similar reasoning he can bring it about that a blind man, while remaining blind, sees, and that the affirmation and negation of a proposition are simultaneously true. As a consequence, he can do all impossible things.

7. It is more difficult to join disparate substantial forms than to join disparate accidental forms. But God has joined in one, substantial forms most disparate, i.e. the human and the Divine, which differ as created and uncreated. So much the more can he join two accidental forms into one so that he can bring it about that something is simultaneously black and white. Thus the same conclusion follows. . . .

I answer that according to the Philosopher (*Metaphysics* 5, 12),[2] "possible" and "impossible" are predicated in three ways. In one way, "possible" is predicated in respect of some active or passive potency. Thus it is said that it is possible for a man to walk on account of his ability to walk, but impossible for him to fly.

In a second way, these words are not predicated in respect of any potentiality, but inherently. Thus we say, "What is not possible is impossible," and "What necessarily is not is impossible."

In a third way, "possible" is predicated in respect of some mathematical possibility of geometry, e.g. it is said that a line is potentially measurable because its square is measurable. Omitting this last possibility, we must give consideration to the other two.

It must also be recognized that "impossible" when predicated inherently, and not in respect of any potentiality, is predicated by reason of the mutual exclusion of terms. Furthermore, every exclusion of terms has the nature of some opposition; and every opposition of terms implies affirmation and negation, as is proved in *Metaphysics,* 10, 4.[3] Hence every impossibility implies that an affirmation and a negation of the same proposition are simultaneously true. However, this state of affairs cannot be attributed to an active potency, which is proved as follows.

Every active potency expresses the actuality and entity to which the power belongs. Furthermore every agent naturally acts to produce something like itself. Hence every act of an active potency terminates in being.[4] If at times it terminates in non-being, as is clear in cases of corruption, then the termination in non-being comes to pass only when the being of the one is incompatible with the being of the other, as the being of a hot thing is incompatible with the being of a cold thing. Hence the chief aim of heat is to generate heat, but it destroys cold as a consequence. However, for an affirmation and a negation to be simultaneously true cannot have the nature of being, or even of non-being, because being excludes non-being and non-being excludes being. [Since both being and non-being would be present in a contradictory state of affairs,] it cannot be the terminus of the action of an active potency either principally or as a consequence.[5]

To be sure, "impossible" predicated according to some potentiality can be taken in two ways. In one way because of an inherent defect of power, as a result of which an agent evidently cannot extend itself to some effect, as for example when a natural agent cannot transform some material. In a second way, its inability comes from something extrinsic, as for example, when its power is impeded or restricted.

Thus something is said to be impossible to be done in three ways. In one way on account of a defect of the active power, as in the transmutation of a material or something of the sort. In a second way because something resists or impedes the action. In a third way, because what is said to be impossible to bring about cannot be the terminus of an action. Those things which are impossible in nature in the first and second way, God can bring about, because his power is infinite and suffers no defect, nor is there any matter which he cannot transform at will. For it is not possible to resist his power.

However, God cannot do what is impossible in the third way, since God is the supreme actuality and principal end. Hence his action can terminate only at being principally, and at non-being only secondarily. Thus it is not possible for the affirmation and negation of a proposition to be true simultaneously, nor for anything to be true in which this impossibility is implied. Nor is this impossibility said to be dependent upon a defect of God's power, but on a lack of possibility, since it departs from the concept of the possible. On account of which fact, it is said by some that God can do everything except what cannot be done. . . .

Reply to the Second Objection: The principle that it is impossible for an affirmation and negation of a proposition to be true simultaneously is implied in any possibility you will. However, those states of affairs which are impossible because of a defect of a natural power, as for example that a blind man see, or others of this kind, since these states are not impossible in themselves, do not imply any inherent impossibility. They are impossible in relation to a natural power for which they are impossible. Thus if we should say, "Nature can make a blind man see," this state is impossible because the power of nature is bounded at a certain point, beyond which point is the impossibility which is attributed to it.

Reply to the Third Objection: The impossibilities of philosophical reasoning are not due to some lack of potency, but are inherently impossible, because those impossibilities which are the results of philosophical reasoning are not dependent on anything material or on any natural potency. . . .

Reply to the Sixth Objection: What is now true God does not destroy, because he does not bring it about that what was true should not be true. Rather, he brings it about that some proposition should not be true and that some other proposition should be true. As a result, when he raises someone from the dead, he brings it about that "He is dead" is not true, and that some other proposition is true. Furthermore, it can be said that the objection does not rest on a real similarity. From the fact that God does not implement a promise, it follows that God is not trustworthy, not that he has destroyed one of his effects. For he has not ordained that some one of his effects should remain forever as he has ordained that his promises should be implemented. . . .

Reply to the First Objection to the Contrary: "Word" is predicated not only of what is uttered orally, but also of what is mentally conceived. However, that an affirmation and negation be simultaneously true cannot be mentally conceived, as is proved in *Metaphysics* 4, 3.[6] As a consequence, anything containing a contradiction cannot be conceived. Therefore, since, according to the Philosopher, contradictory opinions are made up of contradictory propositions, it would follow that one and the same person holds simultaneously contradictory opinions [which is impossible.] Hence it is not contrary to the message of the Angel if it is said that God cannot violate the law of non-contradiction.

Reply to the Second Objection: The power of God is not able to accomplish the impossibility mentioned above because it departs from the nature of the possible. Hence the power of God is not said to be limited even though it cannot bring about this impossibility.

Reply to the Third Objection: God is said not to be able to violate the law of non-contradiction as if he were inhibited from a free choice, as the objection supposes, but because the state of affairs cannot be the terminus of the action of any active power. . . .

Reply to the Sixth Objection: Virginity is not opposed to parturition as blindness is to vision, but is opposed to sexual intercourse with a man, without which nature cannot bring about a birth. However, God can bring about a virgin birth.

Reply to the Seventh Objection: The opposites, created and uncreated, were not in Christ in respect of a unity of substantial forms, but in respect of the two natures. Hence it does not follow that God can make opposite accidental forms inhere in the same identical substance.

Notes

1. Q. 2.
2. Aristotle, 1019a, 35–1019b, 14.
3. 1055b, 3–7.
4. See below, "How the Omnipotent God Is Said To Be Unable To Do Certain Things," Selection 8.
5. *Ibid*.
6. 1005b, 23–34.

5

The Divine Power and
the Creature

PAUL TILLICH

The Meaning of Omnipotence: God is the power of being, resisting
and conquering nonbeing. In relation to the creature, the divine power
is expressed in the symbol of omnipotence. The "almighty God" is
the first subject of the Christian credo. It separates exclusive mono-
theism from all religion in which God is less than being-itself or the
power of being. Only the almighty God can be man's ultimate concern. A very mighty God may claim to be of ultimate concern; but he
is not, and his claim comes to naught, because he cannot resist nonbeing and therefore he cannot supply the ultimate courage which con-
quers anxiety. The confession of the creed concerning "God the Father almighty" expresses the Christian consciousness that the anxiety
of nonbeing is eternally overcome in the divine life. The symbol of
omnipotence gives the first and basic answer to the question implied in
finitude. Therefore, most liturgical and free prayers begin with the invocation "Almighty God."

This is the religious meaning of omnipotence, but how can it be
expressed theologically? In popular parlance the concept "omnipotence" implies a highest being who is able to do whatever he wants.
This notion must be rejected, religiously as well as theologically. It
makes God into a being alongside others, a being who asks himself

From *Systematic Theology,* Vol. I, Chicago, The University of Chicago Press, 1951,
pp. 272ff. Reprinted with the permission of The University of Chicago Press. Copyright
© 1951 by The University of Chicago Press.

which of innumerable possibilities he shall actualize. It subjects God to the split between potentiality and actuality—a split which is actually the heritage of finitude. It leads to absurd questions about God's power in terms of logically contradictory possibilities. Opposing such a caricature of God's omnipotence, Luther, Calvin, and others interpreted omnipotence to mean the divine power through which God is creative in and through everything in every moment. The almighty God is the omniactive God. There is, however, a difficulty in such an interpretation. It tends to identify the divine power with actual happenings in time and space, and thereby it suppresses the transcendent element in God's omnipotence. It is more adequate to define divine omnipotence as the power of being which resists nonbeing in all its expressions and which is manifest in the creative process in all its forms.

Faith in the almighty God is the answer to the quest for a courage which is sufficient to conquer the anxiety of finitude. Ultimate courage is based upon participation in the ultimate power of being. When the invocation "Almighty God" is seriously pronounced, a victory over the threat of nonbeing is experienced, and an ultimate, courageous affirmation of existence is expressed. Neither finitude nor anxiety disappears, but they are taken into infinity and courage. Only in this correlation should the symbol of omnipotence be interpreted. It is magic and an absurdity if it is understood as the quality of a highest being who is able to do what he wants.

With respect to time, omnipotence is eternity; with respect to space, it is omnipresence; and with respect to the subject-object structure of being, it is omniscience. These symbols must now be interpreted. Causality and substance in relation to being-itself were discussed in the symbol of God as the "creative ground" of being, in which the term "creative" contained and transcended causality, while the term "ground" contained and transcended substance. Their interpretation preceded the interpretation of the three other symbols because the divine creativity logically precedes the relation of God to the created.

SOME LIMITATIONS ON GOD'S OMNIPOTENCE

6

God Will Not Act Wickedly

THE BOOK OF JOB

Therefore, hear me, you men of
understanding,
   far be it from God that he
     should do wickedness,
   and from the Almighty that he
     should do wrong.
For according to the work of a man
   he will requite him,
  and according to his ways he will
    make it befall him.
Of a truth, God will not do
   wickedly,
   and the Almighty will not per-
    vert justice.
Who gave him charge over the
   earth
and who laid on him ^{w} the whole
   world?
If he should take back his spirit ^{x}
   to himself,
  and gather to himself his breath,
all flesh would perish together,
   and man would return to dust.

^{w}Heb lacks *on him*
                             ^{x}Heb *his heart and his spirit*

7

God Though Omnipotent
Is Not a Despot

T. C. VRIEZEN

. . . The Old Testament proclaims first and foremost God's absolute power to act according to His holy will.

Remarkable is the occasion when this principle of God's absolute power is stated: when Moses asks God to reveal Himself to him (Exod.xxxiii.18) and when God does so, in so far as He can reveal Himself, He says: "I will be gracious to whom I will be gracious and will shew mercy on whom I will shew mercy." God's grace is infinitely abundant, but He Himself decides who shall be admitted to this grace. It is not to be wrung from Him. More than once we find in the prophets (Amos v. 15*b*; Joel ii.14; Zeph.ii.3) the idea that God may forgive; for them, too, Yahweh remains the only one who can dispose of His favour. Yahweh may, therefore, decline a prayer of penitence (Amos vii.7 f., viii. 1 f.; Hos.vi.1 ff.; Jer.xiv.10 ff.), or accept it (Amos vii.1 ff.; Joel ii.18 ff.).

Here God reveals Himself as the Holy One, who in His majesty has the right to decide. Our human understanding seems to discover a great tension between God's love and His mysterious holy Being. This tension is realized quite clearly in the Old Testament and even transferred to God, for however clearly the Old Testament may proclaim

From T. C. Vriezen, *An Outline of Old Testament Theology*, Charles T. Branford Co., Newton Centre, Mass. 02159. Copyrighted by H. Veenman & Zonen B. V., Wageningen, Holland, 1960. Reprinted with the permission of H. Veenman & Zonen B. V.

Yahweh's omnipotence and accepts all its consequences, it never makes Him an arbitrary despotic Ruler but always regards Him as a God who sympathizes with man; this is depicted most profoundly in the hesitation of Yahweh, who takes counsel with Himself on what is to be done in Hosea (vi.4; xi.8), and in the fact that Yahweh repents of certain deeds. On the other hand this tension makes itself felt in human life and its problems, particularly the problem of suffering.

Most profoundly it is realized by Job who appeals to God his Redeemer, against God whose hand has struck him (Job xix.21 ff.). This problem of life will always remain for the faithful who live before the Holy One, with God who is Goodness. As long as the holiness and the love of God are the central conceptions in faith there must be insoluble spiritual conflicts in thought and life. Even Jesus Christ, when He suffered on the Cross, spoke the words: "Why hast Thou forsaken me?"

8

How the Omnipotent God Is Said To Be Unable To Do Certain Things

ST. THOMAS AQUINAS

From the foregoing, it can be admitted that although God is omnipotent, nonetheless he is said to be unable to do certain things.

It has been shown above[1] that there is active power in God, while it has also been proved above in Book I[2] that there is no passive potency in him. (On the contrary, we are said *to be able* with respect to each of these potentialities.) Therefore, God is not able to do those things whose possibility depends on a passive potentiality. What such things are must now be investigated.

First: Unquestionably an active potency concerns potentiality for *acting,* while a passive potency concerns potentiality for *being.* Consequently, there is potentiality for being only in those things which have matter subject to contraries. But since there is no passive potency in God, he has no potentiality with respect to anything which pertains to his being. Therefore, God cannot be a body or anything of this kind.

Second: Motion is the actuality of passive potentiality.[3] Therefore, God, to whom passive potency does not belong, cannot be moved. One can further conclude that he is not able to be moved in any of the

From St. Thomas Acquinas, *Summa Contra Gentiles,* lib. II, cap. 25, Leonine Edition, Rome, 1918. Translation and notes by Linwood Urban.

kinds of change. Therefore, he cannot be augmented, nor diminished, nor altered, nor generated, nor corrupted.

Third: Since to fail is a kind of corruption, God can fail in nothing.

Fourth: Every deficiency is the result of some deprivation. But the subject of a deprivation is the potentiality of the matter. Therefore, in no way can God be deficient.

Fifth: Since fatigue results from a defect of power, and since forgetfulness results from a defect of intellect, it is clear that God can neither tire or be forgetful.

Sixth: Neither can he be overcome or suffer violence. These conditions can be actualized only in what is by nature movable.

Seventh: Neither can he repent, or be angry, or be sad since all these indicate passion or defect.

Another line of argument is the following. Because the object and effect of an active potency is a *made thing,* no potency is operative when the cause of the object or effect is lacking. Thus sight is inoperative in the absence of the actuality of something visible. Therefore, it follows that God is said not to be able to do something which is contrary to the nature of *being* as being, or the nature of a *made thing* as made. We must examine what these things are.

First: Whatever destroys the nature of an entity is contrary to the nature of that entity. Therefore, the nature of an entity is destroyed by its opposite, just as the nature of man is destroyed by its opposite or the opposite of its parts. Now the opposite of being is non-being. Consequently, God is not able to act so that one and the same thing be and not be simultaneously, because it is contradictory for it both to be and not be at the same time.[4]

Second: The simultaneous predication of contraries or privative opposites implies a contradiction. Thus it follows that if something is black and white, that it is white and not white, and that if someone is seeing and blind, that he is seeing and not seeing. Hence for the same reason, God cannot make opposites to be simultaneously and in the same respect in the same object.

Third: The removal of the thing itself follows the removal of an essential principle of the thing. Thus if God is unable to make it that a thing both be and not be at the same time, neither can he make it that an essential principle be absent from the thing and that the thing remain, e.g. that a man exist and not have soul.

Fourth: Since the principles of certain sciences, e.g. logic, geometry, and arithmetic, are derived solely from the formal principles of things, upon which the essences of those things depend, it follows that God cannot establish the contraries of those principles, e.g. that genus should not be predicable of species, or that lines drawn from the center to the circumference should be unequal, or that the three angles of a rectilinear triangle should not be equal to two right angles.

Fifth: It is thus evident that God is unable to make the past not to have been. For this state of affairs also includes a contradiction. For it is necessary for a thing to be while it is, and for it to have been while it was.

Sixth: There are also some things which are inconsistent with the nature of a made thing as made. These inconsistent things God cannot create, for whatever God makes must be something made.

Seventh: From this it is clear that God is unable to make God. For it is the nature of a made being that its being depend upon some cause. Such a condition is contrary to the nature of him who is called God, as is clear from what is said above.[5]

Eighth: For the same reason, God cannot make anything equal to himself. For a thing whose being does not depend upon another is greater in being and in other perfections than a thing which depends upon another, which belongs to the nature of a created thing.

Ninth: Likewise, God is unable to bring it about that something is conserved in being without him. For the preservation of any entity depends upon its cause. Hence it is evident that if the cause is removed, the effect is removed. Therefore, if anything possibly could exist which is not preserved by God, it is not his effect.[6]

A third line of argument is as follows. Because God is a voluntary agent,[7] he is unable to do anything which he cannot will. It can be conceded that he is unable to will something if it is also admitted that there is necessity in the Divine Will. For what necessarily is cannot not be, and what is impossible to be necessarily is not.

First: Thus it is evident that God cannot make himself not to be, or not to be good and happy, because he necessarily wills himself to be good and happy as is shown in Book I. [8]

Second: It has also been shown above that God is unable to will anything evil. Hence it is evident that God cannot sin. [9]

Third: Likewise it has been shown above that the will of God cannot be mutable. [10] Therefore God cannot bring it about that what is willed by him should not be implemented.

Note that it ought to be understood that for God *to be unable* in this last instance is said in a different sense than in the earlier examples. For God simply cannot will or do what was discussed earlier. In the present case, God can be said to will or do a thing if we consider his absolute will or power, not however if we assume that he wills the opposite. For with respect to creatures, the will of God has only hypothetical necessity, as has been proved in the First Book. [11] And therefore all locutions like "God cannot make the contrary of what he has willed to make," although said without qualification, are to be understood as compound statements. Thus they imply hypothetically that the Divine Will is directed to the opposite. However, if these compound statements are taken disjunctively, they are false because each of the disjuncts falls within the scope of God's absolute power and will.

Finally, just as God acts by will, so he also acts by intellect and knowledge, as has been shown above. [12] By similar reasoning, he cannot make what he did not foreknow that he would make, or omit to make what he did not foreknow that he would not make. Wherefore he is unable to make what he does not will to make or omit what he wills. And in the same way as in the last paragraph, each of two contradictory assertions is conceded and denied. As a result the just mentioned states of affairs are said to be impossible, not however absolutely, but conditionally and hypothetically.

Notes

1. Chap. 7.
2. Chap. 16.
3. Chap. 17, II *Physics,* I, 6.
4. See above, "Are Those Things Which Are Impossible in Nature Possible for God?" Selection 4.
5. Chap. 13.
6. For a treatment of a related issue, see below, William of Ockham, "God's Causality," Selection 27.
7. Chap. 23.
8. Chap. 80.
9. Bk. I, chap. 95.
10. Bk. I, chap. 82.
11. Chap. 81. Absolute necessity is the necessity which is determined by the nature of the thing in question. "A number must be odd or even," hypothetical necessity is the necessity of an "If . . . then . . ." assertion. "If Socrates is sitting, he cannot walk." St. Thomas argues that God is bound by absolute necessity with respect to his own being, but only by hypothetical necessity with respect to creatures. For discussion of a related issue see below, William of Ockham. "God's Absolute and Ordained Power," Selection 11.
12. Chap. 24.

9

On Divine Omnipotence

ST. PETER DAMIAN

To Dom. Desiderius, Most Reverend Rector of the Monastery at Monte Cassino, and to all the Holy Brotherhood, Peter, monk and sinner, sends the Kiss of Peace in the Holy Spirit. . . .

I. As you may remember, we were once discussing at supper an informal remark of the Blessed Jerome. "Fearlessly, I say," he said, "that although God can do all things, he is not able to restore a virgin after her ruin. He is certainly able to free her from punishment, but he cannot restore a woman who has been contaminated to her pedestal." . . .

I confess that this remark has never pleased me. I do not attend to him who said it, but to what is said. Surely it appears excessively ignoble to attribute an impossibility to him who is able to do all things so lightly, unless it be ascribed with a mystical meaning by a higher intelligence. On the contrary, you replied: "What Jerome said is reasonable and sound enough. Obviously, God cannot restore a virgin after she has been ruined."

Then when you had covered much ground in lengthy and tedious arguments, you were led to this closing of your case: "Nothing is impossible to God except because he does not will it." To this I reply: "If God can do none of those things which he does not will, he does nothing except what he wills. Therefore, he is not able to do anything whatever which he does not do. As I freely admit, the consequence of

Selections from *De Divina Omnipotentia etc.*, J. P. Migne, *Patrologia Latina*, Vol. 145, Cols. 595–622. Translated by Linwood Urban.

your position is that God does not make it rain today because he is not able, that he does not heal the sick because he is not able, that he does not strike down the unjust because he is not able, and that he does not deliver the saints from the latter's oppression because he is not able. These and many other things God does not do because he does not will them. And because he does not will them, he is not able to do them. It follows, therefore, that whatever God does not do he is in no way able to do.''

Clearly this conclusion seems so absurd, so ridiculous as to be in no way consistent with an omnipotent God, nor does it even appear consistent with human frailty. Many are the deeds which we do not do and yet are able to do. Therefore, when we meet in the Scripture one of the following passages, we ought to receive it in a mystical and allegorical way, rather than to interpret it recklessly and without restraint in a literal manner. Such is the passage in which Lot, who was approaching Segor, is addressed by an Angel. "Make haste," he said, "and escape to that place, because I will not be able to do anything before you have arrived there" (*Genesis* 45:22). And "It grieves me to have made man" (*Genesis* 6:6). And likewise, "Because God foresees the future, he ought to be touched inwardly with sadness of heart''; and many other similar passages.

Therefore, if such statements appear in the divine pages, they ought not to be published far and wide quickly, recklessly, and presumptuously to the shameless, but rather they ought to be interpreted with the disciplined constraint of sober learning. If it is spread abroad among the vulgar that God is impotent with respect to anything (which ought never to be said), the uneducated common man is confounded; and unless great acuity of mind is employed, the Christian faith is perturbed.

For the same reason that it is said that God cannot do something, it can also be said that he is ignorant of some matters. Since he cannot do anything which is evil, he does not know how to do it. Therefore, it is not possible for him either to think evil, or to swear falsely, or to do anything which is bad in spite of the fact that the Prophet says: "I have formed light and created darkness, making peace and creating evil" (*Isaiah* 45:7). . . .

The foregoing condition ought not to be attributed to God's ignorance
or to an impossibility, but to the rectitude of his eternal will. It is correctly said that he does not know evil because he does not will it, and
hence that he cannot do anything which is evil. Nevertheless, whatever he wills, he is undoubtedly also able to perform, as is attested by
Scripture: "You, the Master of power, judge with tranquility, and
treat us with great respect. For power is yours when you will" (*Wisdom of Solomon* 12:18).

II. Obviously the will of God is the cause of the existence of all things
whether visible or invisible. Just as the form of each of the species antecedently precedes its visible embodiments, so also the visible embodiments live essentially in the will of the Maker. "What comes to
be," says John, "had life in him" (*John* I:4). The same point is made
in the Apocalypse where the four and twenty elders testify by saying:
"Worthy are you, O Lord our God, to receive glory and honor and
power. Because you have created all things, and on account of your
will, they are and were created" (*Revelation* 4:11). Note, this passage
first says "because they are" and afterwards says "they were created." For before anything whatever can be embodied outwardly and
in public view, it must even now exist in the foreknowledge and counsel of the Creator. Just as the will of God is a cause so efficacious that
those things not yet constituted come to be for the first time, so also
that cause is so efficacious that the things which perish return to the
order of his being. " 'Have I any pleasure that the wicked shall die,'
says the Lord, 'And not that he shall be converted and live?' " (*Ezekiel*
18:23).

Let us return to the discussion of the previous question. "For what
reason is God unable to restore a virgin after defloration? Is he unable
to do something because he does not will it; and he does not will it
because it is evil, as has been said: 'To think evil, to swear falsely,
and to do anything unjust, God neither wills nor is capable?' " . . .

III. That a virgin may be restored to purity after her fall can be understood in two ways, either according to the degree of merit, or according to the integrity of her flesh. Let us see whether God has power
with respect to each of these alternatives. According to merit, the
Apostle calls the community of the faithful a virgin when he says to

the Corinthians: "For you are betrothed to one man so that I may present you a chaste virgin in Christ" (II *Corinthians* 11:2). Certainly there were not only virgins among the people of God, but also many married women, and those who after the loss of their virginity were continent. Through the Prophet, the Lord has said: "If a man dismiss his wife, and departing she takes another man, shall the first return to her again? Is not the woman called polluted and contaminated? You, therefore, are a whore with many lovers. Return unto me, says the Lord" (*Jeremiah* 3:1). This passage clearly implies a complete restitution by God as far as the quality of merit is concerned. The whore is made whole from corruption; from prostitution she is restored to virgin status. Again the same speaker says: "And I will remember your sins no more" (*Jeremiah* 31:34). . . .

Therefore, fearing no words to the contrary from contentious cavilers, I say plainly and steadfastly assert: "Because the omnipotent God can act to restore a polygamous woman to virgin status, so he can also restore the sign of incorruption in her flesh so that she is just as she was when she emerged from her mother's womb." I say this, not out of disrespect for the Blessed Jerome who is cited in sacred writings, but that I may refute by invincible reasons of faith those who on account of his words call God impotent.

IV. Finally, guided by your judicious sanctity, I see how an issue in our discussion ought to be treated, although many find my answer controversial. For they say: "If, as you assert, God is omnipotent with respect to everything, can he act in such a way that what is made should not have been made? Certainly he can destroy something which is made, but by no means does it seem possible to see by what power he can bring it about that what was made should not have been made. Obviously it is possible that Rome should exist as of now, and then later on that it should not exist, but no one believes that Rome could now not have been founded in ancient times."

In this matter I place myself under the guidance of God's inspiration. In the first place, I see that my speculations ought to be tempered by the words of Solomon: "Do not inquire into that which is too much for you, and do not search out that which is too high for you" (*Ecclesiastes* 3:22).

Next, it ought to be said that because what God does is something, what God does not do is nothing. Relevant passages from Scripture include the following: "All things were made by him, and without him was nothing made" (*John* 1:3); "He maketh those things which are future" (*Ecclesiastes* 3:11); "He who dwells in eternity has created all things at once" (*Ecclesiastes* 18:3); and the Apostle says: "He made those things which are not" (*Romans* 4:17). The following points are attested plainly by these passages: that God made things which are not, that he has not destroyed what was, that he has constituted the future, that he has not forgotten the past. Furthermore, it is wisely narrated that God has the power to destroy a thing so that he could produce something better. The world was deluged by water (*Genesis* 8). The Five Cities were burned by fire (*Wisdom of Solomon* 10:6). By these actions he certainly took away their being and future being, yet by no means did he take away their having been.

However, as regards the merit of the depraved men who were destroyed in these catastrophes, if you study the matter with intelligence, you must see that since they were vain and inane sheep, and since they had no merit, they tended not to being, but to non-being. It is on this account that the Spirit tenderly laments them. The Scripture testifies: "Our life is short," say such men, "and tedious, and in the death of a man there is no remedy; neither has there been any man known to have returned from the grave. For we are born from nothing; and we shall be hereafter as though we had never been" (*Widsom of Solomon* 2:1f). "We shall be," say they, "as if we had never been," because although they seem to exist at present, they tend rather to nothingness than to true being. " 'I,' " he says " 'am He Who Is;' and say this to the children of Israel: 'He Who Is has sent me to you' " (*Exodus* 3:14). Therefore, for the one who departs from Him Who truly Is, it follows necessarily that he does not have being because he tends toward nothingness. . . .

Countless similar passages are found in Scripture, in which impious men either are compared to most miserable and most vile things, or are even now said to be nothing, although they seem to have a potentiality for being.

XV. Therefore, when the question is put: "In what way can God act so that what came about should not have come about?", the Brother of sound faith ought to answer: "If what came about was evil, it was not something, but rather nothing. Furthermore, it ought to be said not to have been, because it did not have the wherewithall for existing since the Creator of all things has not commanded it to exist. However, if what came about was good, God certainly created it." "He spoke and they were made; he commanded and they were created" (*Psalms* 33:6 and 148:5). "All things were made by him, and without him was not anything made" (*John* 1:3).

Similarly the following question is put: "How is God able to make it so that what was made was not made?" And if it is asked "Can God act so that what he himself did he did not do?", as surely can it also be said "What God has made, he did not make."

Despicable is he who makes such assertions and not worthy of a response, but he is rather fit for the branding iron. Yet these calumnies ought to be committed to memory in order to refute the wicked, which the passages cited above amply do. These we omit here in order to proceed briefly lest excessive care in narration generate tediousness of style. We propose to write a letter not a book.

Among the many other things which we discussed, this one is easily called to mind. Since every ability is coeternal to God who is the Creator of all things, just as all possible things are known to him, so every time, past as well as present and future, is included in the scope of his wisdom. He directs and creates perpetually so that nothing new can ever be added to his being, nor can anything be subtracted from him at a later time. Yet, what is that strength, that power by which God is able to do everything? What is that wisdom by which he knows all things? We shall ask the Apostle. "Christ," he says, "is the power of God and the wisdom of God" (I *Corinthians* 1:24). Here surely is true eternity. Here is true immortality. Here now is that eternity which never changes. Here is that everlasting present and that contemporaneity which is fixed perpetually by such stability that he does not know how to change, much less change himself in the past in any way. Therefore, in order to overcome the impudence of those sarcastic men to whom the solution of this problem given above is not satisfactory, we can properly say that God can so act in his invariable and most constant everlastingness that what had been done in our transient state of affairs was not done. So we say: "Surely God *can* bring it about that Rome which was founded in ancient times was not founded." The assertion "surely he *can do* it" is said consistently in the present tense as far as the changeless eternity of the omnipotent God is concerned; but with respect to us, where is continual mobility and perpetual change, we more naturally say "He *could have* done so," as is customary. The assertion "God can so act that Rome was not founded" is to be understood as regards him for whom "is no change nor shadow of turning" (*James* 1:17). Yet surely for us the assertion means "God was able." As far as his eternity is concerned, whatever God could have done, even now he can do. His present is never turned into his past, nor his today into tomorrow, nor is he changed in anything by the circumstances of time; but he always is what he is. Therefore, whatever he is, he always is. On account of this fact, we can correctly say: "God *could* have made it so that Rome which was created in the past should not have been created." Nonetheless, we can also consistently say: "God *now has* the power to act so that Rome after it was made should also not have been made." "He *was able*" according to our way of speaking. "He *is able*" according to himself. That same power which God had before Rome was created, he preserves always immutable and unchanging according to his eternity. Furthermore, we can also say the same concerning anything whatever. Because God could have done it, we can also say that God can do it because his power, which for him is everywhere coeternal, is always fixed and immobile. . . .

That power, therefore, which God then had is neither changed nor given up, but just as he himself always is what he is, so his power is not able to be changed. He is the one who through the Prophet said: "I am God, and I do not change" (*Malachi* 3:6). And in the Gospel he said: "Before Abraham was, I am" (*John* 8:56). He does not change, as seems to be our state of affairs, from future existence to present existence, or from present existence into past existence; but he is always the same and always is what he was.

Therefore, just as God is always one and the same and is always indefectible and intransitive, so for him all things are possible. And as we can truly say, without the least contradiction, that because God now and always is what he was before all ages, so we can just as surely say that because God now and always is, he is able to do now what he was able to do before all ages. Therefore, if God can do all things which from the beginning he was able to do before all ages, so that what now is might have been as nothing, he is now able to act so that a created thing should be trifling.

His power is therefore fixed and eternal, so that whatever at one time he was able to do, he is always able to do. Neither does his eternity contain any place for vicissitude or variation of time. But just as he always is the same which he was in the beginning, so also he is able to do the whole of what he was able to do before all ages.

The conclusions of these disputed propositions ought to be stated thus:

1) If every power is coeternal with God, God is able to make it so that what was done was not done.
2) But every power is coeternal with God.
3) Therefore, God can make it so that what was done was not done.

It ought to be steadfastly and faithfully maintained that because God is said to be omnipotent, he has complete and entire control over all things, both those which were made and which were not made. This passage from the *Book of Esther* is placed as a sacred seal at the conclusion of this little work.

> O Lord, King Omnipotent, all things are placed together in your power, and there is no one who is able to resist your will. . . . For you have made heaven and earth and whatever is contained in the circle of the heavens. You are Lord of all things, nor is there anyone who can resist your Majesty (*Esther* 13:9–11).

10

Whether God Can Make the Past Not To Have Been?

ST. THOMAS AQUINAS

Objection 1. It seems that God can make the past not to have been. For what is impossible in itself is much more impossible than that which is impossible accidentally. But God can do what is impossible in itself, as to give sight to the blind, or to raise the dead. Therefore, all the more can He do what is impossible accidentally. Now for the past not have been is impossible accidentally: thus, for Socrates not to be running is accidentally impossible, from the fact that his running is a thing of the past. Therefore God can make the past not to have been.

Obj. 2. Further, what God could do, He can do now, since His power is not lessened. But God could have effected, before Socrates ran, that he should not run. Therefore, after Socrates has run, God could bring it about that he had not run.

Obj. 3. Further, charity is a more excellent virtue than virginity. But God can restore charity that is lost: therefore also lost virginity. Therefore He can bring it about that a person who has lost her virginity did not lose it.

On the contrary, Jerome says: *Although God can do all things, He cannot bring it about that a woman who was seduced was not se-*

Summa Theologica, I, q. 25, a. 4. From *The Basic Writings of Saint Thomas Aquinas,* edited and annotated by Anton C. Pegis, New York, Random House, 1945, Vol. I., pp. 265f. Reprinted with the permission of Random House, Inc.

duced.[1] Therefore, for the same reason, He cannot bring it about that anything else which is past should not have been.

I answer that, As was said above, nothing that implies a contradiction falls under the scope of God's omnipotence.[2] Now that the past should not have been implies a contradiction. For just as it implies a contradiction to say that Socrates is sitting and not sitting, so does it to say that he sat and did not sit. But to say that he did sit is to say that it happened in the past. To say that he did not sit is to say that it did not happen. Whence, that the past should not have been, does not come under the scope of divine power. This is what Augustine means when he says: *Whosoever says, If God is almighty, let Him make what is done as if it were not done, does not see that this is to say: If God is almighty let Him effect that what is true, by the very fact that it is true, be false.*[3] And the Philosopher says: *Of this one thing alone is God deprived—namely, to make undone the things that have been done.*[4]

Reply Obj. 1. Although it is accidentally impossible for the past not to have been, if one considers the past thing itself (as, for instance, the running of Socrates), nevertheless, if the past thing is considered as past, that it should not have been is impossible, not only in itself, but absolutely, since it implies a contradiction. Thus, it is more impossible than the raising of the dead, in which there is nothing contradictory, because this is reckoned impossible in reference to some power, that is to say, some natural power; for such impossible things do come beneath the scope of divine power.

Reply Obj. 2. As God, in accordance with the perfection of the divine power, can do all things, and yet some things are not subject to His power, because they fall short of being possible; so, also, if we consider the immutability of the divine power, whatever God could do, He can do now. Some things, however, were at one time in the realm of possibility, while they were yet to be done, which now fall short of being possible, since they have been done. So God is said not to be able to do them because they themselves cannot be done.

Reply Obj. 3. God can remove all corruption of the mind and body from a woman who has been seduced; but the fact that she had been seduced cannot be removed from her. In the same way, it is impossible that the fact of having sinned and lost charity can be removed from the sinner.

Notes

1. *Epist.* XXII (PL 22, 397).
2. A. 3; q. 7, a. 2, ad 1.
3. *Contra Faust.*, XXV, 5(PL 42, 481).
4. *Eth.*, VI, 2 (1139b 10).

11

God's Absolute and Ordained Power

WILLIAM OF OCKHAM

I say that God is able to do some things by his ordained power and some things by his absolute power. This distinction is not to be taken to mean that there are really two powers in God, one of which is the ordained power, the other the absolute, because the power in God directed toward things outside himself is one and that power is himself in every way. Nor should the distinction be so understood that God can do some things ordinately and some absolutely and not ordinately; for God can do nothing inordinately. Rather it is to be understood that his power to do something is sometimes to be accepted according to the laws which he has ordained and instituted; and in this way God is said to be able to act by his ordained power. Alternatively his power means his ability to do everything which does not include a contradiction, whether God has ordained that it should be done or not, because God can do many things which he does not will to do, according to the Master of the Sentences [Peter Lombard], book one, distinction forty-three; and this is called his power by his absolute power.

From William of Ockham, *Quodlibeta Septem,* Strasbourg, 1491. (Reprinted Louvain, 1962), VI, q. 1. Translated by Linwood Urban.

AN OVERVIEW OF THE ISSUES

12

Omnipotence

J. L. MACKIE

I. Introduction

I propose to discuss what meaning can be given to the term "omnipotent," and whether there is one or more than one defensible concept of an omnipotent being, where "defensible" means both that the concept is internally coherent and that we could have some reasonable ground for asserting that there is such a being.

There is one sort of meaning which I shall dismiss at once. In recent years it has often been suggested that religious language should be interpreted not as having descriptive meaning, not as making literal claims about existence, but rather as having a special sort of meaning, perhaps expressive of some feeling or attitude, perhaps an appropriate accompaniment to certain activities. An older variant of this view is that epithets applied to God are to be taken in a merely honorific sense, not as making any positive claims about properties possessed by God. It is clear that if the word "omnipotent" were taken in any of these ways, there could, without any doubt or question, be an omnipotent being; there could be something to which someone might adopt whatever attitude we propose that "omnipotent" should express. But it is equally clear that this is trivial and of no theological interest.

I shall also dismiss a rather more subtle suggestion which, I believe, comes to the same thing in the end. A philosopher influenced by Wittgenstein might say that there are many language games, each of

This article first appeared in *Sophia*, 1, 2, 1962. Reprinted with the permission of *Sophia* and the author, who has made a few changes in the text.

them autonomous in the sense that it cannot be reduced to or translated without loss into any other. This would mean that such a language game, or any essential part of one, could not be criticised within any *other* language game, and since neither it nor any essential part of it could be criticised within this language game itself, it would follow that neither a language game nor any essential part of one could be criticised at all. Such a philosopher might say that "omnipotent" has its place within a religious or theological language game, that within the game it is applied descriptively to a being whose existence cannot be questioned within that game, and whose omnipotence is also an essential feature of that game. So within the religious language game it is impossible to question whether there can be an omnipotent being, and if we step outside the religious language game we automatically change the use, and so the meaning, of "omnipotent," and no answer that we then give is relevant to religion or theology.

I maintain, however, that this view is both false and pernicious; it would prevent any proper consideration of fundamental philosophical questions. Even if a certain use of a certain term is essential within a language game, we can ask from outside, about that game as a whole, what sorts of linguistic activity it comprises, and how it is related to the things that simply exist, to the facts that just are so.

For example, positional astronomy might be considered as a language game that speaks of stars, planets, and so on as located on the celestial sphere; within that language game it would be impossible to speak of one planet passing behind another, and it would be nonsensical to ask how big the sphere itself is; in this language game the question of radial distance does not arise. But of course we can characterise the language game itself as a two-dimensional description of what is really a three-dimensional situation, and as being an adequate description for some purposes but not for others.

Again, ethics might be considered as a language game within which such words as "right" and "wrong" are essential and within which they are used as descriptive and as prescriptive at the same time. Within the ethical language game it is as absurd to question whether anything is right or wrong as it is to ask whether to do what is wrong.

But this in no way precludes a philosophical enquiry about the status of ethics itself, and it is still open to a philosopher to argue that no objective quality is in itself prescriptive, that no simple facts command us to act in one way rather than another.

Or, to come back to a theological example, when Norman Malcolm argues (*Philosophical Review,* LXIX (1960), pp. 41–62) that a necessary being is both possible and essential within the theological language game, this in no way settles or precludes the philosophical question whether there is or can be, simply and absolutely, a necessary being.

I maintain, therefore, that there is a real question whether there can be an omnipotent being, a question which cannot be answered by merely describing the role of the word ''omnipotent'' in a certain languge game and which cannot be dismissed by arguing that the language game is autonomous. If this is so, then to refuse to discuss this real question and to attend solely to the role of the word within the language game would be to evade the philosophical issue, and to assert that all we *can* study is the role of the word in the language game would be to abandon the claim that this word can be used in an objectively descriptive way. That is why I say that this more subtle suggestion about the autonomy of language games comes to the same thing in the end as the simpler statement that the divine epithets, including ''omnipotent,'' can be used only in some expressive or honorific sense. But if this were so, the statement that there is, or can be, an omnipotent being would be of no philosophical or theological interest.

I also set aside any empirical study of the role of the term ''omnipotent'' within the actual body of religious usage. The findings of such a study would belong to history, not to philosophy or theology. They might indirectly throw light on the philosophical and theological questions, simply because what people have thought and believed may contain suggestions for the solution of our problem; but these would be no more than suggestions, they could have no authority. To work through them would be to take the long way round, and at the risk of being philosophically old-fashioned I prefer to tackle the problem more directly.

II. Analysis of the Concept of Omnipotence

1. *The definition of "omnipotent."*

I shall begin by trying to decide what would count as a concept of omnipotence, and shall approach this decision by setting upper and lower
limits to the concept.

A view that could conceivably be held is that "omnipotent" means
"able to do absolutely anything whatever," or (as Mr. Geach has put
it neatly in conversation) that "God is omnipotent" means that every
(affirmative) statement beginning "God can . . ." is true. In particular, this view would include the claim that an omnipotent being could
do things which are logically impossible. Now if anyone holds that
there is an omnipotent being in this sense, then he need never be dis-
turbed by any reasoning or any evidence, for if his omnipotent being
could do what is logically impossible, he could certainly exist, and
have any desired attributes, in defiance of every sort of contrary consideration. The view that there is an absolutely omnipotent being in
this sense stands, therefore, right outside the realm of rational enquiry and discussion; once held, it is so unassailable that it is a waste
of time to consider it further. We must set it aside, and we can do so
with the less reluctance because it is not, I believe, a theologically rep-
utable view. For our purposes, then, "omnipotence" will at any rate
mean something less than this.

On the other hand, "omnipotence" means something more than what
McTaggart (in *The Nature of Existence* Vol. II. p. 176) calls "supremacy"; McTaggart, laying down criteria which a being must satisfy if he is to be called God, says that he must be "supreme," that is
he "must be, at least, much more powerful than any other self, and so
powerful that his volition can affect profoundly all that exists." As
McTaggart says, to satisfy this requirement is not to be omnipotent;
whatever "omnipotent" means, it must mean more than this.

A satisfactory definition then must lie somewhere between these
limits, and we might suggest that "God is omnipotent" means that
God can do anything that is logically possible. However, we may not
wish to confine God's power to *doing,* to actions in any narrow sense,

and so we might say rather "do or make to be" and we might take this to include not-doing and not-making-to-be. But this is still not quite right. "God is omnipotent" cannot imply that God could make it to be that X wherever X itself is logically possible, for it might be that while X itself was logically possible, making-it-to-be-that-X was logically impossible. It is logically possible that the law of contradiction should hold; but it is logically impossible to *make* it hold. It is logically possible that there should be a thing that is not made to be; but it is logically impossible to make such a thing to be. So omnipotence includes the power to make X to be only where there is no contradiction *either* in X itself *or* in making X to be.

In support of this definition it could be pointed out that the restrictions of omnipotence so far introduced are really not restrictions at all. A logical contradiction is not a state of affairs which it is supremely difficult to produce, but only a form of words which fails to describe any state of affairs. So to say, as we are now saying, that "God is omnipotent" means "God can do or make to be X, for any X provided that doing X or making X to be is not logically impossible" would be to say that if God is omnipotent every coherently describable activity or production is within his power.

However, a further restriction may be needed. Does "God is omnipotent" entail "God can make it to be that X in all cases where making-it-to-be-that-X involves no contradiction, even where *God's-* making-it-to-be-that-X *would* involve a contradiction?

I shall show later that there are such cases. If, therefore, we said that "God is omnipotent" does entail this, we should have to say that "God is omnipotent" is false, for it would entail that God can make it to be that X even in those real cases where God's-making-it-to-be-that-X is logically impossible. On the other hand, if we say that "God is omnipotent" does not entail this, but entails only that God can make it to be that X in all cases where God's-making-it-to-be-that-X involves no contradiction, we are in danger of writing down unduly the claim made by the term "omnipotent." On this interpretation, any thing would be omnipotent if it could do all that it was logically possible for that thing to do. That is, a thing's being omnipotent would mean only that practical possibility, for that thing, coincided with logical possibility and this might hold where both sorts of possibility were extremely limited.

However, if we are not to falsify at once the claim that God is omnipotent, we must adopt this second alternative and say that God's omnipotence includes only the power to make it to be that X wherever God's making it to be that X involves no contradiction. Let us see what this restriction means, that is, in what ways God's-making-it-to-be-that-X could be contradictory although making-it-to-be-that-X would not in itself be contradictory.

First, there are paradoxical examples: that God is not making anything to be is logically possible, and perhaps making-it-to-be-that-God-is-not-making-anything-to-be is logically possible; but it is logically impossible that God should be making it to be that God is not making anything to be. But we need not waste time on such puzzles as this.

Secondly, it may be argued that since God is good, it is logically impossible for him to bring about something evil, and in general that there are aspects of God's nature which are incompatible with *his* making it to be that X in many cases where making-it-to-be-that-X is in itself logically possible. If, however, we included here contingent aspects (if there are any) of God's nature, we should fall into the trap mentioned above, we should have so written down the claim made by the term "omnipotent" that anything at all might be omnipotent, since anything at all might be able to do anything that was compatible with its contingent nature. To keep any force in the term "omnipotent," we must therefore include here only logically necessary aspects of God's nature.

Summing up, then, we must say that God's omnipotence includes only the power to make it to be that X in all cases where X, and making-it-to-be-that-X, are logically possible and where God's-making-it-to-be-that-X is neither paradoxical nor incompatible with logically necessary aspects of God's nature.

2. *Ethical limitations of omnipotence*

Does this principle support the view that if God is good as well as omnipotent he may be *unable* to bring about what is evil? It does so only if we make certain further assumptions.

First, we should have to assume that God's being good was a logically necessary aspect of his nature, not a contingent one. Secondly, we should have to assume that bringing about evil was logically incompatible with being (wholly) good. These two assumptions would be sufficent both to show that God is unable to bring about evil and to allow that despite this inability he may nevertheless be omnipotent. If, however, it were a contingent fact that things of such-and-such sorts are evil, we should have to allow that an omnipotent God would be able to bring these things about, provided that he also made them not to be evil. On the other hand if the evilness of things with such-and-such features were logically necessary the conclusion would be that a necessarily good God is unable to bring about things of the sorts that are evil, and yet that he may, despite this inability, be omnipotent in accordance with our definition.

3. *The meaning of "power"*

I believe that the notion of "power," as it is used in the concept of omnipotence, can be made more precise, and its implications displayed more clearly, if we draw an analogy with the notion of legal power; but I am, of course, aware of the danger of pressing an analogy too far.

We might use the phrase "legal power" in a purely negative sense, in which a man has a legal power to do something if the law does not prevent him from doing it. But this would be better called a legal right to use some power of another sort. A man has a legal power in a positive sense if and only if the law positively enables him to do something which he could not otherwise do. It is in this sense that a man may have a legal power to bequeath property; this power presupposes a law that gives effect to a man's wishes when he is dead. Now for the concept of omnipotence we require the notion of positive power, not merely that of negative power, of something's not being forbidden or prevented, and the legal analogy suggests that a positive power always rests upon a law of some kind, each exercise of the power being an application of the corresponding law.

Thus in the causal realm a man has the power to raise his arm if there is a set of causal laws which, along with certain facts, enable him to do this; the laws and facts together constitute a derivative law or lawlike entity of which his raising his arm on any occasion is an application; whenever he chooses to raise his arm, it is raised. I need not enter into the disputed question whether this is all that is meant by saying that he *can* raise his arm: I am concerned with the notion of power, not with that of freedom. It is true that with regard to voluntary bodily movements we do not usually pay attention to the laws they exemplify, and we do not use the derivative law-like statement as a recipe; but that there is such an entity is brought out by contrast with the lack of power when the arm is paralyzed, and it is plain that remoter powers, like an angler's power to pull in a fish, rest in this way on causal laws.

In general, then, where a person A has the power to make it to be that X, we can assert the non-material conditional that if A so chooses it is or will be that X, and such a non-material conditional is sustained by some law or set of laws (cf. my note on "The Sustaining of Counterfactuals" in *Aust. Jnl. of Philosophy* Dec. 1961, and also pp. 114–19 of my *Truth, Probability, and Paradox* (Oxford, 1973)). The powers that we ordinarily speak of are sustained by causal laws together with structural facts. But a power would not exist if there were anything to interfere with it: a man has not the power to raise even a healthy arm if it is tied down. Therefore any ordinary power rests not only on the laws and facts that positively enable its exercise but also on the non-interference of all other laws and facts.

4. *The placing of omnipotence in relation to causal law.*

Powers being thus sustained by laws and facts, the question arises where we are to place God's powers, if God is omnipotent, in relation to causal laws. I think it would be generally agreed that God's powers are not sustained, like ordinary powers, by the whole system of causal laws and structural facts; it would be felt that a power thus sustained, however extensive, would fall far below omnipotence.

We might, indeed, try to establish this view by the following argument, which I shall refer to as "Argument A."

Suppose that not-X is a causal law. Then X is logically possible, making-it-to-be-that-X is logically possible, and God's-making-it-to-be-that-X is neither paradoxical nor incompatible with any logically necessary aspects of God's nature. Hence, by our definition of omnipotence, it follows that an omnipotent God has the power to make it to be that X. Thus he has power over the causal law not-X, so that his powers cannot be sustained by and relative to the actual system of causal laws.

This argument might, however, be challenged by someone who denies that making-it-to-be-that-X is logically possible, if not-X is a causal law. He might argue that if not-X is a causal law, X would also, if it held, have the status of a causal law, and that a causal law cannot be made to be so. However, it is clearly possible to make a derivative causal law hold by using a more fundamental law. I conclude that this objection must be dismissed, and that Argument A is so far unshaken.

But this suggests that God's-making-it-to-be-X would be an application of some more fundamental causal law. That is, God's power would rest on some structural fact about God, or about God and all other things, together with a fundamental causal law.

Can argument A be used to refute this, to show that an omnipotent God has power over *any* causal law, and therefore that his power is not sustained by any causal law, however fundamental? I think not. For suppose that there were a fundamental causal law Y, on which together with certain structural facts, God's powers depended. Now if God made it to be that Y, there would be a vicious circularity, so it is logically impossible that God should make it to be that Y. And it would generate a paradox if God could make it to be that not-Y. Thus on this supposition God's having power over Y would be logically impossible, and therefore, by our definition, his lack of this power is not a departure from omnipotence.

What this shows, in fact, is that Argument A simply does not apply to any law on which God's power depends, and so that to use this argument to show that God's power does not depend on causal law begs the question. For all that can be shown by reference to our definition, then, omnipotent power could be sustained by a set of one or more fundamental causal laws. All that Argument A shows is that no causal laws, other than those on which the omnipotent power depends, can be fundamental. If God is omnipotent, he must have power over all laws other than those which sustain his power.

This discussion has shown only that omnipotence *can* be thus placed as dependent on fundamental causal laws. For all that has been said, it could equally well be placed above all causal laws. But if it were, what kind of law would sustain it? There are two possibilities, that it is sustained by a logically necessary law, and that it is sustained by some law which, though not logically necessary, is in some way superior to causal law. But either of these involves difficulties. I find it very hard to see how a logically necessary law could sustain a positive power of the kind required. And a law that is contingent and yet supra-causal is a sheer mystery: we simply do not know what it could be. Besides, if there is any objection to placing God's power below causal law, would not there be the same objection to placing it below any contingent law?

For the present, however, all three possibilities may be left open. What I have argued is this. If the concept of omnipotence is to fall within the realm of rational enquiry and discussion omnipotence *must* be restricted in the ways outlined; and when it is so restricted, to exclude logically impossible powers, it may be placed either above or below fundamental causal laws.

III. Problems

1. *The paradox of omnipotence.*

In an earlier article ("Evil and Omnipotence," *Mind,* LXIV (1955), pp. 200–212) I stated a "paradox of omnipotence" in these words: "Can an omnipotent being make things which he cannot subsequently control? Or, what is practically equivalent to this, can an omnipotent being make rules which then bind himself?" At that time, I thought that these questions could not be answered satisfactorily either in the affirmative or in the negative, that either answer would commit one to denying that the being in question was omnipotent. I argued that we should distinguish various orders of omnipotence. First order omnipotence would be unlimited power to act, second order omnipotence would be unlimited power to determine what powers to act things should have. (And so on, if you wish.) But then if God has second order omnipotence he may so use it as to give certain things power to act independently of his own power to act, so that he would not have first order omnipotence. I argued, that is, that omnipotences of different orders could be brought into conflict with each other, and that no being, therefore, could have omnipotence of all orders at once.

Subsequent discussion has, I think, shown that my presentation of this problem was wrong. It has been argued (B. Mayo, *Mind,* LXX (1961), pp. 249–250) that since "things which an omnipotent being cannot control" is a self-contradictory phrase, to make such things is logically impossible, and "failure to bring about logical impossibilities does not count against omnipotence." This seems to show that, given the definition of omnipotence that we have been using, the negative answer to the paradox-questions is satisfactory.

I should be happier with this solution if there did not seem to be an equally plausible defence of the affirmative answer. One could argue as follows: if an omnipotent being makes it that certain things are independent, then to control these things is to control things that are omnipotently-made-uncontrollable, and this is logically impossible. Hence, by our definition, even an omnipotent being is unable to control such things, and failure to control them does not count against omnipotence. Thus it would seem that an omnipotent being *can* make things that he cannot control. Thus the paradox is, in a way, reinstated. It is not, as I said in 1955, that neither the affirmative nor the negative answer to the paradox-question is satisfactory. The trouble is rather that when we have restricted omnipotence in the way that we must restrict it if it is to be discussable, *both* answers become satisfactory for similar reasons, and there is no way of choosing between them ("Evil and Omnipotence," *Mind,* LXIV (1955), pp. 200-212). We have here something analogous to what I classified as truth-teller variants of the well-known logical paradoxes in *Truth, Probability, and Paradox,* pp. 240–1, 260–1, and 298.

We can put this problem in terms of the various orders of omnipotence. If we start by saying that God has first order omnipotence, then we infer that he can control anything, and hence that his second order omnipotence, his power to assign first order powers, does not enable him to assign a power that would infringe his first order omnipotence, and yet it still is second order omnipotence. But if instead we start by saying that God has second order omnipotence, we infer that he can assign first order powers that limit his own, but that his first order powers thus limited can still count as omnipotence.

There is, however, a further comment that can be made. Even if we argue in the second way, in favour of an affirmative answer to the paradox-question, the conclusion is only that God can make beings which are beyond control by his first order power. Their independence, being constituted by an exercise of second order power, is still subject to this.

This comes out more clearly in terms of the other formulation of the question: can an omnipotent being bind himself? Our second line of argument suggests that his second order power can bind his first order power (the latter remaining omnipotent none the less) but his second order power cannot bind *itself*.

If this is correct, then if we take "control" to include the exercise of second order powers, the case for a negative answer is the stronger: we can after all solve the paradox and say that an omnipotent being *cannot* make things that he cannot control. But I should like to note how this paradox came up in my discussion of the problem of evil. I was arguing that the solution of that problem which says that evil is due to human freewill can be maintained only on the assumption that God has made men so free that he *cannot* control their wills. Our present solution of the paradox of omnipotence would show that if God is omnipotent he cannot make men as free as this, and therefore, if the rest of my argument was sound, it would show that the problem of evil cannot be solved by reference to human freewill. (cf. my note on "Theism and Utopia" in *Philosophy,* April, 1962.)

2. *Does omnipotence entail omnificence?*

If there is an omnipotent being, is everything that happens his doing? Must he also be what we might call *omnificent?*

To show that he must, we might argue as follows. If God can make it to be that X, but it is that not-X, he has chosen to let it be that not-X, and therefore, he has made it to be that not-X. Anything that God could have made otherwise, but leaves as it is, he in effect makes as it is. Therefore, for all things that are in God's power, whichever way they are he has made them so. Of course, if we are using a restricted definition of omnipotence we must use a similarly restricted definition of omnificence, but as long as the terms are correspondingly interpreted it will follow that if God is omnipotent he is also omnificent.

Against this, it may be argued that there is a clear everyday distinction between positively bringing something about and merely letting it happen when we could have prevented it. To let a person die whom we could have rescued is not the same as killing him. Some moralists have held that the two are equally reprehensible, that letting something happen is tantamount to bringing it about. But this is a moral judgment, it expresses a decision to regard the two actions alike, it cannot deny the simple fact that in themselves, prior to any moral judgment, they are different.

This must, indeed, be admitted as an everyday distinction, but we can ask on what ground the distinction rests. If we bring something about, we exert effort, but if we merely allow it to happen we do not, in fact we spare ourselves the effort it would have cost to prevent it. Also, allowing something to happen, even if we know that it will, is often associated with some degree of inadvertence; bringing something about commonly involves more conscious attention. But the more completely the matter is within our power, the less clear does the first ground of distinction become. If it is something that we can either bring about or prevent with negligible effort, allowing it to happen is less clearly differentiated from bringing it about. And similarly the more completely the matter is within our knowledge, the less clear does the second ground of distinction become; if it is something we cannot help attending to, allowing it to happen cannot be marked off by the criterion of inadvertence. It seems, then, that as power and knowledge increase, this everyday distinction fades out, and for a being with unlimited power and unlimited vision it would not hold at all.

If so, our counter-argument fails, and we return to our original conclusion that an omnipotent being would also be omnificent. This need not be taken to mean that because God does everything no-one else, and nothing else, does anything. There is nothing in the argument to deny that a man does what we ordinarily take him as doing; it only adds that God also does these same individual acts. It would be a corollary of this that God is responsible for everything that occurs, though this need not be taken to exclude human responsibility. This corollary would have an important bearing on the problem of evil.

3. *Grounds for saying that there is an omnipotent being.*

So far I have been merely examining concepts of omnipotence, seeing whether one or more of these is defensible, and what limitations we can or must admit to the power of a being described as omnipotent. At the end of Section II I left open the three possibilities, that omnipotence is sustained by fundamental causal laws, that it is sustained by a logically necessary law, and that it is sustained by some law intermediate in status between these. If we now ask what sorts of reason there could be for asserting that there is an omnipotent being, we can relate these sorts of reason to the choice between these three possibilities.

First, there could conceivably be scientific evidence for omnificence. It is conceivable that we should learn, by the methods of empirical science, that certain causal laws were fundamental and that all other laws and facts were consequences of the fundamental laws along with the choices of and structural facts about a certain being. That is, there could be evidence of an empirical sort for an omnificent—and *a fortiori* omnipotent—being whose power was sustained by fundamental causal laws. There are, indeed, difficulties in this suggestion, but there is no point in pursuing them, because it is surely obvious that we do not actually possess evidence of this sort. And, as I shall argue, it is only by evidence of this sort that we could support the view that there is an omnipotent being whose power is sustained by causal laws.

Secondly, we could conceivably discover that it is logically necessary that God should exist and should be omnipotent. If we did establish this, presumably by some variant of the ontological argument, it is clear that the omnipotence thus established would be sustained by a logically necessary law. However, I think it is equally obvious that we are not in possession of any sound argument of this sort. This remains true despite recent work on the ontological argument by Alvin Plantinga in *The Nature of Necessity* (Oxford, 1974), pp. 196–221. See my paper, "The Riddle of Existence," *Aristotelian Society Supplementary Volume* XLX (1976).

Thirdly, it is conceivable that we could use some variant of the cosmological argument, arguing that things being as they are requires that something should make them to be so, and that while particular facts are made to be so by other particular facts in conjunction with causal laws, there must be something that makes those other facts, and the causal laws, to be so. And so on. Now anyone who uses an argument of this sort finds something unsatisfactory in the self-subsistence of ordinary contingent facts. He could, therefore, not consistently accept, as the final answer to the series of questions of the form "What makes it to be that X?", a structural fact along with a fundamental but contingent causal law which together entail God's omnipotence. Anyone who uses an argument of this sort can consistently be satisfied only with an account of God's omnipotence as sustained by something more necessary than causal laws. And when we have rejected the other two conceivable reasons for holding that there is an omnipotent being, this, as far as I can see, is the only remaining possibility.

It is true that this argument does not commit its user to the view that God's omnipotence is logically necessary, but only to the view that it is necessary in whatever sense being necessary contrasts with the contingency that he finds unsatisfactory in a self-subsistent contingent fact. But until someone can explain further what this contingency is, and therefore what non-logical necessity would make up for it, this remains an empty possibility.

I conclude, then, that the only ground which it might be plausible to say that we have for asserting that there is an omnipotent being would lead to the view that his omnipotence is sustained by something superior to a causal law. But I confess that I am quite unable to see *either* how a logically necessary law could sustain positive powers of the kind required for the notion of omnipotence, *or* what other sort of necessity there could be that is not logical necessity and yet is above causal law. It seems to me that the notion of omnipotence acquires its real force and the term "omnipotent" derives all its positive meaning for us, from an interpretation in terms of powers sustained by causal law, but that although this interpretation is consistent with our definition of omnipotence it is not consistent with any reason that we can plausibly claim to have for saying that there is an omnipotent being.

IV. Conclusion

This survey as a whole indicates that such difficulties as there are in the concept of omnipotence are peripheral rather than central. Once we have decided that omnipotence is not to include the power to achieve logical impossibilities—and it must not include this, if it is to be discussable—there cannot be any contradiction within the concept itself, for we have so defined the concept that anything that turns out to be contradictory is not covered by it. The problems arise when we try to fill in this concept and to relate it to other concepts and to our reasons for applying it.

Problems on which I have touched are these. First, our definition leaves it open that omnipotent power may be sustained by causal law or by logically necessary law or by something between the two, and if we say that there is an omnipotent being we must choose somehow between these possibilities. Secondly, if we survey the possible grounds that we might have for saying that there is an omnipotent being, the only ground that seems at all plausible would indicate that omnipotence is sustained not by causal law but in some much more obscure way. Thirdly, there is the question whether an omnipotent being would have to be omnificent also, whether he would have to make to be everything that is. Fourthly, there is the paradox of omnipotence; it can perhaps be solved, but in a way that makes the problem of evil more acute. We could, of course, pursue much further questions about the problem of evil and about the relation between omnipotence and human freedom. A question on which I have not touched at all is whether omnipotence entails omniscience, and whether omniscience in turn raises further problems.

CAN IT BE PROVED THAT THERE IS BUT ONE OMNIPOTENT BEING?

13

The Unicity of God

DUNS SCOTUS

Natural reason cannot demonstrate [God's unicity] from omnipotence, it seems, for omnipotence—as Catholics conceive of it—cannot be proved from natural reason, as will be shown later; neither is it implied by the fact that [God] has infinite power.[1]

Nevertheless, if one accepts omnipotence on faith, then he can argue his thesis in this way. If A is omnipotent, A can make anything else be or not be. Hence, A could destroy B and thus render B incapable of doing anything. It follows then that B is not God.

Some claim this argument is invalid, since B is not an object of omnipotence, for the scope of omnipotence is the possible [i.e. something that can but need not exist]. B, however, is assumed to be just as necessary as A.

Consequently, the argument is rephrased, by interpreting Richard of St. Victor's reasoning in *De Trinitate* [I, chap. 25] as follows: Just as the Omnipotent by his will can produce anything possible, so he can impede or destroy every possible thing. But if A is omnipotent, A can will that everything other than himself exist, and thus by his own volition produce it in existence. It is not necessary, however, that B will all those things that A wills, for B's will is related only contingently to what A wills, just as A's will is so related to what B wills, assuming both to be God. But if B wills that none of those things exist, none will. Hence, if there were two omnipotent beings, each of them would

Translation and note by A. B. Wolter, from the Ordinatio I, distinction 2, nn. 178–81 (Vatican ed. vol. II, pp. 234–36).

render the other impotent, not by destroying the other, but by an act of nolition, preventing the existence of what the other wills to exist.

And if you were to say, arguing sophistically, that they voluntarily agree to act in unison by a pact, as it were, even though there be no need to do so, I still prove that neither will be omnipotent. For if A is omnipotent, A could produce everything possible by so willing it to exist, and thus B could produce nothing by his own volition. Consequently, B is not omnipotent. That this follows is clear from what was said [earlier, namely], that it is impossible for one and the same effect to have two total causes, for if it is completely caused by one, it is impossible that it should be caused by the other.

Notes

1. Infinite power, as the philosophers postulate it, implies only that God can do anything possible either directly or at least through the intermediacy of other creatures he has created. Catholics, says Scotus, hold that God can do immediately whatever he can do in cooperation with secondary or created causes. Confer A. B. Wolter, "The 'Theologism' of Duns Scotus," *Franciscan Studies* 7 (1947), 376–77, and *John Duns Scotus: God and Creatures* (transl. F. Alluntis and A. B. Wolter), Princeton University Press, 1975, pp. 162–63.

14

Reply to Duns Scotus

WILLIAM OF OCKHAM

Whether It Can Be Proved by Natural Reason That God Is One

An article of faith cannot be evidently proved; but that there is only one God is an article of faith; therefore, etc. . . .

Wherefore to the arguments of Scotus to the contrary I reply: . . . To the last (the seventh way), I say that it is not possible to demonstrate that God is omnipotent, but this is held by faith alone. I argue this: It is possible to say that the will of the one is naturally conformed to the other and concurs with it, and that whatever the one wills naturally, the other wills necessarily. Therefore, if *A* wills something to be, *B* is not able not to will it to be, or to will it not to be, because it can not be demonstrated that it wills that thing freely and contingently and indifferently. Therefore, it does not follow that *A* can make *B* powerless. . . .

Quodlibeta Septem, Strasbourg, 1491. (Reprinted Louvain, 1962), I, q. 1. Translated by Linwood Urban.

15

Some Omnipotent Beings

LOUIS WERNER

This is a limited defense of the claim that (1) there could be more than one omnipotent being (ob).[1,2] The defense is limited in three respects. First, it is a rebuttal of only a single argument against (1). The single argument is, however, the natural argument, or a version of the natural argument,[3] that leads to widespread doubt of (1).[4] Secondly, the statement of the rebuttal takes for granted the correctness of a certain approach to the paradox of the stone, a paradox that some persons take to show that there could not be even one ob. Indeed, the most important suggestion in the paper probably is that the question whether there could be a plurality of ob is apparently amenable to a treatment that is commonly recommended for the paradox of the stone. But because the relevant approach to that paradox is not defended at length here, one may say that I mainly seek to show, not that (1) is true, but that *if* there could be one ob despite the paradox of the stone, *then* there could be more that one ob despite the natural objection to this latter claim. Thirdly, I have no way to show that I have canvassed all of the objections to my central contention. I certainly feel there ought to be some convincing objection to it. Still, in a search for one, it should be kept in mind that I am at most defending the view that there could be, not the view that there probably are, two or more ob. (For simplicity's sake, I shall henceforth write as if we were concerned to determine only whether there could be two ob, and not whether there could be more than two.)

From *Crítica*, Vol. V, no. 14, 1971, pp. 55–69. Reprinted with the permission of *Crítica*, publication of the Instituto de Investigaciones Filosóficas of the Universidad Nacional Autónoma de México, and the author.

The Natural Argument

The natural argument against (1), or the version of that argument to be discussed here, rests heavily on the assumption that (if there were or could be two ob) the wills of two ob might conflict. On this supposition, the argument purports to reduce (1) to absurdity. One might try to put the argument thus:

Suppose

    (a)   there are two ob;
    (b)   if anything is an ob, its will cannot be frustrated;[5]
    (c)   if there are two ob, their wills may conflict.

Then

    (d)   unless (b) or (c) is false, (a) is false.

For

    if (by (c)) the wills of (say) x and y, may conflict, then the will of at least one of them might be frustrated; but (by (b)) the will of x (y) could not be frustrated, if x (y) were an ob. So, x (y) is not an ob.

For numerous reasons, however, this is not a valid *reductio* of (1). Most significantly at this point, (a) is not (1): (a) states that there are two ob, whereas (1) asserts that there could be two ob; to deny (a) is not to deny (1). Nevertheless, if the preceding argument were to yield the conclusion that (a) is not just false but is necessarily false, then the argument would demonstrate that (1) is false. But the argument does not entail that (a) is necessarily false. (a), (b), and (c) do entail, if you like, both (a) and not-(a) are true, and since it is necessarily false that (a) and not-(a) are both true, we may infer that it is necessarily true that some premise or other is false (because the conjunction of the premises is necessarily false). But this is not to say that the premises contain among themselves any particular member that is necessarily false, let alone that (a) is that premise or is such a premise.

One might, though, put the natural argument in this way:

Suppose

(1)   it is possible that there are (be) two ob;

(b')   it is necessarily true that if something is an ob, its will cannot be frustrated;[5]

(c')   it is necessarily true that if there are (were) two ob, their wills may (might) conflict.

Then

(d')   unless (b') or (c') is false, (1) is false.

For

if (in accord with (*c'*)) the wills of (say) *x* and *y* may conflict, then the will of at least one of them might be frustrated; *and* if (c') [that is, if it is necessarily true that if there are or were two ob their wills may or might conflict], then it is necessarily true that the will of at least one of them might be frustrated; *but* (by (b')) if something is an ob, its will cannot be frustrated; *so* it is necessarily true that at least one of the pair, *x* and *y,* is not an ob; so it is not possible that both *x* and *y* are (be) ob.

It is noteworthy that (c') differs from (c). With (c) and without (c') one could conclude (from (1) and (b')) that at least one of the pair, *x* and *y*, is not an ob, but one could not conclude that it is necessarily true that at least one of them is not an ob. The weaker of these two conclusions implies only that *x* and *y* are not ob, whereas the stronger implies that it is not possible that both *x* and *y* are (be) ob.

Four Replies

Despite the allure of the natural argument, at least four replies to it are available; one of these is, I think, especially interesting. First, one may simply say that the argument is not a conclusive argument against (1). For it is not at all plain why one should take the argument to be a *reductio* of (1), and not (say) a *reductio* of (c') or even of (b'). (b') may look analytic or at least indisputable at first glance; and at first glance (c') may look more plausible than (1). But if the natural argument is to be shown to deserve its popularity, the preferability of (c') and (b') over (1) will have to be demonstrated.

Secondly, of the only two arguments for (c') that have occurred to me, one is a *non sequitur* and the other begs the question. The former is that an ob presumably is an abstract entity, and thus presumably could not be distinguished from another ob by, say, spatio-temporal location; but there must be something that distinguishes one from the other, and this probably is the contents of their wills. There are obvious difficulties in this argument, but I want to state just one: the argument shows at most that the wills of two ob (would) have to be different (in at least one respect), and does not show that their wills (would) ever have to be in conflict or even that they may (or might) conflict. I shall leave the question-begging defense of (c') till later.

Thirdly, there is an independent argument to show that (c') is false. Let us make the traditional assumption[6] (among others) that an ob is, in one sense, necessarily omniscient: the assumption, that is, that (2) if (say) x is an ob, then it is necessarily true that x is omniscient. Now, if (2) is true, then it is necessarily true that (if there is an ob, x) x never wills anything that would require the frustration of the will of an ob. The reasoning is: if (2) is true, then it is necessarily true that x knows whether anything he might will would require the frustration of the will of an ob; also, if (2) is true, it is necessarily true that x knows it is logically impossible to frustrate the will of an ob; finally (—and not I hope, too controversially—), it is necessarily true that no one knowingly wills what he knows to be logically impossible.

Whatever is to be said about this argument against (c'), there is a fourth, and much more interesting, reply to the natural argument. This reply shares a presupposition with a familiar response to the paradox of the stone. The presupposition is (3) that an ob cannot do the logically impossible (*i.e.,* cannot bring it about that a self-contradiction be true), but that this inability does not detract from his omnipotence (*i.e.,* does not entail that the (putative) ob is not (or is not really) an ob). According to this reply: if there were two ob, their wills could conflict, but could conflict only in certain ways; furthermore, if their wills were to conflict in these certain ways, the resultant inefficacy of their wills would not detract from their omnipotence; lastly, the inability of their wills to conflict in other ways does not detract from their omnipotence.

More explicitly, it is suggested that two ob can have contrary wills but cannot have contradictory wills; that if they have contrary but not contradictory wills, neither can enact his will, but the reason why his will

is ineffective is *merely* that he has, *in effect,* willed the logically impossible; that the reason why they cannot have contradictory wills is
merely that it would be logically impossible for two ob to have contradictory wills.

Two beings have contrary wills, for our present purposes, just in case
(i) one wills that some proposition p be true and the other wills that
some other proposition r be true, (ii) it is not possible that both p and r
be true, (iii) it is possible that both p and r be false, and (iv) it is possible that both p and r fail (in Strawson's sense) to refer. Two beings
have contradictory wills, for our present purposes, just in case (i) one
wills that some proposition p be true and the other wills that some
other proposition r be true, (ii) it is not possible that both p and r be
true, (iii) it is *not* possible that both p and r be false (unless both fail to
refer, and unless failure of reference produces falsehood), and (iv) it is
not possible that both p and r fail to refer.

Suppose, next, the two ob were to have contrary wills. Each would, in
effect, be willing something that is logically impossible: namely,
something contrary to the will of an ob. For example, if one ob were
to will at some time (or perhaps timelessly) that, at time t, all physical
objects be red all over, but another ob were simultaneously (or timelessly) to will that, at t, all physical objects be blue all over, then neither would have his way. One ob would in effect be willing that, contrary to the will of an ob, every physical object be red all over at t,
whereas, the other ob would in effect be willing that, contrary to the
will of an ob, every physical object be blue all over at t. Although neither would have his way, it would not follow that each or either is not
an ob (if (3) is true).

Before considering questions about these remarks, and before going on
to discuss the impossibility of contradictory wills, we should pause to
look at two arguments that closely resemble the natural argument
against (1). Both differ from that argument in that they purport to
reduce to absurdity the proposition that there could be one ob. One of
them is, loosely stated, that the will of an ob might be inconsistent
with itself, and that therefore the will of even a solitary ob could be
frustrated. More strictly, this argument is:

Suppose

(1')   it is possible that there is (be) an ob;
(b')   it is necessarily true that if something is an ob, its will cannot be frustrated;
(c')   it is necessarily true that if there is (were) an ob, its will may (might) be inconsistent with itself.

Then

(d')   unless (b') or (c') is false, (1') is false.

This argument, like the natural argument against (1) is open to at least four replies. First, one may remark that, without further proof, the argument might with equal justice be taken as a *reductio* of (c') (if not of (b')). Secondly, one may reject arguments for (c'). Thirdly, one might argue, on independent grounds, that (c') is false. (Suppose again that (2) if (say) x is an ob, then it is necessarily true that x is omniscient. From this supposition, it may be argued that it is necessarily true that the will of an ob is always consistent with itself.) Fourthly, one may hold that an ob can will that contraries be true but cannot will that contradictories be true; that if he wills contraries, the reason why his will is not done is merely that, in effect, he wills the logically impossible; that the reason why he cannot will contradictories is merely that it would be logically impossible for an ob to do so.

(*Perhaps* we can imagine an ob who is somewhat forgetful. Picture him at t willing that p be true, and then observing that p is not (or does not become) true. He checks his diary, and discovers that before t he had willed that not-p be true. If, in the circumstances, he (perhaps justifiably) feels less than omnipotent, we should attribute his difficulty to his memory and not, for example, to a loss of strength or to increasing recalcitrance of the world external to him.)

Next, consider this argument:

Suppose

(1')   it is possible that there is (be) an ob;
(b')   it is necessarily true that if something is an ob, its will cannot be frustrated;

(c'')   if there could be an ob, there could be a stone too heavy for anyone to lift, for an ob could create such a stone.

Then

(d'')   unless (b') or (c'') is false, (l') is false

For

if there could be (as (l') and (c'') imply) a stone too heavy for anyone to
lift, then, contrary to (b'), the will of an ob might be frustrated; he
might will to lift that stone or such a stone, but if he willed this, his will
would be frustrated.

One well may reply to this that, if there were an ob, a stone too heavy
for anyone to lift would, *in effect,* be a stone too heavy for an ob to
lift; that a stone too heavy for an ob to lift is logically impossible; and
that it is compatible with omnipotence to be unable to create such a
stone.[7]

Now, having briefly displayed two arguments that resemble the one on
which we are focusing, and having in the process, I hope, enhanced or
exposed the acceptability of a certain sort of reply to such arguments, I
may ask us to return to the distinction between contrary and contradictory wills. The point of drawing this distinction in the present context is probably obvious: if the wills of two ob are merely contrary,
then even though neither has his way, there is still something (else)
that can happen; but if two ob will exhaustive and mutually exclusive
alternatives, then nothing (else) can happen. I think, in this light, that
it is logically impossible for there to be two ob with contradictory
wills. But nothing obvious seems to compel us to conclude from this
that there cannot be two ob, or to conclude that it is logically impossible for there to be two ob with merely contrary wills.

At this point one may raise the question-begging defense of (c') that I
mentioned above. According to it, the wills of an alleged ob is limited
in the ways we have envisaged, the being does not deserve to be called
omnipotent. This objection warrants expansion, and we shall look at it
more closely below. But the short reply to it is, of course, that the
concept of omnipotence is not clear, that we are trying to clarify it,
and that at this point it should be an open question whether to abandon

(1) or whether to give up (c'). In seeking an answer to the question, one may again observe that we probably accept various limitations on ob, and should not be astonished to find another. Again, too, I am anxious to add, the issue before us is not whether it is likely that there are two ob, but only whether it is logically possible.

An Objection[8]

The handling of the paradox of the stone that I endorse is not universally accepted. I am less concerned to answer objections to it than to show that they, and the reply to them, pertain both to the paradox and to the question of a plurality of ob. Brief consideration of one objection may, however, further my restricted aims.

According to that objection, there are crucial disanalogies between the impossibility of (e.g.) round and square objects and the impossibility of (e.g.) stones too heavy for anyone to lift. These disanalogies are obscured by the use of expressions like "in effect, logically impossible." Round square objects are, without qualification, logically impossible. But the stones are logically impossible only if there is an ob. It may clearly be no limitation on an ob that he cannot create objects that are (at once, in the same respect, etc.) both round and square. But objects that are logically impossible only if there is an ob seem to impose on an ob limitations that are peculiarly his own. And these limitations look incompatible with omnipotence. Things that are logically impossible only if there are two ob, and only if they will this or that, seem to be even less firmly impossible, and even less compatible with omnipotence.

But in fact the logical impossibility of stones too heavy for anyone to lift is absolute, or rather it is as absolute as the impossibility of round square objects.[9] The impossibility of round square objects may be taken to amount roughly to this: it is necessarily true that, if anything is a square object, then that thing is not (at the same time, etc.) round. There is, we should observe, no urge to say that the impossibility of round square objects is only conditional on there being square objects.

Focus next on stones too heavy for an ob to lift. Such stones are, without qualification, logically impossible. It is necessarily true that if there is an ob, and if there are any stones, the ob can lift those stones. This is so regardless of whether there are any ob or stones.

In speaking, though, of stones too heavy for anyone to lift, we find the word, "anyone," causes us needless trouble. If it ranges only over humans, then regardless of whether there are ob, or humans, or stones, it is logically possible for there to be stones too heavy for anyone to lift. (Boulders are stones, I presume.) If, however, "anyone" applies to both humans and ob, then we are concerned with stones too heavy for anyone, including ob, to lift. Regardless of whether there are ob, humans, or stones, it is logically impossible that there be such stones.

(It is possible, though, to take "anyone" to mean "anyone existent" or to mean "anyone possible." Reading it in the former of these two ways, we might judge contingent the question whether stones too heavy for anyone to lift are impossible. But this would be to beg important questions, because it might be necessarily true that some ob does exist. If, on the other hand, "anyone" is understood to mean "anyone possible," and if we held that ob are logically impossible, we might arrive at still another view of stones too heavy for anyone to lift. But this too would beg important questions. It seems best, therefore, to treat "anyone" as "anyone, including ob" (or as "anyone possible," if we do not just assume that ob are logically impossible).)

It is on these grounds that I have been holding that stones too heavy for anyone to lift are, unconditionally, logically impossible. It remains merely to apply our reasoning directly to the question whether there might be more than one ob. We need only comment that regardless of whether there is any ob, regardless of whether there are two or more ob, and regardless of what, if anything, an ob wills, it is necessarily true that if there is an ob, and if he wills that some proposition be true, that proposition is (or will be) true (—if it does not involve some logical impossibility).

Two More Objections

Two further specifiable objections should be discussed here. The first of them is a development of the defense of (c') that I called question-

begging. It may be said, then that although it is compatible with omnipotence to be unable to do some things that are logically impossible,
it is not compatible with omnipotence to be unable to do certain other
things that are logically impossible. In particular, it may seem, it is
not compatible with omnipotence to be unable to frustrate the will of
another ob, because it is not compatible with omnipotence to be hampered in any way by the will of another being of any sort.

This objection, as I have claimed, begs the question. Part of our
problem is to determine what an ob would be. Although one may have
used to feel, and may still feel, that an ob could not be hampered in
any way by the will of any other being, it does seem that at this point
one may equally well feel that, after all, there is *one* way in which an
ob can be hampered by the will of another being. For a being seems
just as weak (or as not-weak) when unable to make round square objects as when unable to frustrate the will of a being whose will cannot
be frustrated.

A second objection to our reply to the natural argument is that if there
were two beings that might hamper each others' wills, then neither
would be an ob, because a solitary ob would be more powerful than
either of them, and because an ob could not possibly be less powerful
than some other being.

But it is not obviously true that (4) if there were two (or more) ob,
each would be less powerful than a solitary ob. It is, of course, not
even clear what (4) might mean. Considering, however, the difficulties that arise in the individuation of actions, we would do best to read
(4) in a way that does not require that we be able to count the things
that agents can do. Interpreted acceptably, then, (4) might amount to
(4.1): if there were just one ob, he could do some things that neither of
a pair of ob could do.

In support of (4.1), it might be said that, in any world in which there
is just one ob, the ob can do M and he can do not-M (if neither M nor
not-M is logically impossible), but that, in some worlds in which there
are two ob, one of them cannot do M (or not-M) because the other of
them has already done (or willed) not-M (or M). It is false, however,
that, in any world in which there is just one ob, he can do M and he
can do not-M, because he himself may already have done (or willed)

M (or not-*M*). Admittedly, in such a world, he would be limited by himself and not by another being; but, again, it begs the question to make this difference the basis for ascribing or denying omnipotence.

In support of (4.1), it might further be said that, in some worlds with just one ob, the ob could create a stone too heavy for any-being-but-one to lift, whereas, in any world with just two ob, neither of them could do this. This is true; but it will not support (4), because it is also true that, in any world with just two ob, each could create a stone too heavy for any-being-but-just-two to lift, whereas, in some worlds with just one ob, the ob could not do this. (Some worlds with just one ob differ in an important way from others with just one ob: in some of them, there is also a being that is not omnipotent but that can lift a stone of any weight.)

Perhaps some other way of viewing (4) should be considered; yet in the absence of another interpretation of it, it seems untrue, and we still seem to have no obstacle to believing that there could be more than one ob.

Conciliatory Remarks

I do not know how to explain the unrelenting suspicion that trickery is afoot. But the suspicion might be rooted in one of the following two places.

First, some of us feel that a good thing is better or more admirable if it is unique than it would be if it were one of a pair. (But I doubt the same persons feel that one of a pair would be better or more admirable if the other of them were to disappear or had never existed.) I do not share this feeling. (My objection is not, say, that I like matched pairs: perhaps a matched pair is a single *object*.) My own sentiment is that if there were a perfect (baseball) pitcher, one (say) who struck out on three good pitches every batter he faced, I should admire him, and that if another such pitcher came along, I should then admire each of them as much as I had the first. (On the other hand, I have to admit that if there were a great many pitchers that could, on three good pitches, strike out each batter they met, their ability would not look like much of a skill.)

Secondly, some of us think about omnipotence because we care about religion, but my own interest in omnipotence arises because it poses some puzzles.[10] If my concerns were less narrow, I might want to link together, or to identify, the questions whether there could be two ob and whether the universe could have two sovereigns.[11] Thus, because the answer to the latter question probably is no, some of us may feel my answer to the former is unacceptable. For others of us, however, the notion of omnipotence has in part been severed from its religious ties. For the latter of us, the tentative conclusion of this paper are not blasphemous but merely surprising.[12]

Notes

1. The sign "ob," will stand here sometimes in place of "omnipotent being" and sometimes in place of "omnipotent beings." Also, by "there could be more than one ob," I mean (or mean something like) "it is logically possible that there be .more than one ob," although of course I have no useful analysis to offer for "logically possible." Furthermore, I shall often in this paper write as if I understood (or thought I understood) the words, "the will of an ob," "timelessly," and certain words and phrases related to these. But of course I do not understand them (and do not think I do).

2. On the paradox of the stones, see, *e.g.* G. I. Mavrodes, "Some Puzzles Concerning Omnipotence," *The Philosophical Review,* LXXII (1963), 221–223; H. G. Frankfurt, "The Logic of Omnipotence," *ibid.,* LXXIII (1964), 262–263; C. W. Savage, "The Paradox of the Stone," *ibid.,* LXXVI (1967), 74–79. Some other relevant articles, which I have found after writing most of this paper, are J. L. Cowan, "The Paradox of Omnipotence," *Analysis,* XXV (1965–66), 102–108; I. T. Ramsey, "The Paradox of Omnipotence," *Mind,* LXV (1956), 263–266; S. A. Grave, "On Evil and Omnipotence," *ibid.,* 259–262; G. B. Keene, "A Simpler Solution to the Paradox of Omnipotence," *ibid.,* LXIX (1960), 74–75; B. Mayo, "Mr. Keene on Omnipotence," *ibid.,* LXX (1961), 249–250; G. B. Keene, "Capacity-Limiting Statements," *ibid.,* 251–252; A. F. Bonifacio, "On Capacity Limiting Statements," *ibid.,* LXXIV (1965), 87–88; J. L. Mackie, "Omnipotence," *Sophia,* I:2 (1962), 13–25, esp. 21; A. Olding, "Finite and Infinite Gods," *ibid.,* VI:1 (1967), 3–7; S. Gendin, "Omnidoing," *ibid.,* VI:3 (1967), 17–22; J. Cargile, "On Omnipotence," *Nous,* I, 201–205 (1967).

3. In another version of our argument, it is supposed that one of the ob might will that the other ob be destroyed, and it is further supposed that the second ob might will that he not be destroyed. Without this further supposition of a specific conflict of wills, however, one might offer a different argument from ours, based simply on the supposition that one ob might will that the other be destroyed. In either case, however, the reasoning seems to assume that it is logically impossible for an ob to cease to exist. If this is logically impossible, then by the reasoning of this paper, the would-be destroyer does not have his way, but nevertheless he is omnipotent.

It seems possible, though, that an ob cease to exist. The best argument to the contrary probably is that if an ob ceased after *t* to exist, then there would be actions that an ob could not perform, namely all the actions that can be performed only after t. But there probably are no actions that can be performed *by an ob* only after t. An ob could will in advance that an action occur after t.

If an ob could cease to exist, then it is not clear that one ob could not destroy another. Perhaps the best reasoning is that if an ob could be destroyed without warning, he might not think to will in advance that certain actions occur after t, and thus he would be unable to perform those actions. If, on the other hand, he were threatened with destruction, he might object or he might not. If he did not, then he would cease to exist. But if he did, there would be a conflict of wills, and the main body of this paper would apply here.

4. My friends, Hugh S. Chandler and Robert Wengert, have informed me that Scotus and Ockham addressed themselves to the question whether there might be two omnipotent beings, and considered the natural argument. See John Duns Scotus, *Opus Oxoniense,* 1, 2, 3, in *Opera Omnia,* ed. L. Wadding and L. Vivès (Paris, 1891–1895), VIII, 497–498; William of Ockham, *Quodlibeta septem* (Louvain, 1962), Quod. I, q. 1. A translation of the Scotus appears in John Duns Scotus, *Philosophical Writings: A Selection,* trans. A. W. Wolter (Indianapolis, 1964).

5. For one to be an ob, it would not suffice that one's will were never frustrated. If it did, then a person who never willed much might be omnipotent. For the same reason, I believe it would also not suffice that it be necessarily true that one's will were never frustrated.

6. It would suffice to assume that just one ob is, in our sense, necessarily omniscient.

7. In some variations of this argument, the conclusion is that an ob both could and could not lift such a stone, and that an ob could create such a stone but could not lift it. In more important variations, the argument involves, not a stone too heavy for anyone to lift, but a stone too heavy for its creator to lift. I should think that "its creator" functions here in the confusing way that "anyone" does; see below. See also the works cited in note 2.

8. On this objection, see the exchange between Keene and Mayo, cited in note 2 above. For help in understanding this objection, I am indebted to Hugh Chandler.

9. By making some traditional assumptions, we may render the impossibility of stones too heavy for anyone to lift much firmer than that of round square objects. Suppose that *if* (say) x is an ob, *then* (a) it is necessarily true that x exists, (b) it is necessarily true that x is an ob, and (c) if x wills that (say) p, it is necessarily true that x wills that p.

10. See F. C. S. Schiller, "Omnipotence," *Proceedings of the Aristotelian Society,* XVIII (1917–18), 247–270; C. F. D'Arcy, "The Theory of a Limited Deity," *ibid.,* 158–184; W. M. Thorburn, "Omnipotence and Personality," *Mind,* XXIX (1920), 159–185; Ramsey, *op. cit.*

11. See I. Tammelo, "The Antimomy of Parliamentary Sovereignty," *Archiv fur Rechts—und Sozialphilosophie,* XLIV (1958), 495–513; K. J. J. Hintikka, "Remarks on a Paradox," *ibid.,* 514–516.

12. For discussion of the topics of this paper, I am indebted to Hugh S. Chandler and Robert Wengert, whom I have already mentioned, and to Catherine Conner, Robert Stalnaker, Richard Schacht, James Wallace, and John Cooper.

CAN GOD WILL WHAT HE HAS NOT WILLED?

16

The Properties of God

BARUCH SPINOZA

PROP. XVI.—*From the necessity of the divine nature infinite numbers of things in infinite ways (that is to say, all things which can be conceived by the infinite intellect) must follow.*

Demonst.—This proposition must be plain to every one who considers that from the given definition of anything a number of properties necessarily following from it (that is to say, following from the essence of the thing itself) are inferred by the intellect, and just in proportion as the definition of the thing expresses a greater reality, that is to say, just in proportion as the essence of the thing defined involves a greater reality, will more properties be inferred. But the divine nature possesses absolutely infinite attributes (Def. 6), each one of which expresses infinite essence in its own kind (*in suo genere*), and therefore, from the necessity of the divine nature, infinite numbers of things in infinite ways (that is to say, all things which can be conceived by the infinite intellect) must necessarily follow.—Q.E.D.

Corol. 1.—Hence it follows that God is the efficient cause of all things which can fall under the infinite intellect.

Corol. 2.—It follows, secondly, that God is cause through Himself, and not through that which is contingent (*per accidens*).

Corol. 3.—It follows, thirdly, that God is absolutely the first cause.

From *Ethics*, Part I, Propositions XVI & XVII. Reprinted from Benedict de Spinoza, *Ethic Demonstrated in Geometrical Order etc.*, trans. W. H. White, New York, Macmillan & Co., 1883.

PROP. XVII.—*God acts from the laws of His own nature only, and is compelled by no one.*

Demonst.—We have just shown (Prop. 16) that from the necessity, or (which is the same thing) from the laws only of the divine nature, infinite numbers of things absolutely follow; and we have demonstrated (Prop. 15) that nothing can be, nor can be conceived, without God, but that all things are in God. Therefore, outside Himself, there can be nothing by which He may be determined or compelled to act; and therefore He acts from the laws of His own nature only, and is compelled by no one.—Q.E.D.

Corol. 1.—Hence it follows, firstly, that there is no cause, either external to God or within Him, which can excite Him to act except the perfection of His own nature.

Corol. 2.—It follows, secondly, that God alone is a free cause; for God alone exists from the necessity alone of His own nature (Prop. 11, and Corol. 1, Prop. 14), and acts from the necessity alone of His own nature (Prop. 17). Therefore (Def. 7) He alone is a free cause.—Q.E.D.

Schol.—There are some who think that God is a free cause because He can, as they think, bring about that those things which we have said follow from His nature—that is to say, those things which are in His power—should not be, or should not be produced by Him. But this is simply saying that God could bring about that it should not follow from the nature of a triangle that its three angles should be equal to two right angles, or that from a given cause an effect should not follow, which is absurd. But I shall show farther on, without the help of this proposition, that neither intellect nor will pertain to the nature of God.

I know, indeed, that there are many who think themselves able to demonstrate that intellect of the highest order and freedom of will both pertain to the nature of God, for they say that they know nothing more perfect which they can attribute to Him than that which is the chief perfection in ourselves. But although they conceive God as actually possessing the highest intellect, they nevertheless do not believe that He can bring about that all those things should exist which are actually in His intellect, for they think that by such a supposition they would destroy His power. If He had created, they say, all things which are in His intellect, He could have created nothing more, and this, they believe, does not accord with God's omnipotence so then they prefer to consider God as indifferent to all things, and creating nothing excepting that which He has decreed to create by a certain absolute will. But I think that I have shown with sufficient clearness (Prop. 16) that from the supreme power of God, or from His infinite nature, infinite things in infinite ways, that is to say, all things, have necessarily flowed, or continually follow by the same necessity, in the same way as it follows from the nature of a triangle, from eternity and to eternity, that its three angles are equal to two right angles. The omnipotence of God has therefore been actual from eternity, and in the same actuality will remain to eternity. In this way the omnipotence of God, in my opinion, is far more firmly established. My adversaries, indeed (if I may be permitted to speak plainly), seem to deny the omnipotence of God, inasmuch as they are forced to admit that He has in His mind an infinite number of things which might be created, but which, nevertheless, He will never be able to create, for if He were to create all things which He has in His mind, He would, according to them, exhaust His omnipotence and make Himself imperfect. Therefore, in order to make a perfect God, they are compelled to make Him incapable of doing all those things to which His power extends, and anything more absurd than this, or more opposed to God's omnipotence, I do not think can be imagined.

17

Can God Do What He Does Not?

ST. THOMAS AQUINAS

I answer that the error that God cannot do other than what he does has two sources. First, it has been asserted by several philosophers that God acts from a necessity of nature. If this were the case, since nature is determined to one end,[1] the Divine power could not extend itself to any other agenda than what he actually does.

Second, this error is derived from the reasoning of several theologians. They have been saying that God cannot omit to make those things which he has made since they are made according to his Divine justice and wisdom. They have continued in this line of reasoning so that they say that God cannot do anything except what he does. This error is imputed to Peter Abelard.[2]

We must inquire into the truth or falsity of these positions. To the major premise of the first opinion, I say that it is plain that God does not act from natural necessity. For every agent acts for an end because all things tend toward the good. Now in order to be suited to an end, the action of the agent must be adapted and adjusted to the end, which cannot be done except by some intelligence which recognizes the end, the nature of the end, and the relation of the means to the end. Otherwise the adjustment of the means to the end would be adventitious. However, an intellect ordering means to ends sometimes is joined to the agent or mover, as in a man walking, or sometimes is separated, as

From *Quaestiones Disputatae, De Potentia Dei,* q. 1, a. 5, Parma, 1856, p. 10. Translation and notes by Linwood Urban. Material in [ ] is added for clarification. For a similar discussion see *Summa Theologica,* I, q. 19, a. 3; *Summa Contra Gentiles,* Bk. II, chaps. 23, 26, & 27.

in an arrow which is directed to a definite target, not by an intellect joined to it, but by the intellect of the man aiming it. Therefore it is impossible for an agent which acts from natural necessity to direct itself to its own end, because an agent of the latter kind acts of itself. An agent or mover which acts of itself has the capacity in itself to act or not to act, to be moved or not to be moved, as is stated in *Physics* 8, 4.[3] This ambivalence is not consistent with an agent moved by natural necessity since the latter is directed to only one end. Hence it is necessary that everything which acts from a necessity of nature be directed to an end by another which must be intelligent. On account of this fact, philosophers say: "The work of nature is the work of intelligence."

Hence, if sometimes a body is naturally joined to an intellect, as is clearly the case in man, in those actions for which his intellect determines the end, nature obeys the will, as for example in walking. However, in those actions where the will does not determine the end, nature does not obey the will, as in the processes of nourishment and growth. From these considerations, it follows that what acts from natural necessity cannot be the principal agent, since its end is determined for it by another. [Since God is the principal agent,] it is clear that it is impossible for him to act from natural necessity. Thus the root premise of the first position is false.

It remains to investigate the second position about which it ought to be recognized that something is said to be impossible for something in two ways. In one way, it is said to be impossible absolutely, when one of the principal causes necessary to the action does not extend to the action, e.g. "If a foot is broken, a man cannot walk." In another way some action is said to be impossible hypothetically. When the opposite of the action is posited, the action cannot come to pass, e.g. "I cannot walk while I am sitting." Because God is a voluntary and intellectual agent, as was proved,[4] we must reflect upon three sources of action in him: first, the intellect, second, the will, and third, the power of nature.

As I was saying, the intellect directs the will; and the will rules the power by which the will is executed. But the intellect does not move the will unless it proposes to it something desirable, so that the total power of the intellect to move resides in the will. Now God is said to be absolutely unable to do something in two ways. In one way, God is said to be unable when the power of God does not extend to the effect. Thus we say that God cannot make the affirmation and negation of a proposition to be true simultaneously, as is clear from what was said above.[5] However, this inability does not imply that God can do only what he has done. For the fact remains that the power of God can extend itself to many other things.

In regard to the second way of saying that the will of God cannot extend itself to something, it is necessary to point out that whatever will you name has some end which it wills naturally and of which it cannot will the contrary, e.g. that man naturally and of necessity wills beatitude and cannot will misery. Since what the will wills necessarily is its natural end, it also wills of necessity the means necessary to achieve the end, if these means are known. Therefore, it also wills those things which are adapted to the end, e.g. "If I will life, I will food." To be sure, means which are not adapted to the end, the will does not will of necessity.

Now, the end of the Divine will is his goodness which he cannot help but will. But creatures are not necessary to this end so that without them the Divine goodness could not be manifested, which manifestation was God's intention in creation. Hence, as the Divine goodness is manifested by those things, and the order of those things, which now exist, the Divine goodness could be manifested by other creatures and by their being ordered in a different way. Thus the Divine will, without prejudice to his goodness, justice, and wisdom, can extend itself in other ways than it does. And in this were the heretics deceived. For they thought the order of creatures to be almost necessary to the Divine goodness as if he could not depart from that order.

Therefore, it is clear that absolutely God can do other than what he has done. But because he is unable to make contradictory propositions to be true simultaneously, hypothetically one can say that God cannot do other than he has done, on the supposition that he does not wish to do otherwise, or because he has foreseen that the alternative will not come to pass. Thus "He is unable to do otherwise" is to be interpreted as an implicit conjunctive compound statement and not as a disjunctive compound statement.[6]

Notes

1. See below, William Ockham, "God's Causality," notes 3, 4, 5, 6, p. 181.
2. *Intro. ad Theol.*, III, 5 (*PL* 178, 1093).
3. *Passim.*
4. Qs. 1 & 2 *passim; Summa Con. Gen.*, Bk. II, Chap. 24.
5. Q. 1, a. 3, "Are Those Things Which Are Impossible in Nature Possible for God?" Selection 4 above.
6. For another discussion see "How the Omnipotent God Is Said To Be Unable To Do Certain Things," Selection 8 above.

18

Whether God Can Do What He Does Not?

ST. THOMAS AQUINAS

Objection 1. It seems that God can do only what He does. For God cannot do what He has not foreknown and pre-ordained that He would do. But He neither foreknew nor pre-ordained that He would do anything except what He does. Therefore He can do only what He does. . . .

On the contrary, It is said: *Thinkest thou that I cannot ask My Father, and He will give Me presently more than twelve legions of angels?* (*Matt.* xxvi. 53). But He neither asked for them, nor did His Father show them to refute the Jews. Therefore God can do what he does not.

I answer that, In this matter certain persons erred in two ways. Some [1] laid it down that God acts from natural necessity in such way that, just as from the action of natural things nothing else can happen beyond what actually takes place—as, for instance, from the seed of man, a man must come, and from that of an olive, an olive; so from the divine operation there could not come forth other things, nor another order of things, than that which now is. But we showed above that God does not act from natural necessity, but that His will is the cause of all things; [2] we showed also that the divine will is not naturally and from any necessity determined to these creatures. Whence in no way is

Summa Theologica, I, q. 25, a. 5. From *The Basic Writings of Saint Thomas Aquinas,* edited and annotated by Anton C. Pegis, New York, Random House, 1945, Vol. 1, pp. 266 ff. Reprinted with the permission of Random House, Inc.

the present scheme of things produced by God with such necessity that other things could not come to be.

Others,[3] however, said that the divine power is restricted to this present scheme of things because of the order of the divine wisdom and justice, without which God does nothing. But since the power of God, which is His essence, is nothing else but His wisdom, it can indeed be fittingly said that there is nothing in the divine power which is not in the order conceived by the divine wisdom; for the divine wisdom comprehends the power of God in its entirety. However, the order established in creation by divine wisdom (in which the notion of His justice consists, as was said above[4]), is not so equal to the divine wisdom that the divine wisdom should be restricted to it. For it is clear that the whole nature of the order which a wise man puts into the things made by him is taken from their end. So, when the end is proportionate to the things made for that end, the wisdom of the maker is restricted to a definite order. But the divine goodness is an end exceeding created things beyond all proportion. Therefore, the divine wisdom is not so restricted to any particular order that no other scheme of things could proceed from it. Hence we must say absolutely that God can do other things than those He has done.

Reply Obj. 1. In ourselves, in whom power and essence are distinct from will and intellect, and in whom intellect is distinct from wisdom, and will from justice, something can reside in our power which cannot reside in a just will or in a wise intellect. But in God, power, essence, will, intellect, wisdom and justice are one and the same. Whence, there can be found nothing in the divine power which cannot also be found in His just will or in His wise intellect. Now, because His will cannot be determined from necessity to this or that order of things, except upon supposition, as was said above;[5] and because the wisdom and justice of God are likewise restricted not to this present order, as was shown above; for this reason, nothing prevents there being something in the divine power which He does not will, and which is not included in the order that He has established in things. Furthermore, because power is considered as *executing,* will as *commanding,* and intellect and wisdom as *directing,* what is attributed to His power considered in itself God is said to be able to do in accordance with His *absolute power*. Of such a kind is everything which verifies the nature of being, as was said above. On the other hand, what is attributed to the divine power, according as it carries into execution the command of a just will, God is said to be able to do by His *ordained power*. In this manner, we must say that by His absolute power God can do other things than those He has foreknown and pre-ordained to do. But it could not happen that He should do anything which He has not fore-known and not pre-ordained that He would do. For his doing is subject to His foreknowledge and preordination, though His power, which is His nature, is not. For God does things because He so wills; yet He is able to do so, not because He so wills, but because He is such in His nature. . . .

Notes

1. Cf. Maimonides, *Guide,* II, 20 (p. 189).—Cf. also St. Thomas, *De Pot.,* q. 3, a. 4.
2. Q. 19, a. 3.
3. Peter Abelard, *Introd. ad Theol.,* III, 5 (PL 178, 1093).—Cf. St. Thomas, *De Pot.,* I, 5.—Cf. also St. Albert, *In I Sent.,* d. xliv, a. 2 (XXVI, 391).
4. Q. 21 a. 2 and 4.
5. Q. 19, a. 3.

19

God Is Omnipotent

FRIEDRICH SCHLEIERMACHER

In the conception of the divine Omnipotence two ideas are contained: first, that the entire system of Nature, comprehending all times and spaces, is founded upon divine causality, which as eternal and omnipresent is in contrast to all finite causality; and second, that the divine causality, as affirmed in our feeling of absolute dependence, is completely presented in the totality of finite being, and consequently everything for which there is a causality in God happens and becomes real.

I. Since the natural order is naught but the twofold mutually determined sum of the finite causing and the finite caused, the first part of our proposition first of all implies that each finite given as such, in virtue of its foundation in the divine omnipotence, effects everything which the causality implanted in it makes it capable of effecting in the sphere of universal causality. It is, however, equally implied that every effect within the natural order is also, in virtue of its being ordained by the divine causality, the pure result of all the causes within the natural order, according to the measure in which it stands in relation with each of them. As now everything that we can regard as a separate thing for itself within the totality of finite being must be 'cause' as well as effect, there is never anything of any kind which can begin to be an object of the divine causality, though previously—hence somehow independent of God and opposed to Him—in existence. Rather on such a view (whether it be that the activity of the divine omnipotence as such begins in this way, or that by such opposi-

From F. Schleiermacher, *The Christian Faith,* Eng. trans. of second German edition, edited by H. R. Macintosh & J. S. Stewart, Edinburgh, T. & T. Clark, 1928, pp. 211–19. Reprinted with the permission of T. & T. Clark.

tion its activity is interrupted, whether seldom or often matters not), the foundation feeling of religion would thereby be destroyed. If this is not the immediate result, it at once appears when we extend our self-consciousness to cover the whole of finite being and so represent that object also; for then there would no longer be absolute dependence but only partial dependence.

Further, since divine omnipotence can only be conceived as eternal and omnipresent, it is inadmissible to suppose that at any time anything should begin to be through omnipotence; on the contrary, through omnipotence everything is already posited which comes into existence through finite causes, in time and space. Similarly, because a thing can be recognized as having happened through finite causation, it is not on this account the less posited through the divine omnipotence, nor is that which cannot be traced to finite causation the more on that account to be referred to divine omnipotence. Thus the divine omnipotence can never in any way enter as a supplement (so to speak) to the natural causes in their sphere; for then it must like them work temporally and spatially; and at one time working so, and then again not so, it would not be self-identical and so would be neither eternal nor omnipresent. Rather everything is and becomes altogether by means of the natural order, so that each takes place through all and all wholly through the divine omnipotence, so that all indivisibly exists through One.

2. The second part of our proposition rests upon the fact that in our sphere we only come to the idea of the divine omnipotence through the conception of the feeling of absolute dependence, and we lack any point of connexion for making demands upon the divine causality which extend beyond the natural order embraced by this feeling. As against this it seems as though it might be said that what we call 'all' consists of the actual and the potential, and omnipotence must therefore embrace both of these; but that if it presents itself completely and exhaustively in the totality of finite being, then it includes only the actual but not also the potential. But how little the difference between actual and potential can exist for God will appear very clearly, if we only notice in what cases we ourselves chiefly apply it. We conceive, in the first place, much to be possible in a thing by virtue of the gen-

eral conception of the species to which it belongs, which is not actual, however, because excluded by its special character; whilst in the case of other individuals of the same species other determinations, possible in virtue of the idea of the species, remain excluded for the same reason. Here, however, something appears to us as possible only because we find that the particularity of the individual is a problem we are never fully in a position to solve. But with regard to God such a distinction between the general and the individual is not applicable; in Him the species exists originally as the sum-total of its individual existences, and these in turn are given and established together with their place in the species, so that what does not hereby become actual, is also, so far as He is concerned, not potential. In the same way, we say that much is possible by virtue of the nature of a thing (when we take together its determinations by its species and as an individual being), which yet does not become actual because it is hindered by the position of the thing in the sphere of general interaction. We rightly make this distinction and attribute truth, as in the former case, to that which is thought of in this way as being possible, because it is only by this indirect method that we pass from the unfruitful sphere of abstractions and put together a view of the conditioned development of individual existence. On the other hand, if we could have taken into account for each point the influence of the whole system of interaction, we should then have had to say that what was not actual was also not possible within the system of nature. In God, however, the one is not separated from the other, that which exists for itself having one ground and the system of interaction another, but both these are grounded with and through each other, so that in relation to Him only that is possible which has its foundation in both equally. But every case which has any validity for us, may be reduced under one of these heads. The idea of a potentiality outside the sum of the actual[1] has no validity even for our minds; for not only does the religious self-consciousness not lead us to such a point, but, in addition, however we arrived at it, we should then have to accept a self-limitation of the divine omnipotence which can never be given in experience. Nor can we conceive any ground for such a self-limitation, unless that which is thought of as potential could enter into existence, not as an increase, but only in some way or other as a diminution of the actual, whereby the whole assumption is destroyed.[2]

3. Since in relation to God no distinction between the potential and the actual can be allowed, it is easy to pass judgment on the popular explanation of God's omnipotence, which has often been adopted even in scientific discussions, namely, that it is the attribute in virtue of which God is able to effect all that is possible, or all which contains no contradiction in itself. If, of course, contradiction is taken *realiter* and that is called contradictory which can find no place in the whole of existence, this is perfectly correct; for all the compossible is certainly produced by the divine omnipotence. Objection might still be made to the one point of saying that, in virtue of omnipotence, God *can* effect, not *does* effect, everything; for thereby a distinction is made between 'can' and 'will,' and the explanation comes near to another, namely, that omnipotence is the attribute by which God can do what He will. There is, however, as little distinction between 'can' and 'will' in God, as between the actual and the possible.[3] For whichever is greater than the other, the will or the ability, there is always a limitation, which can only be done away with if both be made equal in range. Moreover the very separation of each in itself, as though, that is, ability were a different condition from will, is an imperfection. For should I think of an ability without will, the will must proceed from an individual impulse, and so also always from a caused impulse; and should I think of a will without ability, the ability cannot be grounded in the inner power, but must be given from without. And if, since in God there is no willing through individual impulses, and no ability given from without, waxing and waning, the two in God cannot be separated even in thought, so also, since 'can' and 'will' together are necessarily doing, neither willing and doing are to be separated, nor 'can' and 'do,' but the entire omnipotence is, undivided and unabbreviated, the omnipotence that does and effects all. But it is useless to say anything further on this view on account of its inevitable separation between 'can' and 'will.'[4]

4. With the misunderstanding just exposed there are connected many distinctions within the divine omnipotence, as well as divisions of it, given currency especially by the scholastics, which can be ruled out without loss. To these belongs, in the first place, the contrast between a mediate and immediate, or absolute and ordered, exercise of the divine omnipotence, *i.e.* between cases when it acts without or with

intermediary causes. Now when individual effects are referred some only to the former and some only to the latter, the distinction is false. For everything which happens in time and space has its determinations in the totality of that which is outside it in space and before it in time, however much they may be hidden, and so far come under the ordered power; and if some, to the exclusion of others, be referred back to the immediate power, the whole order of nature would be abrogated. If, however, we think not of the individual but of the world itself as the effect of the divine omnipotence, we have no choice but to recur to its immediate exercise. Hence in so far as we can apply the idea of creation in detail, we apply at the same time and equally the idea of the absolute exercise of omnipotence; but in so far as we use the idea (rightly understood) of concurrence or preservation,[5] in this aspect of it, everything is referred to the ordered exercise of power which establishes the dependence of each individual on the totality of existence eternally, and for the maintenance of the general interaction makes use of the forces of individual things. There is no point, however, which we can relate only to the absolute (which by way of stricter contrast we ought to call not 'unordered' but 'ordering') exercise of omnipotence and not to the ordered exercise and conversely.

The case is similar with the distinction almost everywhere drawn between the divine will as absolute and as conditioned. It is clear that on this view ability is still made greater than will, because in the former no such distinction is drawn; and there arises a gradation, so that of what God can do some things He wills absolutely, some under conditions, and still others not at all. But it is by no means the case that God wills some things absolutely and others conditionally; just as with regard to every event there is something of which one can say, if this were not then that event would not be; so with regard to every individual thing—the fact that it exists and that it exists in this way—we can say that God wills it conditionally, because everything is conditioned by something else. But that whereby something else is conditioned is itself conditioned by the divine will; indeed in such a way that the divine will upon which the conditioning rests, and the divine will upon which the conditioned rests is not different in each case, but one only and the same; it is the divine will embracing the whole framework of mutually conditioning finite being: and this naturally is the absolute will, because nothing conditions it. In this way everything individual would be willed by God conditionally, but the whole willed absolutely as a unity. On the other hand, if for once we take an individual out of the order, and relate it *so* to the divine will, we shall have to say that each individual existing for itself, so far as we regard it not as conditioned by, but as co-conditioning the whole, is so fully willed by God as what it is, that everything else must be so, and cannot be otherwise than as follows from its action; which is as much as to say that it is absolutely willed by God. In this respect, therefore, it can be said that every individual, so far as it must be affected by the rest, is also only conditionally willed by God; but, of course, not as though on that account it were any the less willed, or any the less came to reality. Everything, however, so far as it is itself effective, and in various ways conditons other things, is absolutely willed by God.

But the whole idea of the divine omnipotence appears most endangered, when an active and an inactive, and a free and a necessary, divine will are set one over against the other. The *necessary* will would be related to what God wills in virtue of His essence, the *free* to that which, so far as His essence is concerned, He could just as well not will;[6] where it is assumed that it does not belong to His essence to reveal Himself. Thus by means of the necessary will God wills Himself, and by means of the free will He wills what is other than Himself. But a 'self-willing' of God is always a most awkward formula, and almost inevitably raises the hair-splitting question whether, just as the world exists by reason of His free will, so also God exists because, by reason of His necessary will, He wills Himself, or whether He wills Himself because He is. Or, to express it rather differently, whether this self-willing is more in the way of self-preservation, or more in the way of self-approval, or (if both are taken together) after the manner of self-love.[7] Now since self-preservation can scarcely be thought of as a real will unless there is something to be striven for or averted,[8] and self-approval almost necessarily implies a divided consciousness, it is easily seen that this self-willing can mean nothing but the very existence of God posited under the form of will. But this, which is in God purely inward and related solely to Himself, can never come into our religious self-consciousness. In any case, therefore, this necessary will of God, as in no way belonging here, would fall under speculative theology. Moreover, it seems that this contrast cannot be applied to God at all, and what has been brought under the contrasted heads respectively is not really separable. For where such a contrast exists the necessary must be unfree, and the free be grounded in no necessity, and so arbitrary. Each, however, is an imperfection; and consequently this contrast has its place solely in that existence in which each being is co-determined by the rest. We must therefore think of nothing in God as necessary without at the same time positing it as free, nor as free unless at the same time it is necessary. Just as little, however, can we think of God's willing Himself, and God's willing the world, as separated the one from the other. For if He wills Himself, He wills Himself as Creator and Sustainer, so that in willing Himself, willing the world is already included; and if He wills the world, in it He wills His eternal and ever-present omnipotence, wherein willing Himself is included; that is to say, the necessary will is included in the free, and the free in the necessary. Obviously, too, there is nothing in the way in which God comes into our religious self-consciousness which corresponds to this contrast, and it lacks dogmatic content.

And finally as to the contrast between the *active* and *inactive* divine will: it first of all contradicts the generally recognized proposition that the divine will extends no further than divine ability.[9] For how should a true and real will be inactive unless it lacked the ability? But it is to be noted that the one all-embracing divine will is identical with the eternal omnipotence; and if then, as eternal, it is timeless, the content of no definite time can quite correspond with it, and so from this point of view the divine will is always inactive. But it is also always active, because there is no fraction of time which does not pass in fulfilment of it, and what seems to resist or repress the divine will is always simply co-operating in its temporal fulfilment.[10] If, then, we hold this fast and distinguish between will and command, it is quite unnecessary to deal with the idea of a precedent and a consequent will, expressions which again suggest the appearance of a change in the will of God.

Postscript: The Independence of God

If the feeling of absolute dependence comprises a reference to divine omnipotence, it is no longer necessary to bring out the independence of God as a special attribute. For if one remains at all true to the derivation of the word, it is, as the opposite of that dependence in which we find ourselves, simply a negative attribute and, as it were, a shadow-picture of omnipotence, and only states that God has no foundation or cause of His being outside Himself, which coincides with the scholastic 'aseitas,' virtually 'existence-from-self.' If, now, this be changed into a formula of quite similar content, namely, that in relation to God there can be no question of a ground, one sees at once how this is already completely contained in our two main conceptions, eternity and omnipotence. But, of course, the term independence is dealt with in very different ways. Some include in the idea that God is Lord over all.[11] But Lordship is connected with independence only on the presupposition that the independent is at the same time in need of something, for otherwise one can be completely independent without having even the slightest Lordship. Thus if the divine attributes are to be separated at all, this combination is not practicable. Then if 'indebted to no one' has only a moral sense, and denies the applicability of the conception of obligation in relation to God, the conception is thereby divided, and there is, according to the usual procedure, a physical and a moral independence. About the latter we have nothing to say here; and since 'to be Lord over all' can be only an expression of omnipotence (if, that is, we leave out in advance the moral consideration which here too enters, that God as Lord cannot be obligated, i.e. can stand under no law), we have nothing left but the above-mentioned 'existence-from-self' of God—a speculative formula which, in the dogmatic sphere, we can only convert into the rule that there is nothing in God for which a determining cause is to be posited outside God. But this is so clearly defined in our first explanation,[12] that it is unnecessary to bring it up specially here.

Notes

1. Statements such as that of Basil, *hom. I. in hexaëm.*: τὸν τοῦ παντὸς τούτου δημιουργὸν οὐχ ἑνὶ κόσμῳ σύμμετρον ἔχειν τὴν ποιητικὴν δύναμιν, ἀλλ' εἰς τὸ ἀπειροπλάσιον ὑπερβαίνουσαν, we must explain by the limits of contemporary knowledge of the universe, in contrast to which we have already arrived at the ἀπειροπλάσιον·

2. Abelard rightly says, *Introd.* iii. 5 : Potest, quod convenit, non convenit quod praetermittit, ergo id tantum facere potest, quod quandoque facit. Cf. August., *En-*

chirid. 24 : Neque enim ob aliud veraciter vocatur omnipotens, nisi quoniam quicquid vult potest.

3. Joh. Damasc., *d. fid. orth.* i. 8, calls God indeed δύναμιν οὐδενὶ μέτρῳ γνωριζομένην, μόνῳ τῷ οἰκείῳ βουλήματι μετρουμένην· But this is only meant to bring out one side, for he says, i. 13: πάντα μὲν ὅσα θέλει δύναται, οὐχ ὅσα δὲ δύναται θέλει·

4. This is true of all such formulæ as Deus absoluta sua potentiâ multa potest, quae non vult nec forte unquam volet; or Nunquam tot et tanta efficit Deus, quia semper plura et majora efficere possit (cf. Gerh., *loc. theol.* i. pp. 132 f.).

5. Cf. § 38, 1 and § 45, *Postscript.*

6. Gerh., *loc. th.* iii. p. 203: *Ex necessitate naturae* vult quae de se ipso vult, nulla re sive extra se sive intra se permotus. *Libere* vult, quae de creaturis vult, quae *poterat* et velle et nolle.

7. Wegscheider, *Institt.*, §67: Voluntas necessaria, *i.e.* actus voluntatis quae e scientia necessaria promanare dicitur, amor nimirum quo Deus . . . se ipsum complecatatur necesse est.

8. Many, of course, still describe the divine will in this way, *e.g.* Mosheim, *Th. dogm.*, p. 277: actus appetendi quae bona sunt et aversandi quae mala sunt.

9. Cf. Gerh., *loc. th.* i. p. 154; Praeter voluntatem non indiget aliqua potentia.

10. On this are also based the formulæ of Augustine, to which we must always come back, *Enchirid.* 26: Omnipotentis voluntas semper invicta est—nec nisi volens quicquam facit, et omnia quaecunque vult facit. 27: dum tamen credere non cogamur aliquid omnipotentem Deum voluisse fieri, factumque non esse.

11. Reinhard's *Dogm.*, p. 106: Independentia est illud attributum, quo nemini quicquam debet, et ipse solus est omnium rerum dominus.—Joh. Damasc., *de orth. fid.* i. 19, can scarcely have regarded αὐτεξούσιος (which, for the most part, corresponds to *independent*) as forming one predicate together with αὐτοκρατής and ἀνενδεής·

12. Cf. § 4, 4.

CAN GOD CREATE A STONE TOO HEAVY TO LIFT?

20

Some Puzzles
Concerning Omnipotence

GEORGE I. MAVRODES

The doctrine of God's omnipotence appears to claim that God can do anything. Consequently, there have been attempts to refute the doctrine by giving examples of things which God cannot do; for example, He cannot draw a square circle.

Responding to objections of this type, St. Thomas pointed out that "anything" should be here construed to refer only to objects, actions, or states of affairs whose descriptions are not self-contradictory.[1] For it is only such things whose nonexistence might plausibly be attributed to a lack of power in some agent. My failure to draw a circle on the exam may indicate my lack of geometrical skill, but my failure to draw a square circle does not indicate any such lack. Therefore, the fact that it is false (or perhaps meaningless) to say that God could draw one does no damage to the doctrine of His omnipotence.

A more involved problem, however, is posed by this type of question: can God create a stone too heavy for Him to lift? This appears to be stronger than the first problem, for it poses a dilemma. If we say that God can create such a stone, then it seems that there might be such a stone. And if there might be a stone too heavy for Him to lift, then He is evidently not omnipotent. But if we deny that God can create such a stone, we seem to have given up His omnipotence already. Both answers lead us to the same conclusion.

From *The Philosophical Review,* LXXII, 1963, pp. 221–23. Reprinted with the permission of *The Philosophical Review* and the author.

Further, this problem does not seem obviously open to St. Thomas' solution. The form "x is able to draw a square circle" seems plainly to involve a contradiction, while "x is able to make a thing too heavy for x to lift" does not. For it may easily be true that I am able to make a boat too heavy for me to lift. So why should it not be possible for God to make a stone too heavy for Him to lift?

Despite this apparent difference, this second puzzle *is* open to essentially the same answer as the first. The dilemma fails because it consists of asking whether God can do a self-contradictory thing. And the reply that He cannot does no damage to the doctrine of omnipotence.

The specious nature of the problem may be seen in this way. God is either omnipotent or He is not.[2] Let us assume first that He is not. In that case the phrase "a stone too heavy for God to lift" may not be self-contradictory. And then, of course, if we assert either that God is able or that He is not able to create such a stone, we may conclude that He is not omnipotent. But this is no more than the assumption with which we began, meeting us again after our roundabout journey. If this were all that the dilemma could establish it would be trivial. To be significant it must derive this same conclusion *from the assumption that God is omnipotent;* that is, it must show that the assumption of the omnipotence of God leads to a *reductio*. But does it?

On the assumption that God is omnipotent, the phrase "a stone too heavy for God to lift" becomes self-contradictory. For it becomes "a stone which cannot be lifted by Him whose power is sufficient for lifting anything." But the "thing" described by a self-contradictory phrase is absolutely impossible and hence has nothing to do with the doctrine of omnipotence. Not being an object of power at all, its failure to exist cannot possibly be due to some lack in the power of God. And, interestingly, it is the very omnipotence of God which makes the existence of such a stone absolutely impossible, while it is the fact that I am finite in power that makes it possible for me to make a boat too heavy for me to lift.

But suppose that some die-hard objector takes the bit in his teeth and denies that the phrase "a stone too heavy for God to lift" is self-contradictory, even on the assumption that God is omnipotent. In other words, he contends that the description "a stone too heavy for an omnipotent God to lift" is self-coherent and therefore describes an absolutely possible object. Must I then attempt to prove the contradiction which I assumed above as intuitively obvious? Not necessarily. Let me simply reply that if the objector is right in this contention then the answer to the original question is, "Yes, God can create such a stone." It may seem that this reply will force us into the original dilemma. But it does not. For now the objector can draw no damaging conclusion from this answer. And the reason is that he has just now contended that such a stone is compatible with the omnipotence of God. Therefore, from the possibility of God's creating such a stone it cannot be concluded that God is not omnipotent. The objector cannot have it both ways. The conclusion which he himself wishes to draw from an affirmative answer to the original question is itself the required proof that the descriptive phrase which appears there is self-contradictory. And "it is more appropriate to say that such things cannot be done, than that God cannot do them." [3]

The specious nature of this problem may also be seen in a somewhat different way. [4] Suppose that some theologian is convinced by this dilemma that he must give up the doctrine of omnipotence. But he resolves to give up as little as possible, just enough to meet the argument. One way he can do so is by retaining the infinite power of God with regard to lifting, while placing a restriction on the sort of stone He is able to create. The only restriction here, however, is that God must not be able to create a stone too heavy for Him to lift. Beyond that the dilemma has not even suggested any necessary restriction. Our theologian has, in effect, answered the original question in the negative, and he now regretfully supposes that this has required him to give up the full doctrine of omnipotence. He is now retaining what he supposes to be the more modest remnants which he has salvaged from that doctrine.

We must ask, however, what it is that he has in fact given up. Is it the unlimited power of God to create stones? No doubt. But what stone is it that God is now precluded from creating? The stone too heavy for Him to lift, of course. But we must remember that nothing in the argument required the theologian to admit any limit on God's power with regard to the lifting of stones. He still holds that to be unlimited. And if God's power to lift is infinite, then His power to create may run to infinity also without outstripping that first power. The supposed limitation turns out to be no limitation at all, since it is specified only by reference to another power which is itself infinite. Our theologian need have no regrets, for he has given up nothing. The doctrine of the power of God remains just what it was before.

Nothing that I have said above, of course, goes to prove that God is, in fact, omnipotent. All I have intended to show is that certain arguments intended to prove that He is not omnipotent fail. They fail because they propose, as tests of God's power, putative tasks whose descriptions are self-contradictory. Such pseudo-tasks, not falling within the realm of possibility, are not objects of power at all. Hence the fact that they cannot be performed implies no limit on the power of God, and hence no defect in the doctrine of omnipotence.

Notes

1. St. Thomas Aquinas, *Summa Theologica,* Part 1, Q. 25, Art. 3.
2. I assume, of course, the existence of God, since that is not being brought in question here.
3. St. Thomas, *loc. cit.*
4. But this method rests finally on the same logical relations as the preceding one.

21

The Logic of Omnipotence

HARRY G. FRANKFURT

George Mavrodes has recently presented an analysis designed to show that, despite some appearances to the contrary, a certain well-known puzzle actually raises no serious difficulties in the notion of divine omnipotence.[1] The puzzle suggests a test of God's power—can He create a stone too heavy for Him to lift?—which, it seems, cannot fail to reveal that His power is limited. For He must, it would appear, either show His limitations by being unable to create such a stone or by being unable to lift it once He had created it.

In dealing with this puzzle, Mavrodes points out that it involves the setting of a task whose description is self-contradictory—the task of creating a stone too heavy for an omnipotent being to lift. He calls such tasks "pseudo-tasks" and he says of them: "Such pseudo-tasks, not falling within the realm of possibility, are not objects of power at all. Hence the fact that they cannot be performed implies no limit on the power of God, and hence no defect in the doctrine of omnipotence."[2] Thus his way of dealing with the puzzle relies upon the principle that an omnipotent being need not be supposed capable of performing tasks whose descriptions are self-contradictory.

Now this principle is one which Mavrodes apparently regards as self-evident, since he offers no support for it whatever except some references which indicate that it was also accepted by Saint Thomas Aquinas. I do not wish to suggest that the principle is false. Indeed,

From *The Philosophical Review*, LXXIII, 1964, pp. 262–63. Reprinted with the permission of *The Philosophical Review* and the author.

for all I know it may even be self-evident. But it happens to be a principle which has been rejected by some important philosophers.[3] Accordingly, it might be preferable to have an analysis of the puzzle in question which does not require the use of this principle. And in fact, such an analysis is easy to provide.

Suppose, then, that God's omnipotence enables Him to do even what is logically impossible and that He actually creates a stone too heavy for Him to lift. The critic of the notion of divine omnipotence is quite mistaken if he thinks that this supposition plays into his hands. What the critic wishes to claim, of course, is that when God has created a stone which He cannot lift He is then faced with a task beyond His ability and is therefore seen to be limited in power. But this claim is not justified.

For why should God not be able to perform the task in question? To be sure, it is a task—the task of lifting a stone which He cannot lift—whose description is self-contradictory. But if God is supposed capable of performing one task whose description is self-contradictory—that of creating the problematic stone in the first place—why should He not be supposed capable of performing another—that of lifting the stone? After all, is there any greater trick in performing two logically impossible tasks than there is in performing one?

If an omnipotent being can do what is logically impossible, then he can not only create situations which he cannot handle but also, since he is not bound by the limits of consistency, he can handle situations which he cannot handle.

Notes

1. George Mavrodes, "Some Puzzles Concerning Omnipotence," *Philosophical Review*, LXXII (1963), 221–223.
2. *Ibid.*, p. 223.
3. Descartes, for instance, who in fact thought it blasphemous to maintain that God can do only what can be described in a logically coherent way: "The truths of mathematics . . . were established by God and entirely depend on Him, as much as do all the rest of His creatures. Actually, it would be to speak of God as a Jupiter or Saturn and to subject Him to the Styx and to the Fates, to say that these truths are independent of Him . . . You will be told that if God established these truths He would be able

to change them, as a king does his laws; to which it is necessary to reply that this is correct. . . . In general we can be quite certain that God can do whatever we are able to understand, but not that He cannot do what we are unable to understand. For it would be presumptuous to think that our imagination extends as far as His power" (letter to Mersenne, 15 April 1630). "God was as free to make it false that all the radii of a circle are equal as to refrain from creating the world" (letter to Mersenne, 27 May 1630). "I would not even dare to say that God cannot arrange that a mountain should exist without a valley, or that one and two should not make three; but I only say that He has given me a mind of such a nature that I cannot conceive a mountain without a valley or a sum of one and two which would not be three, and so on, and that such things imply contradictions in my conception" (letter to Arnauld, 29 July 1648). "As for the difficulty in conceiving how it was a matter of freedom and indifference to God to make it true that the three angles of a triangle should equal two right angles, or generally that contradictions should not be able to be together, one can easily remove it by considering that the power of God can have no limits. . . . God cannot have been determined to make it true that contradictions cannot be together, and consequently He could have done the contrary" (letter to Mesland, 2 May 1644).

22

The Paradox of the Stone

C. WADE SAVAGE

A.   (1)   Either God can create a stone which He cannot lift, or He cannot create a stone which He cannot lift.

       (2)   If God can create a stone which He cannot lift, then He is not omnipotent (since He cannot lift the stone in question).

       (3)   If God cannot create a stone which He cannot lift, then He is not omnipotent (since He cannot create the stone in question).

       (4)   Therefore, God is not omnipotent.

Mr. Mavrodes has offered a solution to the familiar paradox above;[1] but it is erroneous. Mavrodes states that he assumes the existence of God,[2] and then reasons (in pseudo-dilemma fashion) as follows. God is either omnipotent or He is not. If we assume that He is not omnipotent, the task of creating a stone which He cannot lift is not self-contradictory. And we can conclude that God is not omnipotent on the grounds that both His ability and His inability to perform this task imply that He is not omnipotent. But to prove His non-omnipotence in this way is trivial. "To be significant [the paradoxical argument] must derive this same conclusion *from the assumption that God is omnipotent;* that is, it must show that the assumption of the omnipotence of God leads to a *reductio.*" However, on the assumption that God is omnipotent, the task of creating a stone which God cannot lift is self-contradictory. Since inability to perform a self-contradictory task does not imply a limitation on the agent, one of the premises of the para-

From *The Philosophical Review,* LXXVI, 1967, pp. 74–79. Reprinted with the permission of *The Philosophical Review* and the author.

doxical argument—premise A(3)—is false. The argument is, in consequence, either insignificant or unsound.

There are many objections to this solution. First, the paradoxical argument need not be represented as a *reductio;* in A it is a dilemma. Mavrodes' reasoning implies that the pradoxical argument must either assume that God is omnipotent or assume that He is not omnipotent. This is simply false: neither assumption need be made, and neither is made in A. Second, "a stone which God cannot lift" is self-contradictory—on the assumption that God is omnipotent—only if "God is omnipotent" is necessarily true. "Russell can lift any stone" is a contingent statement. Consequently, if we assume that Russell can lift any stone we are thereby committed only to saying that creating a stone which Russell cannot lift is a task which *in fact* cannot be performed by Russell or anyone else. Third, if "God is omnipotent" is necessarily true—as Mavrodes must claim for his solution to work—then his assumption that God exists begs the question of the paradoxical argument. For what the argument really tries to establish is that the existence of an omnipotent being is logically impossible. Fourth, the claim that inability to perform a self-contradictory task is no limitation on the agent is not entirely uncontroversial. Descartes suggested that an omnipotent God must be able to perform such self-contradictory tasks as making a mountain without a valley and arranging that the sum of one and two is not three.[3] No doubt Mavrodes and Descartes have different theories about the nature of contradictions; but that is part of the controversy.

Mavrodes has been led astray by version A of the paradox, which apparently seeks to prove that *God is not omnipotent.* Concentration on this version, together with the inclination to say that God is by definition omnipotent, leads straight to the conclusion that the paradox is specious. For if God is by definition omnipotent, then, obviously, creating a stone which God (an omnipotent being who can lift any stone) cannot lift is a task whose description is self-contradictory. What the paradox of the stone really seeks to prove is that the notion of an omnipotent being is logically inconsistent—that is, that *the existence of an omnipotent being, God or any other, is logically impossible.* It tries to do this by focusing on the perfectly consistent task of creating a stone which the creator cannot lift. The essence of the argument is that an omnipotent being must be able to perform this task and yet cannot perform the task.

Stated in its clearest form, the paradoxical argument of the stone is as follows. Where x is any being:

B.   (1) Either x can create a stone which x cannot lift, or x cannot create a stone which x cannot lift.
      (2) If x can create a stone which x cannot lift, then, necessarily, there is at least one task which x cannot perform (namely, lift the stone in question).
      (3) If x cannot create a stone which x cannot lift, then, necessarily, there is at least one task which x cannot perform (namely, create the stone in question).
      (4) Hence, there is at least one task which x cannot perform.
      (5) If x is an omnipotent being, then x can perform any task.
      (6) Therefore, x is not omnipotent.

Since x is any being, this argument proves that the existence of an omnipotent being, God or any other, is logically impossible.

It is immediately clear that Mavrodes' solution will not apply to this version of the paradox. B is obviously a significant, nontrivial argument. But since it does not contain the word "God," no critic can maintain that B assumes that God is omnipotent. For the same reason, the point that "a stone which God cannot lift" is self-contradictory is simply irrelevant. Notice also that B is neutral on the question of whether inability to perform a self-contradictory task is a limitation on the agent's power. We can, however, replace every occurrence of "task" with "task whose description is not self-contradictory" without damaging the argument in any way.

The paradox does have a correct solution, though a different one from that offered by Mavrodes. The two solutions are similar in that both consist in arguing that an agent's inability to create a stone which he cannot lift does not entail a limitation on his power. But here the similarity ends. For, as we shall see presently, the basis of the correct solution is not that creating a stone which the creator cannot lift is a self-contradictory task (which it is not). Consequently, the correct solution side-steps the question of whether an agent's inability to perform a self-contradictory task is a limitation on his power.

The fallacy in the paradox of the stone lies in the falsity of the second horn—B(3)—of its dilemma: "x can create a stone which x cannot lift" does indeed entail that there is a task which x cannot perform and, consequently, does entail that x is not omnipotent. However, "x cannot create a stone which x cannot lift" does not entail that there is a task which x cannot perform and, consequently, does not entail that x is not omnipotent. That the entailment *seems* to hold is explained by the misleading character of the statement "x cannot create a stone which x cannot lift." The phrase "cannot create a stone" seems to imply that there is a task which x cannot perform and, consequently, seems to imply that x is limited in power. But this illusion vanishes on analysis: "x cannot create a stone which x cannot lift" can only mean "If x can create a stone, then x can lift it." It is obvious that the latter statement does not entail that x is limited in power.

A schematic representation of B(1)-B(3) will bring our point into sharper focus. Let S = stone, C = can create, and L = can lift; let x be any being; and let the universe of discourse be conceivable entities. Then we obtain:

C.   (1) $(\exists y)(Sy \cdot Cxy \cdot -Lxy) \lor -(\exists y)(Sy \cdot Cxy \cdot -Lxy)$.
      (2) $(\exists y)(Sy \cdot Cxy \cdot -Lxy) \supset (\exists y)(Sy \cdot -Lxy)$.
      (3)—$(\exists y)(Sy \cdot Cxy \cdot -Lxy) \supset (\exists y)(Sy \cdot -Cxy)$.

That the second alternative in C(1) is equivalent to "$(y)[(Sy \cdot Cxy) \supset Lxy]$" schematically explains our interpretation of "x cannot create a stone which x cannot lift" as meaning "If x can create a stone, then x can lift it." It is now quite clear where the fallacy in the paradoxical argument lies. Although C(2) is logically true, C(3) is not. "$(\exists y)(Sy \cdot Cxy \cdot -Lxy)$" logically implies "$(\exists y)(Sy \cdot -Lxy)$." But "$-(\exists y)(Sx \cdot Cxy \cdot -Lxy)$" does not logically imply "$(\exists y)(Sy \cdot -Cxy)$"; nor does it logically imply "$(\exists y)(Sy \cdot -Lxy)$." In general, "$x$ cannot create a stone which x cannot lift" does not logically imply "There is a task which x cannot perform."

For some reason the above analysis does not completely remove the inclination to think that an agent's inability to create a stone which he himself cannot lift does entail his inability to perform some task, does entail a limitation on his power. The reason becomes clear when we consider the task of creating a stone which someone *other than* the creator cannot lift. Suppose that y cannot lift any stone heavier than seventy pounds. Not if x cannot create a stone which y cannot lift, then x cannot create a stone heavier than seventy pounds, and is indeed limited in power. But suppose that y is omnipotent and can lift stones of any poundage. Then x's inability to create a stone which y cannot lift does not necessarily constitute a limitation on x's power. For x may be able to create stones of any poundage, although y can lift any stone which x creates. If y can lift stones of any poundage, and x cannot create a stone heavier than seventy pounds, then x cannot create a stone which y cannot lift, and x is limited in power. But if x can create stones of any poundage, and y can lift stones of any poundage, then x cannot create a stone which y cannot lift, and yet x is not thereby limited in power. Now it is easy to see that precisely parallel considerations obtain where x is both stone-creator and stone-lifter.

The logical facts above may be summarized as follows. Whether $x = y$ or $x \neq y$, x's inability to create a stone which y cannot lift constitutes a limitation on x's power only if (i) x is unable to create stones of any poundage, or (ii) y is unable to lift stones of any poundage. And, since either (i) or (ii) may be false, "x cannot create a stone which y cannot lift" does not entail "x is limited in power." This logical point is obscured, however, by the normal context of our discussions of abilities and inabilities. Since such discussions are normally restricted to beings who are limited in their stone-creating, stone-lifting, and other abilities, the inability of a being to create a stone which he himself or some other being cannot lift *normally* constitutes a limitation on his power. And this produces the illusion that a being's inability to create a stone which he himself or some other being cannot lift *necessarily* constitutes a limitation on his power, the illusion that "x cannot create a stone which y cannot lift" (where either $x = y$ or $x \neq y$) entails "x is limited in power."

Since our discussions normally concern beings of limited power, the erroneous belief that "x cannot create a stone which x cannot lift" entails "x is limited in power" will normally cause no difficulty. But we must beware when the discussion turns to God—a being who is presumably unlimited in power. God's inability to create a stone which He cannot lift is a limitation on His power only if (i) He is unable to create stones of any poundage, or (ii) He is unable to lift stones of any poundage—that is, only if He is limited in His power of stone-creating or His power of stone-lifting. But until it has been proved otherwise— and it is difficult to see how this could be done—we are free to suppose that God suffers neither of these limitations. On this supposition God's inability to create a stone which He cannot lift is nothing more nor less than a necessary consequence of two facets of His omnipotence.[4] For if God is omnipotent, then He can create stones of any poundage and lift stones of any poundage. And "God can create stones of any poundage, and God can lift stones of any poundage" entails "God cannot create a stone which He cannot lift."

Notes

1. George I. Mavrodes, "Some Puzzles Concerning Omnipotence," *Philosophical Review*, LXXII (1963), 221–223. The heart of his solution is contained in pars. 6, 7, and 11.
2. See n. 2, p. 221.
3. Harry G. Frankfurt, "The Logic of Omnipotence," *Philosophical Review*, LXXIII (1964), 262–263. The relevant passage from Descartes is quoted by Frankfurt in a long footnote.

   Mavrodes assumes (on his "significant" interpretation of the paradox) that creating a stone which God cannot lift is a self-contradictory task, and contends that God therefore cannot perform it. This forces him onto the second horn of dilemma A, which he tries to break by arguing that inability to perform a self-contradictory task does not imply a limitation on the agent. Frankfurt also assumes that creating a stone which God cannot lift is a self-contradictory task, but contends with Descartes (for the sake of argument) that God can nevertheless perform it. This forces him onto the first horn of the dilemma, which he tries to break with the following argument. If God can perform the self-contradictory task of creating a stone which He cannot lift, then He can just as easily perform the additional self-contradictory task of lifting the stone which He (creates and) cannot lift. Frankfurt's fundamental error is the same as Mavrodes': both suppose that on any significant interpretation the paradox sets for God the self-contradictory task of creating a stone which God (an omnipotent being who can lift any stone) cannot lift.
4. Mavrodes apparently sees this point in the last three paragraphs of his article. But his insight is vitiated by his earlier mistaken attempt to solve the paradox.

23

The Paradox of Omnipotence

J. L. COWAN

The claim that God is omnipotent is presumably the claim that He can do anything. The most direct way of arguing against such a claim is therefore to attempt to show that there is something God cannot do. Thus it has been argued that even God cannot do self-contradictory things. He cannot, for example, draw a square circle.

That this sort of objection will not really do the job, however, seems clear. The reasons why it will not are essentially those advanced by Aquinas.[1] To put Aquinas' point in a more contemporary jargon, the only thing which gives this sort of objection any plausibility is the frequently convenient but often misleading material mode expression "self-contradictory things." Actually there are no self-contradictory things. It is expressions, statements, phrases, descriptions, or predicates which are self-contradictory or not. Those which are self-contradictory are so constituted that they are logically vacuous, they cannot, as a matter of logic, truly be applied to anything. Thus when we have noted that God cannot draw a square circle we have still not noted any *thing* which God cannot draw. We have still not produced anything which God cannot do. Therefore we have still not provided any valid objection to the doctrine that God can do anything, the doctrine of God's omnipotence.

There are, however, other predicates, predicates which are not self-contradictory and which are thus not logically vacuous as are those we

From *Analysis*, Supplement to Vol. 25, 1964–65, pp. 102–8. Reprinted with the permission of *Analysis*.

have so far been considering, predicates which, indeed, are not vacuous at all, which not only can be but are truly applied, and which yet raise difficulties for the concept of omnipotence. Consider the old question of whether God can create a stone too heavy for Him to lift. There does not seem to be any inconsistency here. The expression "making something too heavy for the maker to lift" is not, like "drawing a square circle," one which we must refuse to apply to any activity whatsoever, but is, rather, one which we readily and correctly apply to many quite simple, homely, everyday activities. I myself have performed such and know many others who have. Can God perform such activities? Can He do what even I have done? Can He make something too heavy for the maker to lift? If He cannot, then He is not omnipotent since there is something (namely this) which He cannot do. If, on the other hand, He can do this, He is not omnipotent since there is something else (namely lift everything) which He cannot do. So in any case He cannot, it would seem, be omnipotent.

It may be argued, however, that in spite of the apparent differences between the present sort of objection to God's omnipotence and that first considered, the sort of response given by Aquinas to the original objection is actually applicable here as well. One might reason that even though a predicate may not itself be self-contradictory, its *predication* of an omnipotent being might be so. This in fact has been the conclusion reached in a series of recent discussions of this ancient (more accurately medieval) paradox.

J. L. Mackie began the series, in a paper on omnipotence and evil, by arguing that even apart from the problem of evil the present paradox poses formidable obstacles for those who would accept the concept of an omnipotent God.[2] Mackie then suggested two "solutions" of the paradox. The first of these would in effect eliminate the concept of omnipotence. The second would in effect eliminate the concept of God. G. B. Keene next suggested a simpler "solution."[3] Keene's idea was that the paradox when suitably phrased proves not to be a paradox at all. B. Mayo then showed that Keene's translation was inadequate and so that his proposed solution would not do the job.[4] Mayo concluded, however, by pointing out that the statement of the paradox contains a self-contradiction and suggesting that it was therefore resoluble along the same lines as that about round squares. Finally, G. I. Mavrodes argued to the same effect in greater detail.[5]

Mavrodes' formulation is the more elaborate. If, he argues, we assume that God is not omnipotent, we can, of course, "prove" that He is not omnipotent. But if we assume that God is omnipotent, then presumably the statement that God can make something too heavy for Him to lift becomes, on analysis, the statement that a being who can lift anything can make something too heavy for Him to lift. But since this statement is self-contradictory and thus vacuous in the sense explained above, God's "inability" to perform the pseudo-task described by the statement can constitute no more objection to His omnipotence than his "inability" to draw a square circle. To ask that God be both omnipotent (as for the purposes of the argument we must assume Him to be) *and* able to make something too heavy for Him to lift, is exactly comparable to asking our friend Smith to be a married bachelor or a teetotaller who drinks Scotch.

This Mayo-Mavrodes argument is an ingenious one, yet it leaves me unhappy. The argument shows that the statement that God is both omnipotent and can make something He cannot lift is self-contradictory and thus does not constitute the description of something God could be expected to do. But the argument does not thereby show that the concept of omnipotence is *itself* self-contradictory and that it therefore constitutes *in itself* something not to be expected of God. But since it is just this which is the real point of the objection to God's omnipotence now under consideration, the present argument, and indeed any argument along the lines taken by Aquinas in response to the sort of objection initially considered, might be taken to support rather than to rebut this second kind of objection to the doctrine of God's omnipotence. I shall argue in this paper that this is in fact the case, that Mayo and Mavrodes are quite correct in holding that the paradox contains a self-contradiction, but that the paradox still constitutes a valid objection to the doctrine of omnipotence since that contradiction stems from the concept of omnipotence itself.

The crux of the entire issue lies in one simple fact. Because of its central importance I shall state this in three ways, in the formal mode as (1a), in the material mode as (1b), and in a simple logical notation as

(1c). These are quite equivalent, however, and I shall refer to them indiscriminately as "(1)."

> (1a) There are perfectly respectable, non-self-contradictory predicates, predicates meaningfully and even truly predicable even of such lowly beings as you and me, predicates which, however, are such that the capacity to have them truly predicated of one logically excludes the capacity to have *other* similarly non-self-contradictory predicates truly predicated of one.
>
> (1b) Some capacities imply limitations; there are things one can do only if one cannot do certain other things.
>
> (1c) $(\exists F)(\exists G)(x)(pFx \supset \sim pGx)$. Here "pFx" means "x can (do or be) F," and the other symbols are as usual except that to rule out all suspicion of having cheated the Mayo-Mavrodes objections we might limit the range of the "F"'s and "G"'s to the non-self-contradictory.

One example of the sort of thing referred to in (1) is the manufacturing ability we have been considering. If one can make something one cannot lift, one cannot lift everything (collectively or distributively) that one can make. It is important to note, moreover, that the existence of such mutually exclusive predicates is a matter of logic. If we did not have them already, we could define some. Thus (1) is not merely true, it is a logical truth in the sense of being true by (following logically from) definitions.

But since there are such mutually exclusive predicates the assumption that God (or anything else) is omnipotent becomes, on analysis, self-contradictory. That God is omnipotent presumably means that He can do anything the description of which is not self-contradictory. He can do F, which is not self-contradictory; He can do G, which is also not self-contradictory; and so on. But since the ability to do F will in some cases logically imply the inability to do G, the claim that God is omnipotent will implicate both the claim that God can do G and the claim that He cannot do G. More formally:

> (1) $(\exists F)(\exists G)(x)(pFx \supset \sim pGx)$ By definition.
> (2) $(F)pFg$ Assumption that God is omnipotent. 'F' again restricted to the non-self-contradictory.

(3)	pFg ⊃~pGg	From (1) by instantiation.
(4)	pFg	From (2) by instantiation.
(5)	~pGg	From (3) and (4) by modus ponens.
(6)	pGg	From (2) by instantiation.

For example, since God is omnipotent and thus can make any kind of thing, He can make something He cannot lift; but since He is omnipotent and thus can lift any kind of thing, He cannot make something He cannot lift.

The same point may be put in a way which confronts even more directly the line of reasoning represented by Mavrodes' argument. This may be done by challenging the basic premiss of this kind of argument. It is *not* necessary to begin a proof that God is not omnipotent either with the assumption that He is not omnipotent or with the assumption that He is. To prove that neither God nor anything else is omnipotent one need assume nothing more than (1). Since there are things one can do only if one cannot do certain other things, it follows that there will be, for everyone (everything), *something* he (it) cannot do. Formally:

(1)	(∃F)(∃G)(x)(pFx ⊃~pGx)	By definition.
(2)	pFx ⊃~pGx	By existential instantiation on F and G, and universal instantiation on x.
→(3)	pFx	Conditional proof assumption.
(4)	~pGx	By *modus ponens* from (2) and (3).
(5)	(∃F)~pFx	Existential generalization from (4).
(6)	pFx ⊃(∃F)~pFx	Conditional proof from (3)–(5).
→(7)	~pFx	Conditional proof assumption.
(8)	(∃F)~pFx	Existential generalization from (7).
(9)	~pFx ⊃(∃F)~pFx	Conditional proof from (7)–(8).
(10)	pFx v ~pFx	Tautology. Horns between which we cannot slip by the Mayo-Mavrodes gambit since no omnipotent being is mentioned.
(11)	(∃F)~pFx	By constructive dilemma from (6), (9) and (10).
(12)	~(F)pFx	By quantifier negation from (11).
(13)	(x)~(F)pFx	Universal generalization from (12).
(14)	~(∃x)(F)pFx	By quantifier negation from (13).
or (14a)	(x)(∃F)~pFx	By quantifier negation from (13).

Since no one can make something he cannot lift unless he cannot lift everything, everyone (including God) will be limited either with respect to his making or with respect to his lifting or both.

Moreover, since (1) is a logical truth, since the existence of mutually exclusive predicates is assured by definition, and since the non-existence of anything omnipotent follows directly from (1) without any further premiss being necessary, that nothing is omnipotent is not merely true, it is a logical truth exactly comparable to the truth that nothing is a square circle. Our concepts of being able to do (or be) things are simply not such that they will all fit together on any one subject. Since being able to do some perfectly legitimate, non-self-contradictory things involves (logically) being unable to do others, nothing can (logically) be able to do everything non-self-contradictory. We would therefore seem to have no choice but to abandon as irrevocably vacuous the concept of omnipotence, to admit that neither God nor anything else can be omnipotent.

I suspect, however, that, clear and cogent as this argument seems, the proponents of the line of reasoning I have been criticizing will not yet be quite satisfied, for I have not yet confronted quite directly enough what must be the basic points at which they are driving, or, as I should prefer to put it, the basic sources of their confusion. Surely, such a proponent might argue, the only things we can show *a priori,* by logic alone, that God cannot do are self-contradictory "things." From this it would seem to follow that we cannot, by logic alone, show that there is any non-self-contradictory thing God cannot do. This in turn would seem to mean that we cannot, after all, show, by logic alone, that God is not omnipotent.

There are two confusions in this short line of reasoning. In the first place, even if we restrict God's omnipotence to the ability to do anything the description of which is not self-contradictory, there is *one* thing which, even if its description *is* self-contradictory, is still relevant to the question of God's omnipotence. That thing is omnipotence itself. Since the concept of being able to do anything not self-contradictory is *itself* self-contradictory, one can indeed, by showing that there is "something" self-contradictory which God cannot do, show that there is something *not* self-contradictory which God cannot do.

A second confusion turns on an ambiguity in the phrase "show that there is something non-self-contradictory which God cannot do." It is true that the only definite, specific things we can logically prove God cannot do are self-contradictory "things." We can, however, still by logic alone, prove that there is *something* non-self-contradictory that God cannot do. We cannot by logic alone say specifically *what* that thing is, but simply proving that it exists is enough to prove that God cannot do everything non-self-contradictory, that He is not omnipotent.

I shall put this point in concrete form once again. There is a perfectly simple, straightforward, entirely non-self-contradictory task which I, who am fairly skilful at making things but not much on muscles, can do. I can make something too heavy for the maker to lift. Our friend Smith, on the other hand, who is quite strong but incredibly inept at making things, can perform another, equally straightforward and non-self-contradictory task. He can lift anything the lifter can make. But no one, not even God, can do *both* what I can do *and* what Smith can do. To ask God, or anyone else, to be able so to do would be to ask for something self-contradictory and thus vacuous, a pseudo-something. So either Smith or I, although we cannot by logic alone say which, can do something even God cannot do. Thus God cannot be omnipotent.

So much for the argument. What does it really establish? After all, whatever I could make, God could make still better; whatever Smith could lift, God could lift this and more. Mavrodes, indeed, feels that the argument, even if accepted, would establish nothing at all. Even if God's ability to make were "limited" by His ability to lift, he reasons, since God's ability to lift would still be infinite, His ability to make would likewise be infinite.

But surely this line of reasoning confuses finitude with limitation and one limitation with another. One might just as well argue that puppy A which cannot catch its own tail is really no more limited than puppy B which, being somewhat more flexible, *can* catch its own tail. After all, one may reason, this places no limitation on how far puppy A may run or how fast. Puppy A might still be able to catch B's tail and might indeed be able to do so even more easily than puppy B can. All this is quite true, but it is also quite irrelevant. The fact remains that puppy A, however splendid his other qualities, lacks a capacity possessed by puppy B.

Perhaps part of the difficulty of grasping the force of this conclusion stems from having, thus far, kept our examples so simple. But consider two possible (theologically interesting) conceptions of a limited God: (a) a God who cannot completely control the development of every universe he can create, and (b) a God who cannot create a universe he cannot completely control. Our argument then shows that the actual God, if there is one, must possess either limitation (a) or limitation (b). He cannot escape both.

The argument also has applications beyond theology. In the United States the founding documents of colleges and universities usually state that their governing boards shall have the power to hire and fire "at pleasure," or "whenever, in the judgment of the board, the interests of the university shall require," or something to this effect. These documents state, in brief, that within this area the governing board is to be omnipotent. Thus the courts have traditionally maintained that any contract for employment at such an institution not terminable at will (let alone a tenure arrangement) was invalid as constituting a limitation on the power to discharge. More recently, however, as the value of contracts and tenure systems has become more apparent, courts have upheld such contracts on the grounds that to deny governing boards the power to enter into them would constitute a limitation on their power to employ. Despite their contradictory conclusions both arguments are, of course, quite correct. The original documents granting omnipotence even within such a limited area are, if interpreted straightforwardly, self-contradictory. The power to hire (for a fixed term for example) cannot be unlimited unless the power to fire can be limited and conversely.[6]

The same argument, moreover, is applicable to other omniconcepts. It is applicable, for example, to omniscience.[7] Does God know how to create a universe the potentialities of which he does not know?

The final upshot of our argument, then, would seem to be that there is more work to be done than some have thought. In the area of law, for example, such blanket empowerings as we have considered, since they are ruled out by logic, 'will have to be replaced by more specific grantings and withholdings whether by statute or by the courts. In theology it would seem that those theologians or philosophers of religion who have explored various conceptions of a limited God have been taking the only consistent course. Rather than trying to cut the Gordian knot of God's nature with impossible concepts like omnipotence and omniscience, we must try to unpuzzle it strand by strand. We cannot have everything, but must be content with the best of all *possible* gods.

Notes

1. *Summa Theologica,* Part I, Q.25, Art.3.
2. "Evil and Omnipotence," *Mind,* Vol. LXIV, No. 254 (April 1955), pp. 200–212.
3. "A Simpler Solution to the Paradox of Omnipotence," *Mind,* Vol. LXIX, No. 273 (January 1960), pp. 74–75.
4. "Mr. Keene on Omnipotence," *Mind,* Vol. LXX, No. 278 (April 1961), pp. 249–250.
5. "Some Puzzles Concerning Omnipotence," *The Philosophical Review,* Vol. LXXII, No. 2 (April 1963), pp. 221–223.
6. For references see W. P. Murphy, "Educational Freedom in the Courts," *A.A.U.P. Bulletin,* Vol. XLIX, No. 4 (December 1963), pp. 309–327.
7. As was pointed out to me by my colleagues R. L. Caldwell and R. D. Milo.

24

The Omnipotence Paradox

DOUGLAS WALTON

Can an omnipotent being create a stone too heavy for him to lift? If not, he is not omnipotent. But if so, he is not omnipotent either, since there is something he cannot lift. Hence there can be no omnipotent being. J. L. Cowan's recent reformulation of this paradox of omnipotence (this *Journal,* vol. III, no. 3, March, 1974) has been sharpened through a number of objections and clarifications,[1] and, in its final form, constitutes a significant problem for the analysis of the concept of an omnipotent agent. I will develop fragments of two systems in which the problem can be defined more exactly, and try to indicate some formal guidelines within which constructive steps towards a solution may be possible. I will argue that the paradox shows the need for a special kind of restriction on omnipotence that can be distinguished from some related restrictions.

It is a common presupposition that there are agents that bring about states of affairs in the world directly through their agency. We could represent this motion in a standard kind of notation by having propositional variables range over states of affairs and introduce an operator to construct sentences like $\ulcorner \delta_a p \urcorner$, to be read "The individual a brings it about directly that p obtains." It is useful to be able to extend this kind of talk such that if p and q are states of affairs, $\ulcorner p \& q \urcorner$, $\ulcorner p \lor q \urcorner$, and $\ulcorner p \supset q \urcorner$ are conjunctive, disjunctive and conditional states of affairs respectively. If we are ontologically permissive enough and

This article is reprinted from Vol. IV, no. 4 (June 1975) of the *Canadian Journal of Philosophy,* pp. 705–15, by permission of the Canadian Association for Publishing in Philosophy.

regard a state of affairs as something that may or may not obtain, we can also have negative states of affairs such as ⌜~p⌝, the state of affairs that obtains just in case p fails to obtain. For those who regard this way of speaking as ontologically lavish, p,q,r, etc. may be thought of as propositions, provided only we restrict ourselves to the kind of propositions that may be made to come to be true or false through human agency. In particular, it is a *desideratum* that δ be regarded as a vacuous operator over tautologies and inconsistent schemata much as a quantifier is vacuous over a schema containing no variables of its type within its scope.[2] Thus sentences like ⌜δ$_a$ (p v~ p)⌝ and ⌜~δ$_a$ (p & ~p)⌝ will all be theorems. A picture of a fragment of a system now begins to emerge, *System* δ, that should have, minimally, as axioms the following pair.

Aδ1: δ$_a$p ⊃ p
Aδ2: δ$_a$(p & q) ⊃ (δ$_a$p & δ$_a$q)

First, δ is truth-entailing. That is, if I directly bring it about that p obtains then it follows that p obtains. Second, δ is closed under conjunction-elimination. If I bring ⌜p & q⌝ about then, severally, I bring it about that p and I bring it about that q.[3]

Means of extending this fragment of System δ towards a theory of action are replete with significant problems. Should we have as a theorem

(1)   (δ$_a$(p ⊃ q) & δ$_a$p) ⊃ δ$_a$q?

If I bring it about that if the light is turned on the prowler is warned, and I turn the light on, do I directly bring it about that the prowler is warned?[4] It seems rather that I warn the prowler in some more indirect sense than through *direct personal* agency, as it were. Other conundrums are suggested by reflecting on iterated schemata such as ⌜δ$_a$ δ$_b$p⌝. Can Al bring it about that Cal pulls the trigger? Again, perhaps only in some suitably indirect sense.

It is a second common presupposition that agents sometimes have opportunities to bring states of affairs about, that sometimes the way is open to doing things. We could represent this notion by iterating an operation M* over the δ-operator of System δ to construct expressions like $\ulcorner M^*\delta_a p\urcorner$, to be read "a has the opportunity to bring it about that p." This notation might also be glossed "a is free to do p," "a has positive control over p" or "a has the power to do p," in the restricted sense that implies only that there is no (physical) obstruction to a's doing p. A picture of a fragment of System $M^*\delta$ (with System δ as a base system) emerges through consideration of the following two minimal axioms for M^*.

$$AM^*\delta 1: \delta_a p \supset M^*\delta_a p$$
$$AM^*\delta 2: M^*\delta_a(p v q) \equiv (M^*\delta_a p \ v \ M^*\delta_a q)$$

This fragment underlies much recent action theory and the philosophical problems associated with it and surrounding it are enormously significant.[5]

Some problems relating to these fragments have to do with omnipotence, as discussed in some recent articles.[6] Initially, one might expect to capture a certain conception of omnipotence by ruling that an agent is omnipotent where each state of affairs is such that he has the opportunity to bring it about, that is, where the following obtains.

(2) $(\forall p)(M^*\delta_a p)$

According to this conception, an omnipotent agent has the power at t, relative to the set of initial conditions at t to bring about any state of affairs $p_{t+\Delta}$, where t is some point or small stretch of time and Δ is some, perhaps very small, interval. We could call this the *nihil obstat* conception of omnipotence. It need not be required, for an agent to be omnipotent in this sense, Descartes to the contrary, that the agent have the power to bring it about that $\ulcorner p \ \& \ {\sim}p\urcorner$ obtain.[7] We remember that $\ulcorner {\sim} \delta_a (p \ \& \ {\sim}p)\urcorner$ is a theorem of System δ.

An important problem is introduced by this anti-Cartesian way of proceeding, since it commits us to the consistency of (2) with

(3) ${\sim}M^*\delta_a(p \ \& \ {\sim}p),$

and thereby seems to unduly restrict the domain of the quantifier in (2) to truth-functionally atomic states of affairs. The problem for M^* here is analogous to the question of what to do about cases where tautologies or inconsistencies come within the scope of the δ-operator. In response to that problem, we followed Fitch in ruling that δ be regarded as vacuous in such instances so that, in M*δ, $\ulcorner \sim\delta_a(p\&\sim p)\urcorner$ will be a theorem. A similar strategy is required for M*—a parallel, and what seems the most appropriate solution, would be to rule that when M* is iterated to the left of a δ-operator that precedes a theorem, the resultant expression is a theorem, and when M* is iterated to the left of a δ-operator that precedes the negation of a theorem, the resultant expression is a negation of a theorem. Hence by double negation, (3) is a theorem. The upshot is that (2), the base conception of omnipotence, is not correct as it stands, assuming we follow the Fitchean route sketched above, according to which no individual, even an omnipotent being, has the power to bring about $\ulcorner p \& \sim p\urcorner$. Accordingly, it is required that in (2) we add a clause restricting the domain of the quantifier to consistent states of affairs. An alternative solution would be to rule that no expressions where δ or M* appear to the left of a tautology or inconsistent schema are well-formed. I will not pursue either of these solutions in depth here,[8] but simply acknowledge the difficulty and pass on to the central locus of Cowan's concern.

It should be contingent in System M*δ whether a given agent has the power to bring it about that p and at the same time the power to bring it about that $\sim$p. The same agent can have both positive and negative control over a state of affairs.[9] *Example:* right now I have the power to make this piece of chalk drop on the floor and also the power to bring about the state of affairs whereby the chalk does not drop. Thus it should not be a theorem of System M* δ that

(4) $(M^*\delta_a p \ \& \ M^*\delta_a q) \supset M^*\delta_a(p \ \& \ q)$

In addition, neither the schema,

$M^*\delta_a p \ \& \ M^*\delta_a \sim p$

nor its negation should be a theorem of System M* δ if common conceptions of agency are to be captured. Oddly enough, however, where we replace *a* in the above schema by *b,* where *a* and *b* are not identical, we get a schema whose negation should be a theorem of System M* δ.

(5) $M^*\delta_a p \ \& \ M^*\delta_b \sim p$

In other words, it should be a theorem of M* δ that

(TM*δ) ($\forall_a$) ($\forall_b$) (a ≠ b ⊃ ~(M*δ_ap & M*δ_b~p))

For assume that (5) obtains. Then

(6)   M*δ_ap

Then *a* has positive control over p. For example, Al has the power to make this piece of chalk drop on the floor. But we also have it from (5) that

(7)   M*δ_b~p

That is, *b* has negative control over p. For example, Cal has the power to bring it about that the chalk does not drop. Thus the state of affairs represented by (5) is what we might call a *control stalemate* or *control clash*.[10] If Al has the power to make the chalk drop then Cal cannot *at the very same time* (or over the same period) genuinely have the power to bring it about that the chalk does not drop. One agent or the other has merely the illusion of control. Without dwelling too long on this very interesting notion of control stalemate, let me simply indicate its relevance to the free will defense. The problem is to determine how it is possible that an omnipotent agent, in the above sense, could fail to be in a situation of control stalemate with every other free agent. At least, I would like to suggest that this is a useful way to formulate the problem initially faced by the free will defense proponent.[11]

The problem of omnipotence that interests Cowan is posed by the observation that there is a certain class of states of affairs such that an agent's bringing one of these states about has the consequence that his control over some state of affairs is negated. My cutting off my hand is an illustrative, if gruesome, member of this class. If I cut off my hand then there is a state of affairs, for example, winning the Golden Gloves, that will thereby no longer be within my power. We might call this class of states of affairs the *self-limiting class,* those where minimally,

(8) δ_ap ⊃ ($\exists$q) (~M*δ_aq)

The state of affairs that there comes to be an object too heavy for its creator to lift is a self-limiting or self-disabling state of affairs. If I create such an object it follows that I cannot lift it. The paradox is posed by asking of a logically consistent self-limiting state of affairs, p, can an omnipotent agent bring it about? If he can, then assume he does. Then by (8), it follows by *modus ponens* that

(9) $(\exists q)\,(\sim M^*\delta_a q)$

But since the agent is omnipotent, we have it for logically consistent states of affairs that

(2) $(\forall p)\,(M^*\delta_a p)$

which contradicts (9). Thus, in general, an omnipotent agent, as defined above, cannot bring about self-limiting states of affairs. But this seems absurd.

Let us digress briefly to show that (8) cannot be regarded as an adequate explicit definition of self-limiting states, but only a necessary condition, for the expressive power of System $M^*\ \delta$ is thereby shown incomplete in this respect. Observe that if there is *anything* that a is unable to do, the consequent of (8) is satisfied, and *every* state of affairs is self-limiting for a. An adequate definition for the self-limiting class would require a supplementary condition, perhaps to the effect that a's bringing about p is the *cause* of his inability to bring about q. It is well known that the material conditional is inadequate to the kinds of conditionals often expressed in strongly tensed or causal contexts, just those contexts most often appropriate to assertions of agency. Thus $M^*\ \delta$ is bound to have significant limitations since it is based in classical truth-functional logic. It is important, nevertheless, I suggest, to study the behaviour of δ and M^* in classical logic as a preliminary means to eventually extending these operators into causal contexts. A fuller, really thoroughgoing understanding of the paradox of omnipotence would need to be strongly causal, or at any rate, would need to study the properties of δ and M^* over non-classical conditionals.

As we will see below, various restrictions on the base notion of omnipotence of (2) are required, but the paradox of omnipotence specifically shows that some restriction banning self-limiting actions is called for. It seems likely that such a restriction will need to be causal, yet it is interesting to try to determine how far some variant in (8) might succeed in doing the job. One proposal might be to make (2) provisional upon the negation of (8), ostensibly ruling that a being is omnipotent where he can bring about any state of affairs provided (among other possible requirements) it is not the case that if he brings about a state of affairs there is a state of affairs that he does not have the power to bring about. Regrettably, this proviso turns out to be demonstrably spurious, as we can see by observing that the negation of (8) is first-order-equivalent to

(10) $\delta_a p \ \& \ \sim(\exists q)\,(\sim M^*\delta_a q)$

Now the first conjunct of (10) is already implied by (2) and the second one is equivalent to (2) by quantifier-interchange. Hence the negation of (8) is a redundant qualification to (2). I have not shown, I hasten to add, that a variant of (8) *cannot* be expressed in $M^*\delta$ that will do the job of coping with the paradox. The paradox can be expressed, usefully I think, as a contradiction in $M^*\delta$, but whether it can be avoided within extensions of $M^*\delta$ I pose as an interesting but unsolved problem.

I would like to suggest, however, that some restriction along the lines of (8) seems consistent with and even required by Christian theology, since it seems inconceivable that Almighty God could be said to bring about a state of affairs that would impair his power. Even this thesis, however, requires qualifications that suggest that multiple, interlocking restrictions on omnipotence are ultimately necessary for theology. For the control of even an omnipotent being over *free* agents must be suitably indirect and have as a consequence a certain loss of direct control.[12] These special qualifications apart, it seems theologically inappropriate to require of an omnipotent deity that he be able to bring about self-limiting states. In short, the paradox poses a genuine problem for theology.

Part of the problem is that there is a feeling that a truly omnipotent being must be capable of doing *literally everything* and therefore that any restrictions at all on the concept of omnipotence is intrinsically contradictory or absurd. Descartes is the extreme proponent of this view, arguing that a perfect agent must even be able to bring it about that $\ulcorner p\, \&\sim p\urcorner$ obtains. However, unless the Cartesian suggestion is that we consider a deviant logic, it is hard to see how it can result in anything but a Kierkegaardian irrationalism that prohibits any consistent account of omnipotence at all. While it is true that we should hardly expect to get a perfect grasp of almightiness, that should not deter us from trying to construct a rational if imperfect model that is at least consistent with what we do know and adequate within reasonable limits.

Yet once we ban $\lceil p \ \& \sim p \rceil$ from the domain of states of affairs that can be brought about, the way is paved for the introduction of further limitations. Consider

$$(11) \quad \delta_a(p \ \& \sim \delta_a p)$$

The state of affairs in parentheses is logically consistent. Example: the door is open but I do not directly bring it about that the door is open. But the negation of the entire schema must be a theorem in System δ, for by A δ 1, we have it from the entire scheme that

$$(12) \quad p \ \& \sim \delta_a p$$

and hence truth-functionally that

$$\sim \delta_a p$$

Whereas by A δ 2 and the same truth-functional step, we have it that

$$\delta_a p$$

Thus (11) is logically false by *reductio*.[13] And since (11) is logically false it cannot come within the range of states of affairs that an agent can control in M*δ p. The schema in parentheses represents a state of affairs that no agent, even an omnipotent one, can bring about, although this state of affairs is logically consistent.

Geach has argued that there is a third class of states of affairs not within the control of even an omnipotent agent, namely, events in the past, and it seems unreasonable not to acquiesce in this restriction.[14] That is, once δp has happened at t, then at $t + \Delta$, p is not within the control of any agent.

$$(13) \quad \sim p_t \supset (\forall_a) \ (\sim M^* \delta_{a, t+\Delta} p_t)$$

Essentially, what this restriction amounts to is that the notion of omnipotence is tensed and future-directed. To say that an agent is omnipotent is to say that given any future, unactualized state of affairs, p, the agent has the power to bring about p (positive control) or $\sim$p (negative control). The tensed aspect is part and parcel of the *nihil obstat* conception of control.

The three restrictions above apply to all agents and hence to an omnipotent agent. In this respect, the restriction necessitated by the paradox of omnipotence is to be distinguished from them. Imperfect controllers can sometimes bring about self-limiting states of affairs, but an ominpotent agent is restricted in this respect, paradoxical though that sounds. Having accepted the principle of conceptual limitations on omnipotence as exemplified in the three restrictions above, however, a fourth restriction may seem less paradoxical. The critic who persists in reserving the term 'omnipotence' for the first definition (the power to do literally everything) can cheerfully be conceded this usage by the theologican, who is free to reserve the term 'almightiness' for the restricted conception.[15] In this idiom, omnipotence, but not almightiness, is demonstrably an incoherent concept.

The heart of the special problem posed by the paradox of omnipotence lies in the search for an adequate characterization of the self-limiting class. The condition proposed above, namely

(8) $\delta_a p \supset (\exists q)\,(\sim M^* \delta_a q)$

can now be shown to be too wide, apart from its other deficiencies, since virtually any state of affairs is thereby ruled self-limiting. Consider a state of affairs, p, that has been brought about by a. p having happened, there will generally be some state of affairs not then within the control of a, namely $\sim$p. We recall having stipulated, following Geach, that events in the past, once having happened in such-and-such a way, are not longer in the control of any agent at ensuing times. Thus some appropriate modification of the consequent is in order. This might be achieved by requiring only that a state of affairs is *self-limiting* only where if an agent brings it about, there will be some future state of affairs he will not be able to bring about. That is, p is *self-limiting* only where

(14) $\delta_a p_t \supset (\exists q_{t+\Delta})(\sim M^* \,\delta_a q_{\,t+\Delta})$

Clearly, if a brings about p at t, his inability to also bring about $\sim$p at t should not ensure that his action is self-limiting. Only if the inability to do $\sim$p tends to persist into the future, as a consequence of his doing p, should such an inability be regarded as truly self-limiting. The state of affairs, "there comes to be an object too heavy for its creator to lift" is self-limiting because, having created this object, the agent cannot *thereafter* lift it. It would not serve the purpose of the paradox to rule that this state of affairs is self-limiting because the agent cannot simultaneously create and lift such an object.

The need for subjoining to a tense logic if self-limiting actions are to be accommodated in M* δ is further confirmed when we consider the class of totally (or ultimately) limiting actions. Let us say an action is *totally self-limiting* only where

(15) $\delta_a p \supset (\forall q) (\sim M^* \delta_a q)$

That is, where it is a consequence of my action that I lose control over all states of affairs. Suicide would be an example of a totally self-limiting action.[16] Similarly an action may be said to be *totally other-limiting* only where if I carry it out, some other individual has no control over any state of affairs whatever.

(16) $(a \neq b) \supset [\delta_a p \supset (\forall q) (\sim M^* \delta_b q)]$

An example of a totally other-limiting action would be murder. Now consider again the requirement of totally self-limiting actions, (15). By a rule of passage for the quantifier and UI, we can infer

(17) $\delta_a p \supset \sim M^* \delta_a p$,

which in conjunction with AM*δ1, yields

$\sim \delta_a p$

That is, it is in general false that any individual brings about totally self-limiting actions. But this consequence is absurd because individuals sometimes do commit suicide. The difficulty can be circumvented, however, by introducing tenses into the definition of a totally self-limiting action above. Thus the modified requirement on totally self-limiting action, just as we introduced tenses into the definition of a self-limiting action reads:

(18) $\delta_a p_t \supset (\forall q_{t+\Delta}) (\sim M^* \delta_a q_{t+\Delta})$

It is therefore doubly confirmed that temporal indices are essential to our understanding of limiting actions. A language strong enough to adequately express, and thereby also possibly avoid, the paradox of omnipotence, will be at least a tensed extension of M*δ. Yet while tensed M*δ does capture some minimal relevant syntax in a helpful way, my deep and dark suspicion is that the paradox of omnipotence is essentially causal and may therefore in large measure outrun the expressive capabilities of M*δ or other classically based logics. Hopefully, further research will allow us to chart the metatheory of M*δ, and more accurately fix the limits of its capacity to subjugate this paradox.

Notes

1. For references, *vide* J. L. Cowan, "The Paradox of Omnipotence Revisited," *Canadian Journal of Philosophy,* vol. III, no. 3, p. 435.

2. For a similar convention in deontic modal systems, *vide* Frederic B. Fitch, "Natural Deduction Rules for Obligation," *American Philosophical Quarterly,* vol. 3, no. 1, January 1966, 27–38. See especially p. 37f. The convention in question carries with it the implication that it is a rule of inference of System δ that if φ is a theorem, δ φ is a theorem, parallel to Fitch's System DM.

3. These two stipulations on δ are suggested by Frederic B. Fitch in "A Logical Analysis of Some Value Concepts," *Journal of Symbolic Logic,* vol. 28, no. 2, June, 1963, 135–142.

4. *Vide* Donald Davidson, "The Logical Form of Action Sentences," *The Logic of Decision and Action,* ed. Nicholas Rescher (Pittsburgh, University of Pittsburgh Press, 1967), 81–95.

5. These two stipulations on the notion of opportunity are suggested by Anthony Kenny in "Freedom, Spontaneity and Indifference," *Essays on Freedom of Action,* ed. Ted. Honderich, (London and Boston, Routledge and Kegan Paul, 1973), 89–104. *Vide* p. 99f. A clear explanation of this notion of opportunity is to be found in Myles Brand, "On Having the Opportunity," *Theory and Decision,* vol. 2, 1972, 307–313.

6. See note 1. A useful article not cited by Cowan is that of James Cargile, "On Omnipotence," *Noûs,* vol. 1, no. 2, May 1967, 201–205.

7. Descartes thought it blasphemous to maintain that God cannot do that which cannot be described in a logically coherent way. See letters to Mersenne, April 15, 1630, and May 27, 1644. These references are found in Harry G. Frankfurt, "The Logic of Omnipotence," *The Philosophical Review,* Vol. LXXIII, 1964, pp. 262–263. See also the discussion in Geach, p. 10f.

8. For some discussion of this problem see Ingmar Pörn, *The Logic of Power,* (Oxford, Blackwell, 1970), p. 7.

9. Nicholas Rescher, "The Concept of Control," *Essays in Philosophical Analysis,* (Pittsburgh, University of Pittsburgh Press, 1969), pp. 327–353.

10. The notion of control stalemate makes it clear that there can be at most one omnipotent agent.

11. To put it bluntly, my argument is that it is a consequence of (TM* δ) that if there is an omnipotent being, in the sense characterized by (TM* δ), then there are no other free agents. This anomaly (like the others adumbrated below) suggests that we need an appropriately qualified characterization of omnipotence. I do not try to propose a workable restriction here, but merely argue for the need of one to complement other restrictions alluded to below and elsewhere (e.g., see Geach, *op. cit.,* note 14).

12. *Vide* note 11. See also Alvin Plantinga, *The Nature of Necessity* (Oxford, Oxford University Press, 1974), ch. 9.

13. Similar proof is found in Fitch. See note 3. See also Selection 28.

14. Peter Geach, "Omnipotence," *Philosophy,* January 1973, vol. 48, pp. 7–20. See also Peter Geach, "An Irrelevance of Omnipotence," *Philosophy,* October, 1973, vol. 48, pp. 327–333. Walton (note 13) argues that some results can be derived from Fitch's theorems that strongly support Geach's thesis that what is past ceases to be alterable even by an omnipotent agent.

15. This is essentially Geach's suggestion.

16. The concept of a totally self-limiting action, and the consequent demonstration of the need for temporal indices in M*δ, are due to J. E. Bickenbach, whose contribution I gratefully acknowledge.

25

A Kenotic Theory
of the Incarnation

CHARLES GORE

A divine motive caused the Incarnation. It was a deliberate act of God
"propter nos homines et propter nostram salutem": it was a "means
devised" for our recovery and for our consummation, a means, therefore, directed and adapted in the divine wisdom, to serve its purpose.
That purpose included on the one side a clearer revelation of God's
mind and being to man in terms intelligible to him, and on the other
hand, the exhibition of the true ideal of human nature. Now for the
first part of the purpose, for the unveiling of the divine character, what
was necessary was that the humanity should reflect, without refracting,
the divine Being whose organ it was made. It could not be too pure a
channel, too infallible a voice, provided it was really human and fitted
to man. Thus in fact, in becoming incarnate, the Son of God retained
and expressed His essential relation to the Father; he received, therefore, as eternally, so in the days of His flesh, the consciousness of His
own and of His Father's being, and the power to reveal that which He
knew. "No man," He said, "knoweth the Son save the Father; neither
knoweth any man the Father" (not, *knew* but *knoweth*) "save the Son,
and he to whomsoever the Son willeth to reveal Him." Limited moreover, as we shall have occasion to remark, as is His disclosure of the
unseen world, what He does disclose is in the tone of one who speaks
"that he doth know, and testifies that he hath seen": for example, "I
say unto you, that in heaven the angels of the little ones do always

From Charles Gore, *The Incarnation of the Son of God,* New York, C. Scribner's Sons,
1891, pp. 169–75.

behold the face of my Father which is in heaven." "In my Father's
house are many mansions; if it were not so I would have told you." [1]
Plainly the continuous personality of the Son carried with it a continuous consciousness, which if the human nature was allowed to subject
to limitation, it was not allowed to deface or to distort. What He
teaches, He teaches so that we can depend upon it to the uttermost,
and the fact is explained by the motive of the Incarnation.

On the other hand, our Lord is to exhibit a true example of manhood—tried, progressive, perfected. For this purpose it was necessary
that He should be without the exercise of such divine prerogatives as
would have made human experience or progress impossible. He could
not, as far as we can see, abiding in the exercise of an absolute consciousness, have grown in knowledge, or have prayed, "Father, if it
be possible," or cried, "My God, my God, *why*"—He could not, that
is, have passed through those very experiences, which have brought
him closest to us in our spiritual trials.

So far the facts of the Incarnation are accounted for by the divine motive which underlay it; but they are interpreted further by the divine
method or principle of action as St. Paul unfolds it to us. He describes
it as a self-emptying.[2] Christ Jesus pre-existed, he declares, in the
form of God. The word "form" transferred from physical shape to
spiritual type, describes—as St. Paul uses it, alone or in composition,
with uniform accuracy—the permanent characteristics of a thing. Jesus
Christ then, in his pre-existent state, was living in the permanent characteristics of the life of God. In such a life it was His right to remain.
It belonged to him. But He regarded not His prerogatives, as a man
regards a prize He must clutch at. For love of us He abjured the
prerogatives of equality with God. By an act of deliberate self-abnegation, He so emptied Himself as to assume the permanent characteristics of the human or servile life: He took the *form* of a servant. Not
only so, but He was made in outward appearance like other men and
was found in fashion as a man, that is, in the transitory quality of our
mortality. The "form," the "likeness," the "fashion" of manhood,
He took them all. Thus, remaining in unchanged personality, He aban-
doned certain prerogatives of the divine mode of existence in order to
assume the human.

Again St. Paul describes the Incarnation as a "self-beggary."[3] The metaphor suggests a man of wealth who deliberately abandons the prerogatives of possession to enter upon the experience of poverty, not because he thinks it a better state, but in order to help others up through real fellowship with their experience to a life of weal. "Ye know the grace of our Lord Jesus Christ, that, though he was rich, yet for your sakes he beggared himself, that ye through his poverty might be rich." This is how St. Paul interprets our Lord's coming down from heaven, and it is manifest that it expresses something very much more than the mere addition of a manhood to his Godhead. In a certain aspect indeed the Incarnation is the folding round the Godhead of the veil of the humanity, to hide its glory, but it is much more than this. It is a ceasing to exercise certain natural prerogatives of the divine existence; it is a coming to exist for love of us under conditions of being not natural to the Son of God. . . .

Is then such a self-emptying intelligible? It is easy to see that it involves no dishonouring of the eternal Son, no attribution to Him of failing powers. "It was not," says St. Leo, "the failure of power, but the condescension of pity."[4] There was conscious voluntariness in all our Lord's self-abnegation; "I have power to lay down my life," He said, "and I have power to take it again": "Thinkest thou that I cannot beseech my Father, and He shall even now send me more than twelve legions of angels."[5] This same deliberateness belongs, we must suppose, to the limitation of consciousness under which our Lord is found. And God declares His almighty power most chiefly in such an act of voluntary self-limitation for the purposes of sympathy. It is physical power which makes itself felt only in self-assertion and pressure; it is the higher power of love which is shown in self-effacement. The power to think one's self into another's thoughts, to look through another's eyes, to feel with another's feeling, to merge one's self in another's interests,—this is the higher power, the power of love, and we owe it to the Incarnation that we know God to possess and to use, not only the power to vindicate Himself, but the power also of self-limitation. . . .

Thus far, however, we can see our way. The Incarnation involves both the self-expression, and the self-limitation, of God. God can express

Himself in true manhood because manhood is truly and originally made in God's image; and on the other hand God can limit Himself by the conditions of manhood, because the Godhead contains in itself eternally the prototype of human self-sacrifice and self-limitation, for God is love.

Notes

1. St. Matt. xviii. 10; St. John xiv.2.
2. Phil. ii. 5–11.
3. 2 Cor. viii. 9.
4. St. Leo, *Ep*. xxviii. 3.
5. St. John x. 18; St. Matt. xxvi. 53.

OMNIPOTENCE AND
HUMAN FREEDOM

26

The Fall of Satan

ST. ANSELM

How God causes evil wills and evil actions; and how they are received from Him.

S. Your argument is so bound together by true, necessary, and clear reasons that I do not in any respect see how what you say can be undone—except that I do see something to be implied which I do not believe ought to be said, but which I do not see how to deny if what you say is true. For if to will to be like God is not nothing or is not an evil but is a good, then this will was able to exist only from Him from whom all existing things come. Therefore, if the angel did not have what he did not receive, then what he had, he received from Him from whom he had it. However, what did the angel receive from Him except what He gave? Therefore, if he had the will to be like God, he had it because God gave it.

T. Why is it strange if just as we say that God leads into temptation when He does not deliver from it, so we say that He gives an evil will by not preventing it when He can—especially since the ability to will anything at all comes only from Him?

S. Put this way, it does not seem to be inappropriate.

T. Therefore, if there is no giving without a receiving, then just as someone who willingly concedes and also someone who permits,

From *The Fall of the Devil, Chap. XX*. Reprinted by permission from *Anselm of Canterbury*, Vol. II, pp. 164–66, edited and translated by J. Hopkins and H. Richardson, published by The Edwin Mellen Press, Suite 918, 225 West 34th Street, New York, N.Y. 10001.

though disapproving, are commonly said to give, so someone who receives what has been conceded and someone who dares to take forbidden things are not incorrectly said to receive.

S. What you say seems to me neither incorrect nor uncommon.

T. Then, what do we say in opposition to the truth if we say that when the Devil willed what he ought not to have [willed] he received this willing from God because God permitted it, and also did not receive it [from God] because God did not consent to it?

S. Nothing here seems to be opposed to the truth.

T. Therefore, when the Devil turned his will to what he ought not to have [willed], that willing and that turning were something. And yet, he had something only from God and [by permission] of God, since he was able to will something or to move his will only by permission of the one who creates all natures—substantial and accidental, universal and individual. For insofar as the will and its turning, or movement, are something, each is a good and is due to God. But insofar as the will lacks the justice which it ought not to lack, it is *something* evil— rather than an absolute evil. And what is evil is not due to God but is due to the one who wills, or who moves his will.

To be sure, injustice is an unqualified evil since it is identical with the evil which is nothing. But a nature in which there is injustice is *something* evil because the nature is something and is something other than injustice, which is an evil and nothing. Therefore, what is something is caused by God and is of God's doing; but what is nothing, or an evil, is caused by someone unjust and is of his doing.

S. Indeed, we must admit that God creates the natures of all things. But who would concede that He causes the particular actions of evil wills—for example, the depraved movement of will by which this evil will moves itself?

T. Why is it strange to say that God causes the particular actions which are done by an evil will? For we say that He causes the particular substances which are made by an unjust will and by dishonorable action.

S. I do not have anything to say against this. Indeed, I am not able to deny that any given action is really something. Nor do I wish to deny that what really has some being is caused by God. Nor does your reasoning in any way accuse God or excuse the Devil; rather, it completely excuses God and accuses the Devil.

27

God's Causality

WILLIAM OF OCKHAM

Question 4:

A   *Whether God is a primary and immediate cause of everything.* 1

Objection 1: No, because from one cause only one effect proceeds.

Objection 2: No, he is not an immediate cause. This conclusion is commended on the grounds that every effect could then be demonstrated from him as it can from an immediate cause. Thus all mediate causes would be superfluous. . . .

B   On the contrary: God contains the causality of every second cause whatever. . . .

F   Concerning the Fourth Question, two things must be done. First, it must be shown whether or not God is an immediate cause of everything by immediate causation. Second, whether or not God creates *simpliciter* 2 everything which he produces.

Concerning the first there is one difficulty: Since God is one, in what way does he produce many effects? It truly appears to be the opinion of the Philosopher that from one cause only one effect can be produced, which is proved from *Physics* VIII 3 and from *On Generation*

From William of Ockham, II *Sententiarum,* qus. 4 & 5, Lyon, 1494–1496, reprinted by Gregg Press Limited, 1962. The translation was made by Linwood Urban. Material in [   ] is added for clarification.

and Corruption II where it is said: "The same cause, provided it remains in the same condition, always produces the same effects. . . . for contrary effects demand contraries as their causes." [4] And with respect to *Metaphysics* XII, the Commentator says: "If the agent be one and the material be one, the effect will be one" and likewise: "From one mover there is only one motion." [5] Second, in *On the Soul* the Philosopher proves distinctions in potentiality through distinctions in operations, and operations are effects. [6]

On the contrary, this opinion is heretical because, according to the faith, God produces many effects immediately. Neither is the opinion consonant with natural reason because the very same will in every way simple and without distinctions is the principle of willing and not willing, of love and of hate.

Second: This same state of affairs is manifest in natural causes because the sun is able to produce many effects and yet the sun in itself does not have distinctions.

Third: If there were as many distinctions in the cause as there are in the effect, then taking two effects, these two effects would be reduced to two causes, and those two causes to two other causes, and thus there would be a regression to infinity or there would be a stop in the regress at the two first causes. Either of these alternatives is false. Or finally there would be a stop in the regress at one first cause of all things. [This is the true opinion, and thus we have the proposition: A single cause may produce many effects.]. . . .

I say, therefore, to the second objection, that God is a primary and immediate cause of everything which is produced by second causes. Moreover, that he is an immediate cause is manifest because a cause is usually said to be immediate to which, when present, the effect can be present, and when not present, the effect cannot be present. [7] But God is a cause of this kind with respect to whatever creature you will, therefore he is an immediate cause of all things. Whence since whatever is properly called a "cause" is "a cause to whose power the effect can be present, and when not present, the effect cannot be present," every cause properly so called can be designated an immediate cause. [8]

From this it follows that a remote cause is not really a cause, because from its potency the effect does not follow. Otherwise Adam could be said to be my cause, which statement is not true because a non-existent being cannot be the cause of a being. Likewise, properly speaking, cause and effect are simultaneous. They are not always so when many partial causes concur in the production of some effect however immediate one of them may be.[9]

If God concurs with a second cause, both are immediate causes. This is proved by *John* I: "All things were made by him."[10] If you say that this statement is true, but that God is always a mediate cause [i.e. a cause of a cause], I say *on the contrary* that according to all the Saints, God is in different ways the cause of goods and evils. He is a mediate cause of evil because he produces and conserves a creature who is the immediate cause of evil. However, he concurs otherwise as far as good is concerned. In this latter case, he appears to be the immediate cause.

Second, an effect depends more greatly upon a first and simply infinite universal cause than upon a finite universal cause.[11] With respect to the senses, we see that an effect depends upon a finite universal cause [e.g. seeing a tree depends upon the light of the sun]. Of course, unless the universal cause [the sun] be present and immediately causing the effect, [the seeing] is not produced. This proposition is proved by the fact that a proximate cause is a cause which is close to the object acted upon. The proximate cause [in this case the tree] is a more inferior cause if it is conserved by the sun.[12] Unless the sun is in due approximation to the object acted upon [in this case the eye], the proximate cause [the tree] cannot produce its effects. This is clear with respect to effects whenever the sun is in a position close to us [i.e. when the sun is overhead, there is light by which to see]. Therefore, it follows that the sun is an immediate cause of any effects whatever produced by the sun. Therefore, so much the more is God [the unlimited universal cause] an immediate cause.

If you say that the potency of the sun and of the primary cause [the tree] are certainly required for the production of an effect, yet on that account neither the one nor the other is the cause, to the contrary, I reply that this conclusion destroys every way for proving anything to be a cause of anything else.

If you say that heat in fire is without doubt the cause of heat in wood, I say that this is not true. First, certainly the presence of the fire is required, but from this fact causality does not follow. Whence you prove not more that heat in fire is the cause of heat in water than that white in a parent is the cause of whiteness in me, unless because the presence of the heat in the water follows the presence of heat in the fire. [Likewise from the presence of whiteness, it does not follow that anything else is white.]

Second, the suspension of the action of the fire in the furnace [containing the three children, Shadrach, Mishach, and Abednego] [13] does not seem to be for any reason except that God did not cooperate immediately in the production of the heat. Surely the substance of the fire was there conserved; but because God did not concur immediately with the fire in causing the effects of fire, the fire was not able to act in this case as it usually does.

Thus it is clear that God is an immediate cause of any effect whatever. Certainly he is the first cause with respect to the primacy of perfection, but not necessarily the primacy of duration. [14] In that instant in which he acts, he acts and the second cause acts, because there is no good reason why God should suspend the action of a second cause in the first instant or in the second or in any other.

From this it follows that God is the partial cause of any effect whatever produced by a second cause. I say that this is true *de facto*.

Because he is able to be the total cause of everything, he is *simpliciter* the principal cause. From this it follows that he is a free cause with respect to any such effects. (Even if he were a natural cause, since he is infinite, he would necessarily totally produce the whole effect. [15]) Thus by his absolute power, he certainly can be the total cause of any one of the absolute effects, whatever his relationship be to the primacy of duration.

This proposition is proved by the fact that whatever agent can be the total cause of anything is certainly a partial cause. This latter is clear because God can keep for himself every causality of a second cause and, as a consequence, is able to supplement his action, and, as a consequence, can produce the effect totally without any other cause.

L   If you ask: "Does God ever concur with a second cause in the produc-
         tion of some indivisible effect?" And reply: "We ought to take it that
         since each of them produces the total effect, each is the total cause,
         because to be the total cause is to produce the total effect." I answer:
         "The total cause is that cause which when present, in the absence of
         anything else, the effect is present if it be a total cause in fact, or that
         can be present if it be a possible total cause." Now whenever God
         concurs with a second cause, albeit he can produce the effect without
         the second cause, and as a consequence can be the total cause, he in
         fact produces it with a second cause and as a consequence is not in
         fact the total cause. Nor is it true what John [Scotus] said: "The total
         cause is that when present, the effect is present, and when not present,
         the effect is not present." [16] For, as was said elsewhere, [17] the same ef-
         fect can have two total causes. If one is destroyed, it nonetheless can
         be caused by the other. But as has been said: "The total cause is that
         which when present, in the absence of anything else, the effect can be
         present."

         Lastly I say, without asserting that it is true in fact, it is possible for
         God to produce a particular thing and for a creature to produce the
         same thing. To which the proof is that a passive creation is nothing
         other than for a creature to be immediately created by God and to
         depend immediately on God and to be referred immediately to God.
         But a creature produced by God through creation can be dependent
         upon a second cause. However, it is impossible for anything to be
         dependent upon anything else except the latter have some causality
         with respect to the former. Since second causes cannot have any cau-
         sality with respect to the said effects except through production, there-
         fore [both God and a creature produce the same thing].

         The assumption is manifest, because should God produce fire by
         means of the sun, then the fire is likewise said to be produced by the
         sun. However, should God first produce the fire and conserve it, and
         not create the sun, and then afterwards produce the sun, then the fire is
         conserved by the sun as if it had been produced by the sun. And like-
         wise, the fire depends essentially upon the sun because although God
         produced the sun after the fire, he gave the sun an action making all
         things possibly producible by the sun dependent upon it. Therefore,

the fire is dependent upon the sun in the same way in which it would have been had it first been produced by the sun. Therefore, it is now produced by the sun, because creation and conservation differ in nothing positive. For "creation" signifies an object by connoting [i.e. referring indirectly to] a negation immediately preceding the thing, and "conservation" signifies the same object by connoting a continuation, which in turn is nothing else but to connote a negation of the interruption or destruction of the essence of the thing. Whence it is not inconsistent [that the sun, though created later than the fire, should produce the fire] although it appears inconsistent in speech. Nor is there any difficulty except with the words "creation" and "conservation" [not, however,] with respect to what they signify.

If, therefore, God should first produce an effect totally and afterwards should conserve it partially with the sun, then the sun would be a partial cause with God of that conservation and, as a consequence, of the effect. Thus it appears that God is a primary and immediate cause of every effect or production by second causes by the immediacy of his causation without any change on his part. The same situation obtains for a natural cause, e.g. the sun. In the same way as God, it is always directed toward things inferior and always produces without any new mutation on its part.

As to the second objection, I say that God is the cause of all things in the class of effects. This claim is proved by the fact that any effect depends no more greatly upon the agent creating it than an accident upon a substance. Since God is able to make in the class of effects an accident without a substance, he is able to make any accident whatever without anything else in the class of effects.[18] He can do the same with regard to other effects. . . .

Furthermore, to the second objection, I say that, according to the meanings of the words, "when God acts by means of second causes or together with them," it is not said that God acts mediately [i.e. as a cause of a cause], or that second causes are in vain. For he is a free and not a necessary agent. If he were not, he would be a necessary agent with respect to anything upon which he acts immediately. A rude example for this has been proposed. One strong man can carry ten heavy bundles, and nobody else can carry them without his help. Even though some weaker fellow, together with the strong man, can carry the ten bundles, nonetheless the strong man is able to carry them just as immediately as is the weaker man. If the strong man should not wish to carry all ten by himself, neither, on that account, is the weaker fellow superfluous. And such is also the case in the proposition: ("God is such an agent that he can be the total cause of the effect without any other thing whatever.") For, according to Augustine, "God so administers things that he allows them to have their proper motions." [19] Therefore, he does not will to produce everything by himself, but cooperates with second causes, although the partial cause may be the principal one. Therefore, God is an immediate cause of all things whenever he acts with second causes just as he is when he acts without them. Nor, on this account, are the second causes superfluous because God does not always act according to the totality of his power.

R   From this it follows that it cannot be demonstrated that any effect is produced by a second cause. Although combustion always follows when a combustible material is placed next to fire, with respect to this fact, it can be maintained that fire is not the cause of the combustion. For God could have ordained that always in consequence of the potentiality of fire that fire alone causes combustion in a proximate passive subject. In like manner, God has ordained, in relation to the church, that the speaking of certain words causes grace in the soul. Whence from no effects can it be proved that someone is a man, especially from effects which appear to us. Everything we see in a man, an angel can cause in a body, such as eating, drinking, etc. This is clear from the example of Tobias and the angel. [20] Therefore, it is not remarkable that it cannot be demonstrated that something is a cause. I say, then, that any being which is said to act by means of second causes, because it cooperates with them or produces what the second cause produces, acts as immediately as do second causes.

Notes

1. An immediate cause is a direct cause that acts without intermediaries. It is to be contrasted with a mediate cause, one which acts by means of intermediaries.
2. "To create *simpliciter*" is "to create without any co-operating matter."
3. This assertion seems to be based on a standard medieval exegesis of 251a:28–35. *Cf.*, St. Thomas Aquinas: "Things which act through nature always move *per se* to one thing." *Commentary on Aristotle's Physics*, Bk. VIII, Lec. 2, trans. R. J. Blackwell, *et al.* London, Routledge & Kegan Paul, 1963, p. 479.
4. 336a:28f and 31f.
5. Averroes, *ed.* Iuntina, VIII, Venetiis, 1552, f.103r.
6. 415a:14–25.
7. *Cf. Exposition super physicam Aristotelis*, f.113c: "An efficient immediate cause is one which, without the use of any other effects caused by it, can cause the effect in question. Thus if fire does not cause any other effect than heat, fire can be the immediate cause of heat." Cited in L. Baudry, *Lexique philosophique de Guillaume D'Ockham*, P. Lethielleux, 1958, p. 38.
8. *Cf.* I *Sent.* d. 45, q. 1, E: "Taking 'cause' properly or strictly, nothing is the cause of anything unless it be its immediate cause." Cited, Baudry, *op. cit., ibid.*
9. Ockham allows many partial conserving, though not producing causes, to be simultaneous with their effects in a hierarchy of essentially ordered causes. *Cf.* P. Boehner, *Ockham: Philosophical Writings*, Nelson, 1957, p. 118ff.
10. v. 3.
11. A universal cause is a cause capable of producing several effects either simultaneously or successively. The sun is a standard example of a finite universal cause.
12. Following Aristotle, Medieval philosophers believed that the sun played a very important role in production and conservation. For example, man is generated both by man and the sun; and fire is conserved in being by the sun.
13. *Daniel,* 3:19–30.
14. It might be the case that not all of God's causality is operative during the whole time his effects are in existence. See below for a theoretical example with respect to God, the sun and fire. See also Boehner, *op. cit.* p. 121f.
15. See Selections 16–19 and 30 for further discussions of the relationship between "natural (necessary)" and "free" causation.
16. Reference unidentified. However, it seems to be presupposed in Duns Scotus's discussion of total causes in Selection 13 above. Ockham's objection to Scotus's definition is that it is counter factual. The same indivisible effect can have two total causes, e.g. a fire can be lit with two matches. If one is destroyed, the other lights just as well. Therefore, the second clause of Scotus's definition is false. Furthermore, Scotus's principle that "Two causes of the same order cannot each be the total cause of the same effect" (*Opus Oxoniense*, I, d. II, q. 3, quoted in *Duns Scotus: Philosophical Writings*, ed. & trans. by Allan Wolter, Nelson, 1962, p. 87) is also false.
17. I *Sent.* d. 11, q. 1, C–G; *Quodlibeta septem*, I, q. 1.
18. "Whatever God produces by means of secondary causes, God can produce and conserve immediately without their aid. . . . God can cause, produce and conserve every reality, be it substance or accident, apart from any other reality." Boehner, *op. cit.*, p. xix; *Cf. Quodlibeta septem*, VI, q. 6 and II *Sent.*, q. 19F.
19. Reference unidentified. However, it is implied in St. Thomas's treatment of *Contra Faustum*, XXVI, 3 in *Summa Theol.* I, q. 105, a. 6.
20. *Tobit* 5:4 & 5.

28

Some Theorems of Fitch on Omnipotence

DOUGLAS WALTON

Frederic Fitch, in a fascinating article,[1] most regrettably ignored by philosophers of religion, proves the following theorem on omnipotence: If for each situation that is the case it is logically possible that that situation was brought about by some agent, then whatever is the case was personally brought about by that agent. This is a mightily perplexing result. It seems to say that an omnipotent agent, in this sense, must personally have brought about every actual state of affairs that obtains. Yet many theologians have held that God is omnipotent while not being a universal agent. The free will defense,[2] for example, seems to require that there should be some actual states of affairs not (personally, at any rate) brought about by God. Whether and how God acts is puzzling in its own right.[3] But in any case it has often been assumed that God is omnipotent, at least minimally in Fitch's sense, without being a universal personal agent.

Let us therefore carefully examine Fitch's proof. We need to establish two preliminary theorems before we can arrive at Theorem 3, the omnipotence theorem. And in order to establish these two lemmas, we must introduce some of Fitch's terminology. A class of propositions is said to be *closed with respect to conjunction elimination* if (necessarily) whenever the conjunction of two propositions is in the class so are the two propositions themselves.[4] For example, the relation of believ-

From *Sophia,* Vol. XV, No. 1, 1976, pp. 20–27. Reprinted with the permission of *Sophia.*

ing (that obtains between an agent and a possible state of affairs) is closed with respect to conjunction elimination because if I believe "p & q" then it follows that I believe p and that I believe q.[5] In symbols,

B (p & q) → (B p & B q)

Thus for any class of operators α that obtain between an agent and a state of affairs, α is closed with respect to conjunction elimination where

α (p & q) → (α p & α q)

for any p and q. Fitch also postulates that the relation of doing (personally bringing it about that p) is closed with respect to conjunction elimination. If I do both p and q then I do p and also I do q.

δ (p & q)→(δ p & δ q)

Here we read "δ p" as "the agent a personally brings it about that obtains."[6] Fitch understands δ as being a truth-entailing, that is,

δ p→p

Defining the general notion, Fitch postulates that a class of propositions is said to be a *truth class* if (necessarily) every member of it is true. Thus, if α is a truth class, we have it that

α p → p

Hence δ is such a truth class. Truth and logical necessity are also obviously truth classes.

We can now approach Theorem 1 which I shall quote below in entirety with its proof.

> Theorem 1. If α is a truth class which is closed with respect to conjunction elimination, then the proposition [p & ~ (α p)], which asserts that p is true but not a member of α (where p is any proposition), is itself necessarily not a member of α.

> Proof. Suppose, on the contrary, that [p & ~ (α p)] is a member of α; that is, suppose (α [p & ~ (α p)]). Since α is closed with respect to conjunction elimination, the propositions p and ~ (α p) must accord-

ingly both be members of α, so that the propositions (α p) and (α ($\sim$(α p))) must both be true. But from the fact that α is a truth class and has $\sim$ (α p) as a member, we conclude that $\sim$ (α p) is true, and this contradicts the result that (α p) is true. Thus from the assumption that [p & $\sim$ (α p)] is a member of α we have derived contradictory results. Hence that assumption is necessarily false.[7]

Formally, the proof of Theorem 1 can be exhibited in five steps as follows.

(1) α [p & $\sim$ (α p)], Assumption
(2) α p (1), Conj. Elim.
(3) α $\sim$ (α p) (1), Conj. Elim.
(4) $\sim$ (α p) (3), α p$\rightarrow$p
(5) α p & $\sim$ (α p) (2), (5) Conj. Intro.

Thus by *reductio* we can conclude that

(6) $\sim$ M α [p & $\sim$ (α p)]

where "M" is read "it is logically possible that."

The second theorem reads as follows.

Theorem 2. If α is a truth class which is closed with respect to conjunction elimination, and if p is any true proposition which is not a member of α, then the proposition, [p & $\sim$ (α p)], is a true proposition which is necessarily not a member of α.

Proof. The proposition [p & $\sim$ (α p)] is clearly true, and by Theorem 1 it is necessarily not a member of α.[8]

We can perhaps see a little clearer how this proof works if we write a "T" in the right upper corner of a proposition (state of affairs) that is true (obtains).[9] The theorem then reads

T 2: $\sim \alpha$ p$^T \rightarrow \sim$Mα [p & $\sim$ (α p)]^T

That the consequent obtains (disregarding the "T") simply follows from the fact that it is an instance of (6), that is, Theorem 1. That the part in brackets of the consequence is true is apparent in that both conjuncts of it follow trivially from the antecedent. By the antecedent, we have it that $\sim \alpha$ p, and since p, according to the antecedent, is true, we have it that p.

Now let us proceed to Theorem 3.

> Theorem 3. If an agent is all-powerful in the sense that for each situation that is the case, it is logically possible that that situation was brought about by that agent, then whatever is the case was brought about (done) by that agent.
>
> Proof. Suppose that p is the case but was not brought about by the agent in question. Then, since doing is a truth class closed with respect to conjunction elimination, we conclude from Theorem 2 that there is some actual situation which could not have been brought about by that agent, and hence that the agent is not all-powerful in the sense described.[10]

Theorem 3 is proven simply by substituting the operator δ (bringing it about) for the general operator α. If we assume:

(1) $\sim \delta \, p^T$

namely that p obtains but was not brought about by the agent in question, then it follows simply by substitution in T 2 that we have

(2) $\sim M \, \delta \, [p \, \& \sim (\delta \, p)]^T$

This asserts that there is an actual state of affairs, represented by the proposition in the square brackets that obtains (note the T in the right corner) but that it is logically impossible for the agent to bring about. Fitch concludes from (2) that

(3) $\sim M \, \delta \, p^T$

For the agent in question, it is not logically possible that he should fail to bring about any actual state of affairs. Necessarily, everything that obtains has been brought about by him. Thus any omnipotent agent (in this sense) is also thereby necessarily a universal agent of actual states of affairs. Formally, this result comes about as follows.

(4) $\sim \delta \, p^T \rightarrow \sim M \, \delta \, p^T$ (1), (3), Conditionalization
(5) $M \, \delta \, p^T \rightarrow \delta \, p^T$ (4), Contraposition

(5) states that for a given agent, if it is possible that he brings about any actual state of affairs then it follows that he personally brings about that actual state of affairs. Any omnipotent being is also a universal agent.

Fitch's theorem may not seem too significant because it is generally felt that God's omnipotence consists not merely in the logical possibility of his doing anything but in the physical possibility of his doing anything. It is not enough that it should be logically possible for God to do anything, but it should be required that there can be no physical obstruction to his action either.[11] For any given state of affairs it could never be the case that a set of antecedent conditions of God's bringing about that state of affairs, taken together with the set of nomic universals, entails the proposition that God does not bring about the state of affairs. There are no physical obstacles to God's action. This sense of "physical possibility" has never been very clearly explained,[12] but what is clear is that something like it, rather than merely logical possibility, is the true sense in which it is possible for God to do anything. Whatever "physical possibility" is, minimally, we can say that it includes logical possibility. That is for this sense of possibility, M*,

(1) $M^* p \rightarrow M p$

And by substitution in (1) we have

(2) $M^* \delta p^T \rightarrow M \delta p^T$ Sub. $[\delta p^T/p]$

Then from Fitch's theorem

(3) $M \delta p^T \rightarrow \delta p^T$

and (2), the transitivity of $\rightarrow$ yields

(4) $M^* \delta p^T \rightarrow \delta p^T$ (2), (3), H.S.

Thus if it is physically possible that an agent brings about every actual state of affairs, that agent has brought about every actual state of affairs. The import of this theorem for philosophical theology is even more evident than Fitch's. If God is omnipotent, in perhaps the most usual or standard sense, then Aquinas' traditional solution to the problem of evil, that God permits rather than brings about evil, cannot be defended. Indeed, if (4) obtains, it is hard to see how any free will defense could possibly succeed.

I cannot pretend that I know definitively what all the implications for philosophical theology are of Fitch's theorem and my corollary of it, although it seems to me that these results must be importantly relevant to the problem of evil and related problems of the notion of omnipotence in a number of ways. I will content myself with adumbrating two primary implications here.

First, Fitch's Theorem 1 provides interesting new grounds for rejecting a claim of Aquinas that God can bring about any state of affairs that is logically possible.[13] Fitch has shown that

$$\sim M \; \bar\delta \; [p \; \& \; \sim (\delta \; p)]$$

even though the state of affairs represented within the brackets is logically possible. It is logically possible that the door is open where God has not brought it about that the door is open (unless it is assumed at the outset that God does everything). Yet it is logically impossible that God personally brings it about both that the door is open and that God does not bring it about that the door is open. Of course this Thomist doctrine has often been rejected,[14] perhaps even by Aquinas himself elsewhere,[15] but so far as I know it has never been rejected on the grounds of anything like Theorem 1.

Second, Theorem 1 and its corollary expose the absurdity of a common but spurious notion of omnipotence. In this sense, to say that God is omnipotent is to say that for any actual state of affairs, God could have been the agent of that state of affairs. To put it another way, let us say that every actual state of affairs is such that either it was brought about by some agent or it just happened. In the latter case, we might say that it was brought about by the null agent. Now to say that God is omnipotent, in this sense, is to say that God is an alternate for any agent. Given any agent of an actual event, even the null agent, God can be put in for this agent. He is the universal agent-substitute. For anything that happened, God can be conceived as being the agent of it.

This notion is demonstrably absurd because if God is omnipotent in this sense, there are no other agents, nor can anything just happen. It follows from the conception of omnipotence that God is the author of literally every state of affairs. Thus the notion that God's power can consist in such agent-substitutability is absurd.

This result, however, by no means implies that all conceptions of omnipotence are inchoate or contradictory. Indeed, I would like to suggest that it indicates that we should concentrate our attention of explicating another quite distinct model of omnipotence while rejecting the above spurious conception. I suggest that we need to think of God's omnipotence not as directed to actual (past) states of affairs, but as directed to unactualized (future) states of affairs. Given any future state of affairs p, God can bring it about that p or bring it about that $\sim$ p. There are no obstacles to his actualization of any possible (that is, unactualized) state of affairs. It should be a *desideratum* of this concept of omnipotence (which we might call the *nihil obstat* conception) that it not be true of every state of affairs that God personally brings it about (or that God will bring it about), except perhaps in some suitably vicarious sense. Importantly, God's power is viewed as being directed to an unactualized future (though he himself is timeless) rather than to the actualized past. Equally importantly, God's power is not the power to substitute for (even future) agents, but the power to bring it about either that p or that $\sim$ p. Even where p has actually obtained at t, God's power is such that only at a previous time, $t - A$, could he have brought it about that $\sim$ p.

It is important to emphasize that the power of an omnipotent agent must not be thought of as extending over actual states of affairs that have occurred, since in this instance otherwise viable accounts of omnipotence are driven to absurdity. Consider Plantinga's view that God is omnipotent just in case God can create any state of affairs p such that God brings it about that p is consistent.[16] On this view, an agent is omnipotent where for that agent

(P) $M \delta p$

But we remember that Fitch's theorem reads

$M \delta p^T \rightarrow \delta p^T$

Obviously if we allow p^T as a legitimate substitution instance of p in (P), we get the undesirable result

δp^T

namely that the agent in question has brought about everything that has happened. The same result is forthcoming on the *nihil obstat* account of omnipotence which asserts that an agent is omnipotent where

$$M^* \ \delta \ p$$

By the corollary to Fitch's theorem we have it that

$$M^* \ \delta \ p^T \rightarrow \delta \ p^T$$

Thus substituting p^T for p yields the same result. The same result is a consequence of a third conception of omnipotence entertained by Duns Scotus, who was concerned to determine whether we can prove that God can produce directly whatever can be caused.[17] We might reconstruct this conception by ruling that an agent is omnipotent in this sense where

$$M^* \ p \rightarrow M^* \ \delta \ p$$

An agent is omnipotent where if a state of affairs is physically possible then it is physically possible that it be brought about by the agent. Here again, if we allow p^T as an instance of p, we have it that

$$M^* \ p^T \rightarrow M^* \ \delta \ p^T$$

But assuming our corollary to Fitch's theorem

$$M^* \ \delta \ p^T \rightarrow \delta \ p^T$$

it follows by hypothetical syllogism that

$$M^* \ p^T \rightarrow \delta \ p^T$$

Since we also have it that any actual state of affairs must be physically possible

$$p^T \rightarrow M^* \ p^T$$

it also follows that every actual state of affairs is an action of the agent in question

$$p^T \rightarrow \delta \ p^T$$

Or to put it more simply,

$$\delta \, p^{\,T}$$

Thus even these otherwise quite plausible accounts of omnipotence are vitiated if we allow the substitution in question, that is, if we allow the agent's power to extend over actual states of affairs.

Our conclusion from Fitch's theorem that omnipotence is best thought of as directed only to unactualized states of affairs is thus doubly reinforced. Even otherwise promising explications of omnipotence, such as the *nihil obstat* conception, admit of Fitch-like consequences if actualized states of affairs are included in the domain of the variables. An omnipotent being is better thought of as having unlimited power over which unactualized states of affairs he will bring about.[18] At least, I would add, that is the conclusion that Fitch's theorems suggest to me. It is not clear to me that this conclusion is the only one that can be unequivocably and finally drawn from Fitch's results. What I would principally like to leave in the reader's mind is the importance of Fitch's theorems in any serious attempt to understand the concept of omnipotence and the problem of evil. Here I leave off and commend them to the attention of philosophical theologians and atheologians.

Notes

1. Frederic Fitch, "A Logical Analysis of Some Value Concepts," *Journal of Symbolic Logic,* Vol. 28, No. 2, June 1963, pp. 135–42.
2. *Vide* J. L. Mackie, "Evil and Omnipotence," *Mind,* Vol. LXIV, 1955. Reprinted in Nelson Pike (ed.), *God and Evil,* Englewood Cliffs, Prentice-Hall, 1964. See also Douglas Walton, "Modalities in the Free Will Defense," Selection 33.
3. Gordon D. Kaufman, "On the Meaning of 'Act of God'," *Harvard Theological Review,* Vol. 61, 1968, pp. 175–201.
4. Fitch, 136f.
5. *Vide* Jaakko Hintikka, "Knowledge, Belief, and Logical Consequence," *Ajatus,* Vol. 32, 1970, pp. 32–47.
6. In Fitch's notation, the usual subscript denoting an individual is dropped. Instead of "$\delta_a p$" we simply have "$\delta \, p$" meaning *"a brings it about that p."*
7. Fitch, p. 138.
8. Fitch, p. 138.
9. This is not used by Fitch.
10. Fitch, p. 138.
11. For an excellent recent discussion and review of various traditional conceptions of

omnipotence, see Peter Geach, "Omnipotence," *Philogophy,* January 1973, Vol. 48, pp. 7–20, and Peter Geach, "An Irrelevance of Omnipotence," *Philosophy,* October 1973, Vol. 48, pp. 327–33. References in the sequel are to the former article.

12. For a helpful discussion, see Myles Brand, "On Having the Opportunity," *Theory and Decision,* Vol. 2, 1972, pp. 307–13.

13. *Summa Theologica,* Ia q. xxv art. 3. *Vide* Geach, p. 12f. What I take to be the same view has been held by Alvin Plantinga (see note 16).

14. *Vide* Wade Savage, "The Paradox of the Stone," *Philosophical Review,* Vol. LXXVI, No. 1, January 1967, 74–79.

15. See the discussion in Geach, p. 12f.

16. Alvin Plantinga, "The Free Will Defense," *Philosophy in America,* ed. Max Black, London, Allen and Unwin, 1965, p. 209.

17. Felix Alluntis and Allan B. Wolter, "Duns Scotus on the Omnipotence of God," *Studies in Philosophy and the History of Philosophy,* Vol. 5, 1970, pp. 178–222.

18. For an illuminating discussion of divine control of past events, see Geach, p. 16f. I take it that our conclusions here strongly support Geach's view that what is past ceases to be alterable even by God (Geach, p. 17).

29

Freedom Within Omnipotence

LINWOOD URBAN and DOUGLAS WALTON

In traditional Christianity, the doctrine that men are free and responsible has two important consequences. First, human freedom and responsibility are necessary conditions for any further doctrine that men can be justly punished or rewarded for their success or failure in leading a good and honorable life. For, if men's decisions and actions are wholly determined, then it is hard to see how they can be said to deserve or merit praise or blame. If human decisions and actions be good, then the creator who predestines them is to be praised. Likewise, if they be evil, then that same creator ought to be blamed.

Second, the doctrine that men are free and responsible and that they can be justly praised or blamed has also played an important role in discussions of the problem of evil. If it is true that a morally excellent and very powerful deity desires to create beings as much like himself as possible, then he would create at least some beings who have as great a measure of freedom and responsibility as can be conferred. If human beings are among those free and responsible beings, then they are to blame for much of the moral evil in the universe and also for the physical evil which results from their free choices. Regrettable as it may be that there is so much evil in the world, at least some of it must be blamed upon man and not upon God. While God is responsible for having created free beings in the first place, he is not responsible for the evil which such beings bring into the world; for they could have chosen and done otherwise.

However, many theologians who believe that the existence of human freedom is at least a partial solution to the problem of evil also hold that God is omnipotent in the sense that he can control every outcome. By this is meant that God, if he so chose, could determine every human decision and could also prevent every evil outcome which might result from those decisions. God does not choose to do so, it is argued, because it is more desirable for human beings to learn of the moral law by themselves than that it should be given them in detail by revelation or that they be programmed to decide and act always in the best way. Hence it is said that although God could control every outcome, he permits men to share control of some events. Thus, men bear responsibility for some events because of the measure of control which they are permitted to exercise.

It will be contended in this paper that attempts to consistently combine the notion of God's omnipotence, taken in the way adumbrated above as the power to determine *every* outcome, with the notion of human freedom to control at least partially some of these outcomes, cannot succeed. What will be shown can be put crudely as follows: an omnipotent agent, so strictly defined, exhausts *all* the power in the universe, leaving no room for other centers of power. An analogy to a more familiar problem may be helpful. It has been argued that if there is an "omniscient" agent, then it is inconsistent to assert that any other agent can do anything freely.[1] If the omniscient agent knows in advance that *a* will do R, then *a* does not do R freely, i.e., *a* cannot do not R. Similarly, it will be shown here that there is a parallel problem for omnipotence: if there is an "omnipotent" agent in the strict sense just characterized, then it is inconsistent to assert that any other agent ever possesses control over any outcome.[2] Our feeling that we do sometimes possess control over some events would thus be merely the illusion of control.

One can easily see that this result is disastrous for those who hope to solve the problem of evil at least partially by placing the blame for some of the evil in the world upon men. For, if God could control every outcome, he is responsible for every outcome. Hence, God must, so to speak, shoulder the full blame for whatever happens in the world. However paradoxical it may seem, it is still within the confines of this definition of "an omnipotent being" and within the scope of the conclusions just reached for men to have enough control to justify praise and blame sufficient to merit rewards and punishments. Part of the paper will discuss this possibility.[3]

Finally, the paper will examine a different concept of an omnipotent being which offers greater hope for a partial solution to the problem of evil.

§1 Partial Control: Explication A

The first project of this paper is to attempt to reconcile the theses that God can control every outcome and that men have or have been given sufficient control to be held responsible for at least their decisions and for the evil which results from them. An initial suggestion might be that both God and men have partial control, in some sense that implies that neither individually has complete control over an evil outcome. However, any claim of this sort depends on what is meant by ''partial control.''

Let us stipulate first that *positive control* is the power to bring about an outcome or result, R, whereas *negative control* is the power to preclude R from happening, that is the power to bring about $\sim$R. Further, let us stipulate that an agent has *partial control* over R when he can bring R about only jointly with some other agent. There are several ways in which partial control might be explicated, but let us take as a relatively sharp instance a physical model: two circuits, where a is at switch A and b is at switch B. We take each controller to be independent from the other. (See figure.)

In the parallel circuit, a has positive control over R, the illumination of the light. Indeed, he has complete, as opposed to partial positive control over R, since he can make the light go on without assistance from b. b also has complete positive control over R. a and b jointly have complete negative control over R—if they both keep their switches open, the light will remain off. But individually, neither has complete negative control over R, because, for example, even if a keeps his switch open, the light will still be on if b closes his switch. If *full control* is the power to make the light go on or off, then neither individually has full control, although jointly they do have full control.

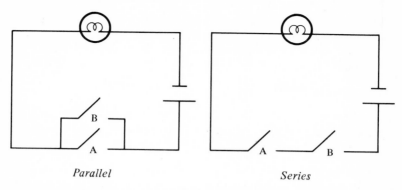

Parallel   *Series*

Conversely, in the series circuit, each has complete negative control, but neither has complete positive control. One can thwart the efforts of the other to illuminate the light by keeping his switch open. Again jointly, but not separately, they have full control. In other words, full control is partial for each. Negative control is complete for each, but positive control is only partial for each.

To summarize the definitions suggested by the model: partial, or shared control, is opposed to complete control, and full control indicates the presence of both positive and negative control. All these notions can be defined in terms of positive control (cont$^+$), taken as primitive.[4]

> Def. cont$^-$: a cont$^-$ R $=_{df}$ a cont$^+$ $\sim$R

Partial (positive) control may initially be defined as shared (positive) control.[5]

> Def. cont^{+P}: a cont^{+P} R $=_{df}$ ($\exists$x) [(x & a cont$^+$ R) & $\sim a$ cont$^+$ R & x $\neq$ y]

As characterized strictly above, an omnipotent agent must have full complete control over all events. If he had only partial control, shared with other agents, his aims could occasionally be frustrated.[6] If a and b each have partial control over moving a large rock, then a's aim to move the rock could be frustrated when b refuses to cooperate. Thus, the model does not appear to provide any way of explicating the notion of partial control in such a way that on the one hand, God can be said to control every outcome, and on the other that human beings can be said to control the effects of their decisions. So far developed, the model does not allow either God or man enough control to satisfy the requirements of the project.

Control Stalemates

The definitions adopted above strongly seem to make the following theses *true,* given our understanding of the physical model we have in mind.

(1) It is logically impossible that a should have complete positive (negative) control over R while b $(a \neq b)$ also has complete negative (positive) control over R, and thus

(2) It is impossible that the omnipotent agent and some human (i.e., non-omnipotent) agent should at the same time have complete full control over some R. Yet surprisingly,

(3) It is logically possible that the omnipotent agent could have complete full control over an R where some human agent has partial (full) control over R. To be sure, some other explication of partial control will have to be given than that afforded by the model of parallel and series circuits. Let us now examine each of these theses. According to (1), we have it that

$$(A) \sim M(a \text{ cont}^+ R \& b \text{ cont}^- R), \text{ where } a \neq b$$

In order to examine (A), we might try to construct a plausible counter-example. Imagine a state of affairs in which a has the power to make a light go on and b can open the circuit to make the light go off. (See figure.)

Let us say that a can close the switch but not open it, and b can open the switch but not close it. Thus apparently, a controls R and b controls $\sim$R. The impossibility of this suggestion, that the one exercises positive control and the other negative control, is made clear when it is made explicit that R refers to a specific state of affairs with a specifiable duration. Consider some future time-interval t_Δ. Who controls R_{t_Δ}? b obviously does not control R_{t_Δ} since he cannot close the switch. a can close the switch before t_Δ, but he cannot completely control R_{t_Δ}

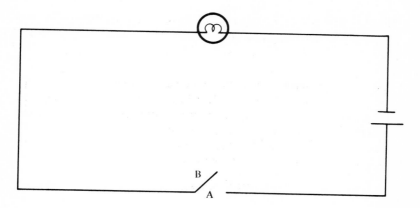

because, provided the interval Δ is long enough, b can exercise his option to open the switch. So a's purported control is recognizably an illusion once we are reminded that a state of affairs is an actual event with a specific duration, even though we have avoided using tense markers up until now for convenience. We recall that a and b are assumed to be *independent* controllers. The state of affairs imagined would be a *control stalemate* where Δ is sufficiently long for one controller to interfere with the other.

Another putative counter-example to (A) might be where a and b, as in the circuit-diagram above, are said to each have full complete control over R_{t_Δ}. But this is absurd. a might think he has complete positive control over R, but this is simply false. By hypothesis b can open the switch. Thus, we seem to be unable to find a conceivable model for the state of affairs represented in the parenthesis in (A), where a has positive control and b has negative control. Oddly enough, however, we do have it that

(B) $M(a \text{ cont}^+ R \ \& \ a \text{ cont}^+ R)$

The part within the parentheses of (B) is simply an instance of full control.

We can summarize by noting that positive (complete) control by a conflicts with negative (complete) control by b ($a \neq b$) and *vice versa*, whereas positive goes with positive and negative with negative. Thus

John and Charles can both compatibly have complete positive control
(or for that matter, negative control) over the illumination of a lamp.
But John's complete positive control must conflict with Charles's complete negative control and *vice versa*. Hence (2) follows as an instance
of (A). The omnipotent agent and some human agent cannot both have
full complete control over some R. Since, as we say, the omnipotent
agent is assumed to have full complete control over R, it follows that a
given human being can, at best, share full control with God over a
given event, as (3) concedes. Let us now investigate what partial control in the sense of shared full control might mean.

§2 Partial Control: Explication B

It is conceivable that *a* might have complete positive control over R
where *b* has only partial (shared) control over R. Where one party's
control is merely shared, positive and negative need not conflict. This
situation can obtain where *b*'s partial control is shared with a full
complete controller *a*. Likewise it can obtain where man shares control
with an omnipotent agent.

This state of affairs can be exemplified in the following circuit diagram where *a* is taken to have full complete control.

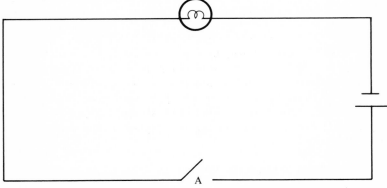

b can still have partial positive control over R. He can, jointly with *a*,
make the light go on. That is, substituting into the definition of partial
control, we have it that

$$(\exists x) (x \,\&\, b \text{ cont}^+ R) \,\&\, \sim b \text{ cont}^+ R$$

The first conjunct obtains since there is a person a such that a and b positively control R. And the second conjunct obtains since it is not the case that b completely controls R. Thus, it is perfectly consistent to say that b partially controls the illumination of the lamp, even though a (fully) controls the illumination and non-illumination of the lamp without requiring the assistance of anyone else. This is exactly the situation envisioned by William of Ockham in his example of the strong man who could carry the ten bundles, but asks a weaker man to carry some of them for him.[7] The strong man could carry all the bundles himself. The weaker man could carry only a few. If the weaker man assists the stronger man, he is a partial agent; however, he does not do anything which the stronger man could not do on his own. To make the example completely parallel to the circuit above, we need only suppose that the strong man is quite capable of preventing the weaker man from carrying any bundles at all if he so chose. William of Ockham was apparently satisfied with this rude example[8] which is intended to show how a God who can determine every outcome could share his agency in the world with men.

But is there not something spurious about the notion that such shared agency amounts to any real control? In both examples, in the circuit diagram and in Ockham's story of the ten bundles, neither b nor the weaker fellow can determine the outcome. "Partial control," by the revised definition, has degenerated into "partial agency" which is no control at all.

§ 3 Partial Control: Explication C

Perhaps a less vacuous concept of partial control might be obtained by requiring that both parties be needed when control is shared. Thus, we might modify the definition to read

> Def. Alt. $cont^{+P}$: $a \ cont^{+P} R =_{df} (\exists x) (x \ \& \ a \ cont^{+} R \ \& \ \sim x \ cont^{+} R \ \& \ \sim a \ cont^{+} R \ \& \ x = a)$

To say then that a has partial control over R is to say that a does not control R but that there is someone else, b, who does not fully control

R either, but who, taken together with *a*, does control R. In short, *a* and *b* need each other.

Unfortunately this definition does not square with the initial project which requires that we conceive of a state of affairs in which there is an omnipotent agent who has full and complete control over every outcome and in which there are also agents who fully control some events. In the new proposed definition, neither *a* or *b* has *enough* control to satisfy these requirements. Since they both need each other to effect an outcome, neither one nor the other can be said to individually control any event. However, there may seem to be one last way out of the impasse.

Picture the following diagram with a bypass.

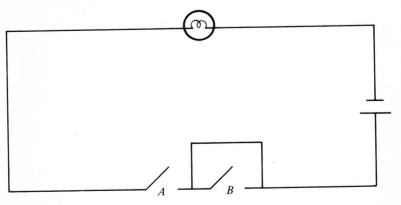

Let us take it that *a* is at switch A and that *b* is at switch B. Now *a* has complete control of both the illumination and the non-illumination of the lamp. *b* has control of neither of these alternatives unless he might be said to have it insofar as *a* cooperates. Thus, if when *b* pushes his switch down, *a* does likewise, the lamp will go on. Similarly if when *b* raises his switch and *a* does the same, the lamp will go off. Thinking along these lines, it might be said that *b* controls the outcome when *a* cooperates, even though it is always possible for *a* to wrest control away from *b* at any time. Again this seems to be exactly the situation envisioned by William of Ockham when he says that God concurs with man in every action willed and done by man; and that unless God cooperated in every action and event along with second causes, the event simply would not take place.[9] Note however that here, *b*'s "control" is precariously thin. For the light is on (off) *if and only if* *a*'s switch is closed (open). What *b* does makes no difference, presuming that it is not the case that *b* exerts control over *a* in some *other* way, not pictured by the model. To say that *b* controls at all postulates the cooperation of *a,* and this violates our assumption that the controllers must be independent of each other.

What is especially interesting about this situation is that it seems to be the only way in which man's partial control of events and God's capacity to fully determine every outcome can be illustrated. At the same time, however, it makes God responsible for every outcome. For every action which a man decides to do, God could prevent by refusing to cooperate with the man in the same way in which *a* could refuse to push his switch down to accommodate *b*. God's omnipotence is maintained and some control is given man by divine permission, but only at the expense of making God responsible for everything. Thus, while a model has been found for reconciling the notions that an omnipotent being can determine every outcome and yet man may also with God's permission determine some outcomes, this solution is of no assistance in helping to solve the problem of evil. For although it can be said that it is man who chooses to sin, still on this model God could have prevented him from sinning since God must concur with every human decision and with every human action if it is to take place.

Nonetheless, it is important to realize that in making his proposal William of Ockham was not really interested in the problem of evil at all. His discussion has a different focus. He was interested in the question: Can God justly condemn a human being for his evil choices in this world?[10] According to Ockham, because men have the freedom to choose alternative courses of action, but do not have the power to determine the outcome of their decisions unless God cooperates with them, human beings are still responsible for their *decisions*. Of course, even though they control their decisions, still, since the desired outcome cannot be wrought except God cooperate, he must bear the ultimate responsibility for its occurrence.

The upshot can be put schematically as follows:

1. God can control every outcome.
2. God permits men to choose certain alternatives.
3. God could override those choices which men make.
4. Men are still responsible for the decisions which they make since they control them *de facto*.
5. Men can be justly punished for their sins.

We can see this situation intuitively in the circuit diagram with the bypass. Although *a* must bear the ultimate responsibility for what happens, since he completely controls both the illumination and the non-illumination of the lamp, still *b* bears some responsibility since he controls how he will decide. Similarly, although man is not ultimately responsible for his decisions or their results, he is responsible *as long as God cooperates with him*. Hence, he can be justly praised or blamed for his decisions. Although this understanding of the relationship between God's agency and man's does not, we think, aid in the solution of the problem of evil, still men can be held accountable for the decision which they have made. However, they cannot be held responsible for the outcome which has occurred.

§4 Another Definition of Omnipotence

Up to this point, it has been assumed that an omnipotent being is a being who can control every outcome. But suppose an omnipotent being is defined as a being who can create at least some creatures over which he has no control. If God has created such beings, then because he cannot control them, he is not responsible for the results of their decisions and actions. He is, of course, still responsible for creating them in the first place. However, if free and responsible beings are more desirable than are automata, then God's moral excellence need not be diminished by having created them. Thus, were God to have created such beings, and were such creative acts consistent with omnipotence, a partial solution to the problem of evil would be logically possible.

The major difficulty with this proposal is that many have concluded that it is logically contradictory to affirm that an omnipotent being can create beings over which he has no control.[11] There is an analogy between this problem and the problem as to whether God can create a stone too heavy to lift. Should one say that an omnipotent being can create such a stone? If he can do so, he seems to fail in omnipotence because there is at least one stone which he cannot lift. However, if it is said that God cannot create a stone too heavy for him to lift, he also seems to lack omnipotence since he cannot do something which even non-omnipotent agents can do. A human being can build a boat too heavy for him to lift. Why cannot God, if he is omnipotent, perform a similar feat? [12]

Suggested solutions to the paradox of the stone have usually proposed that an omnipotent being could not create such a stone.[13] It seems to be assumed that the power to control a world once created is more basic to the notion of omnipotence than the power to create a variety of different kinds of worlds. It will be suggested that in light of the impasse created in §1 to §3 by cleaving to a strict definition of omnipotence of complete, full control, and in light of subsequent developments below, omnipotence is more adequately understood in the latter way, as power to create a variety of different kinds of worlds.

§5 Towards a More Mature Notion of Omnipotence

It must be noted at the outset that a restriction on the notion of omnipotence has generally been accepted. An omnipotent being cannot create a contradictory state of affairs. Such a being need not for example be able to create an object which is black and white all over at the same time. This restriction has usually been thought to obtain for any power whatever. Hence, St. Thomas Aquinas says that it is better to say that such things cannot be done rather than that God cannot perform them.[14]

Second, it has also been affirmed that God cannot make the past not to have been. St. Thomas Aquinas argues against St. Peter Damian that God could not at a later time cause a past event not to have taken place. For such an ability could also violate the law of non-contradiction.[15]

Third, an omnipotent being cannot bring about a state of affairs which cannot be brought about by him. The previous examples only show that an omnipotent being cannot bring about states of affairs which involve a contradiction. However, an omnipotent being cannot bring about every non-contradictory state of affairs. An uncreated world is a non-contradictory state of affairs, but if we accept the further restriction that no power can do that which is contradictory, even an omnipotent being could not create an un-created universe.[16]

These three examples show that it is unreasonable to require that an omnipotent being control *every* outcome. However, there are other examples which further restrict what it is reasonable to require an omnipotent being to perform. An omnipotent being cannot control that portion of the universe governed by chance.

Suppose we take it that certain parts of our world are governed by chance. Present physical theories about the movement of particles and of the mutations of genes assume as much. If there are parts of our universe governed by chance, then even an omnipotent power could not control them. It is contradictory to affirm that they are governed by chance and that they are at the same time controlled.

Take the owner of a gambling casino. He can allow the roulette wheel to run freely, and if he does, then those who bet risk their money to chance. A scurrilous casino czar can "control" the wheel so that a majority of those wagering will more likely lose. Yet, if he does so, he has interfered with the wheel. He has in effect determined the outcome and those who bet no longer have the outcome determined by chance. Suppose God should determine that a particular particle should not follow the chance path which contemporary physics assumes that it does. That particle would no longer be governed by chance, but by the divine will.

The upshot of this brief discussion is the rather obvious conclusion that even an omnipotent being cannot control the outcomes of chance. Were he to do so, the results would not be *by chance,* but by divine intervention. This is not to assert that an omnipotent being could not determine the outcome, but that as long as it is determined by chance, he could not determine it. For it is contradictory we think to assert both that an outcome is determined by chance and that it is determined by an agent.

If the foregoing thoughts are correct, then were God to create a world which is even partially governed by chance, he could not control the outcome of those chance occurrences as long as they are governed by chance. Furthermore, if God has created a world partially governed by chance, he has created a world over which he has imperfect control.

§6 Freedom of the Will

If we apply what has been said to the problem of human freedom, it ought to be said that if God has given men power to determine their choices and the power to act upon them, then God could not control these choices and these actions as long as men possess these powers. Of course, God might intervene to determine the outcomes. However, as long as these decisions and these actions are free decisions and actions, it is not possible for him to do so.

§7 Can God Create Such a World?

Those who hold that an omnipotent being must be able to control every outcome which does not involve a contradictory state of affairs or a state of affairs which could not be controlled by him must insist paradoxically that such a being *could not* create a world governed by chance or by man's free choice. Although the present universe may appear to be ruled partially by chance, in fact it could not be so ruled. Likewise even though it may appear that God does not control the decisions and actions of men, he must in fact do so. However, we will argue here to the contrary, equally paradoxical as it may seem, that a being who can create a world over which he has no control has a greater measure of power than one who is limited to creating worlds over which he has complete control.

Suppose there are two types of very powerful beings. α can create worlds over which he can exercise complete control. He can strictly determine every outcome. β can create all the worlds α can, but he can also create worlds over which he has only partial control. He can create worlds partially governed by chance, and he can create worlds in which there are free beings over which he has no control as long as they are free. Which of these beings has the *greater* power? We think β has. For β can create many different kinds of worlds. The being who can only create worlds over which he has complete control does not have as many abilities as the one who can create worlds of different sorts.

J. L. Mackie argued that there is no rational way to choose between two conceptions of omnipotence. 1) A conception in which the omnipotent being is able to bind himself, to limit his control, or 2) one in which he has not this capacity.[17] But we think this conclusion is incorrect. For a being who can limit himself by creating either worlds in which he has complete control or worlds in which he has only partial control has greater control than one who can consistently with his omnipotence create only worlds in which he has complete control. This is true we think, even though in these latter worlds he has the power to fully determine every outcome which is not a contradictory state of affairs or could not be brought about by him.

A partial explanation can be provided if the reader will forgive another rude example. Suppose Charles has a million dollars. Charles is of such a character that he is able to spend this million only upon goods which will bring him personal pleasure. James also has a million. James's character is such that he can spend his million either upon goods which are of benefit to others or upon his own pleasure. Since both Charles and James each have exactly one million, each has only the same monetary power. Should James decide to spend his money for personal pleasure, he can do no more than Charles. James can buy no more expensive a fleet of yachts than Charles. Nonetheless, James has the greater control over the destiny of the world. For he is not limited as is Charles in the way in which his money is to be spent. He can spend his money for the relief of those who could truly benefit.

If then omnipotence is in part at least to be explicated in terms of control, a being who can both create a world over which he is in complete control and also a world over which he has only partial control has greater general control over the outcome than a being who can create only a world in which he can determine every outcome which does not entail a contradiction and which is such that an omnipotent being could bring about and control. Hence, a being who could create beings over which he has no control has, paradoxical as it may seem, a greater measure of control than one who cannot create free and independent beings. We think that it is possible to consistently understand a truly omnipotent being who creates free beings over which he cannot exercise control as long as he permits them to remain free.[18] Whereas we can find no clear way of modeling the notion of a complete full controller who strictly determines every outcome by an explication that is both consistent and theologically adequate.

Notes

1. *Cf.* Nelson Pike, *God and Timelessness,* Schocken Books, 1970; Linwood Urban, "Was Luther a Thoroughgoing Determinist?'', *Journal of Theological Studies,* 22, Pt. I, April 1971, pp. 113–39.
2. J. L. Mackie, "Omnipotence,'' see above, selection 12, § III, 2.
3. *Ibid.*
4. See also Nicholas Rescher, "The Concept of Control,'' *Essays in Philosophical Analysis,* ed. Nicholas Rescher, University of Pittsburgh Press, 1969.
5. Here we adopt the convention that cont$^+$ denotes *complete* positive control, and similarly for negative control.
6. We will assume that there is at most one omnipotent agent. It will be easy to see that this thesis must obtain according to the conception of omnipotence adopted here when we come to the notion of control stalemate, below.
7. William of Ockham, II. *Sent.* qus. 4 and 5, Q. See above, Selection 27.
8. Rude, but delightfully clear.
9. *Ibid.*
10. William of Ockham, I *Sent.,* d. 17, q. 1, L; *cf.* Linwood Urban, "William of Ockham's Theological Ethics,'' *Franciscan Studies,* Vol. 33, Annual XI, 1973, p. 394f.
11. Cf. J. L. Mackie, *loc. cit.*
12. G. Mavrodes, "Some Puzzles Concerning Omnipotence,'' Selection 20 above.
13. C. Wade Savage, "The Paradox of the Stone,'' Selection 22 above.
14. *De Potentia Dei,* Bk. 1, q. 1, a. 3. Selection 4 above.
15. *Summa Theologica,* I, q. 25, a. 4. Selection 10 above.
16. *Cf.* J. L. Mackie, *op. cit.,* § II, 1. Selection 12 above.
17. *Ibid.,* § III, 2.
18. Mackie's discussion of first and second order causes notwithstanding. *Cf. Ibid.*

30

God's Universal Causality

THOMAS BRADWARDINE

I rarely heard anything of grace said in the lectures of the philosophers
. . . but every day I heard them teach that we are masters of our own
free acts, and that it is in our power to do either good or evil, to be either virtuous or vicious and the like. And when now and then in
Church I heard a passage read from the Apostle which exalted grace
and humbled free will, for example, that text in *Romans* 9, ''Therefore
it is not in him that wills, nor in him that runs, but in God that shows
mercy,'' [1] I had no liking for Paul's teaching, for toward grace I was
still graceless. . . . . But afterwards, and before I had become a student
of theology, the truth of his teaching struck upon me like a beam of
grace. It seemed to me as if I beheld in the distance, under a clear
image of truth, that the grace of God is prevenient both in time and nature to all good works—that is to say, the gracious will of God which
antecedently wills that he who merits salvation shall be saved, antecedently works merit in him—God in truth, being in all movements
the primary Mover. . . .

In the first place, it ought to be most firmly stated that God is most supremely perfect and good to such a degree that nothing is able to be
better or more perfect. This proposition can be evidently shown from
the infinite majesty of his perfection and goodness. Likewise it can be
demonstrated by the many arguments of the philosophers and theologians. The Father of Philosophy, Hermogenes, or Hermes, thrice

De Causa Dei Contra Pelagium, etc., H. Saville, ed., London, 1618, reprinted Min-
erva, Frankfurt am Main, 1964. Selections are from p. 308 C–D; p. 1 D–E & p. 2 A; p.
4 C–D; p. 190 D–E & p. 191 A–B; p. 195 A–C; p. 197 B–D; p. 554 C–E. Material in
[ ] is added for clarification. Translated by Linwood Urban.

Mercury, thrice Trismegistus, thrice greatest among the lovers of wisdom, King of Egypt, Philosopher and Prophet, speaking of God in *On the Word Eternal,* 29, says: "He is complete and perfect totality." Further on in 32 he says: "He is Holy, and incorrupt, and everlasting; and if anything can be shown to be better than such a being, God is that supreme excellence." [2] . . . To which in agreement Anselm in *Proslogion* Chapter 2 addresses God: "We believe that thou art a being than which nothing better can be conceived." [3] And Augustine in *On Christian Doctrine* Book I, Chapter 7 says: "All struggle emulously for the excellence of God, and no one can be found who believes God to be something to which there is a superior. Thus all agree that God is that thing which they place above all things." [4] Whence the Prophet says: "Great is God and highly to be praised, and there is no end of his greatness (*Psalm* 145). [5]

Second, it must be supposed immediately that there is no infinite regress in entities, but that there is in whatever genus you will a single first member. [6] It must be left to others to demonstrate that almost all philosophers and certainly all theologians agree with this proposition. . . .

Thus they ought to apply themselves who deny that whatever power of God you will and whatever good of God you will are simply infinite. Certainly if any of his power and goodness should be ever so little finite, his power or goodness could be increased. The First Proposition condemns this supposition, since nothing can be better than God. . . .

However, I judge that this proposition ought to be added: "The divine will is the efficient cause of everything whatever which is made, moving or the mover of every motion whatever, and universally the generator of every most fond affection and the unified conservor of all things." . . . This statement can be confirmed by several arguments and by the authority of the philosophers and theologians. For according to our second presupposition: "Causes do not proceed to infinity." There is, therefore, one first cause of all things, which is God, as was shown above.

But such causality is not attributed to God according to his absolute essence, since his causality, in so far as it is from his very nature, holds itself equally and indifferently to what is possible, just as much to those possibilities which may never come to pass as to those which ought to be done, as much to the remote future as to the past, and as much to motion as to rest. Therefore these states of affairs would always be similarly and equally possible. So much the more is this true because if anything should be done by God's essence alone without any volition, that thing would be done by way of nature and necessity, just as are all the effects of causation by nature, since liberty can be placed only in the will. And such natural causes whenever they are able always act necessarily, since their actions are owing to a supposed passive disposition. For their causation differs from voluntary causation which participates in reason, as is clear from the *Metaphysics,* Book IX, and likewise in the Commentator. [7]

If God should ever act toward things outside of himself purely naturally, he would act according to the full extent of his power. Since he is necessarily infinite, all his effects would be simply infinite and equal to himself, since every lesser thing can be made greater as the First Proposition shows. . . . Therefore, nothing remains as a sufficient cause unless the divine will is posited. Since whoever does anything freely, does it voluntarily, God also will do freely whatever he does outside himself. [8] It is more perfect to act in this way. Otherwise God's actions of grace would be irrational, and prayers to God would be inane.

Whence it is evident that all things which are made, conserved, or moved, and which were, are, or shall be, were, are, or shall be done by the divine will. . . . If it is necessary that all things done at the present time, are presenty done by the divine will, it is correspondingly necessary that past and future events, whether conservations or movements, be done by the divine will. . . .

However, it consequently remains to be shown that the divine will is universally efficacious, insuperable, and necessary in causation, and cannot be frustrated in any way. . . . Who does not know that it follows most strictly that if God can do anything and wills to do it, he does it; or, since his will and power remain constant, that he shall do it at a predetermined time? For nothing requisite is lacking to him for the doing of it.

Therefore, from these considerations it follows clearly that for God to will to do something, or that it be done through him or in some way through something else, it necessarily follows that it come to pass. . . . From which it is plainly inferred that the will of God is the first free principle. For if something other than God's willing to act is required, his will will not of itself be sufficient for acting, which is contrary to what has been said. . . .

In addition, that the divine will should be the first free principle is clear, because under the Second Proposition, in free principles there is no regress to infinity, but there is some one first principle; and this free principle cannot be supposed to be present in any second cause. . . . Since all second causes in any of their causation whatever are necessarily subordinate to first causes, . . . every bit of the formers' causation is necessarily present in the causation of the first causes. Wherefore, liberty, contingency, and merit totally perish.[9]

Thus it should not be said that in the natural order of causes, inferior and second causes are freer than the supreme first cause. This latter is not possible in any way. The rule in all things and necessarily regulating them is that the first cause subjugates, the second is subject, the former precedent and dominant, the latter ancillary and following in all things. . . . Therefore, the first free principle is God, however, not his essence first of all, because . . . he is necessary being as regards his essence. [Hence his freedom does not lie in his essence.] Nor does his freedom rest in his intellect, because his intellect necessarily cognizes universals and not particulars. Therefore, God's freedom lies in no other potency than his will. For every other potency is purely natural, and if the will is of this kind, when acting and moving itself, it would act purely naturally and necessarily. Therefore, only liberty in the will can be posited, as the first cause *simpliciter* in the first being *simpliciter,* which is God.

Whence this conclusion is most easily elicited: Whatever the created will effects, it is necessary that the uncreated will also effect it, and whatever shall have been done by an Angelic or human will, it is necessary that the divine will shall have co-operated with it, and that every act of a created will, the whole of it the created will effects and likewise the whole of it the uncreated will effects. This corollary . . .

can be demonstrated most easily. For if God is necessarily required for co-effecting and co-working every act of the created will, and God does not [necessarily] do anything or [necessarily] operates outside himself, surely his action is not possible purely naturally or from his thought processes alone. God's uncreated will and efficacy is necessarily required. Wherefore the Prophet says, "Incline my heart O God to your testimonies" (*Psalm* 119)[10] and in a later poem, "Incline my heart to doing your just works."[11] . . . Thus Bernard in *On Grace and Free Will,* Chapter 14(47), speaking of grace has written: "It itself excites free will; when it brings forth thought, it heals; when it transforms affection, it invigorates as it brings it forth to action; it keeps watch lest the will feel defection. Moreover, grace so works together with free will that in the beginning it is prevenient, in later actions it is concomitant. Wherefore everywhere it is prevenient, as even now it co-operates successively with free will. Therefore, what by grace alone is attained, equally by both grace and free will is perfected, as mixed and not singular; not victoriously through one of the two is an effect produced, not part grace and part free will, but both complete the whole this and the whole that by a single individual operation; both complete the whole action as the whole in it and the whole from it."[12]

Notes

1. v. 16.
2. [Ipse] totus est plenus ateque perfectus. *Corpus Hermeticum,* A. D. Nock & A. J. Festugière, eds., Paris, Société D'Édition, "Les Belle Lettres," vol. II, 338: [Ipse] sanctus et incorruptus et sempiternus est, et si quid potest melius nuncupari [Deus enim summum bonum.] *Ibid.* p. 340. For an account of this literature and of its supposed author see *The Encyclopedia of Philosophy* under "Hermeticism."
3. *Saint Anselm: Basic Writings,* trans. S. W. Deane, La Salle, Ill., Open Court Pub. Co., Second Edition, 1962, p. 7.
4. *On Christian Doctrine,* trans. D. W. Robertson, Jr., Indianapolis & New York, Bobbs-Merrill, 1958, p. 11f.
5. v. 3.
6. Proposition Two as stated should be taken as a summary statement of the longer principle found in the writings of St. Thomas Aquinas, *Summa Theologica,* I, I, q. 2, a. 3, and in *Summa Contra Gentes,* Bk. III, Ch. 17, which can be put as follows: "In every genus where there are degrees, there is a maximum of the genus; and the maximum is the cause of everything in the genus." St. Thomas uses this principle to establish the existence of a Supreme Good and of a Supreme Being, which is

God. Bradwardine will use the principle to establish a Most Free Being (see below).

7. Aristotle, 1047b 31–1038a 11.

8. It is a common principle of Medieval theology that God is necessitated only with regard to himself. He acts freely with regard to everything else. For example, God necessarily loves only himself. He freely loves his creatures. *Cf.* F. Copleston, *History of Philosophy*, Westminster, Md., The Newman Press, 1955, Vol. II, p. 364ff.

9. See note 6 above.

10. v. 36.

11. Ps. 141:4.

12. Migne *Patrologia Latina,* Vol. 182, col. 1026f. Bradwardine elsewhere characterizes free human actions as those actions dictated by reason. (*Cf.* Book II, Chap. 2, pp. 444ff.) If reasons are causes, then there is no inconsistency in affirming that a human action is both caused by God and freely willed. For according to Bradwardine, God causes us to have reasons which we do.

OMNIPOTENCE
AND THE PROBLEM
OF EVIL

31

Can God Create a World in Which All Men Always Freely Choose the Good?

JOHN HICK

Flew contends, "Omnipotence might have, could without contradiction be said to have, created people who would always as a matter of fact freely have chosen to do the right thing."[1] This is the essence of Flew's argument. It can be concentrated into a single question, If God made us, why did He not make us so that we should always want to do what is right? . . .

I shall, however, endeavour to show by internal criticism the insufficiency of the Flew–Mackie argument and the way in which it points to the need for such a larger conception of freedom. But let us first have before us another statement of the challenge that is to be met. J. L. Mackie formulates it as follows:

> If there is no logical impossibility in a man's freely choosing the good on one, or on several occasions, there cannot be a logical impossibility in his freely choosing the good on every occasion. God was not, then, faced with a choice between making innocent automata and making beings who, in acting freely, would sometimes go wrong: there was open to him the obviously better possibility of making beings who would act freely but always go right. Clearly, his failure to avail him-

Abridged from pp. 268–69, 271–75 in *Evil and the God of Love*, Revised Edition by John Hick. Copyright © 1966, 1978 by John Hick. By permission of Harper & Row, Publishers, Inc.

self of this possibility is inconsistent with his being both omnipotent and wholly good.[2]

In a subsequent reply to critics[3] Mackie notes a progression of three questions that arise; and it will be useful to discuss the problem in the same three stages.

The first question is this: Granted that it is logically possible that one man should on one occasion freely choose the good, it is also logically possible that *all* men should *always* do so? Is there, in other words, any logical contradiction in the idea of all men always acting rightly, and doing so of their own free choice, without external compulsion? Clearly the answer of the Christian theologian must be that this *is* logically possible, since it belongs to the expected fulfilment of God's purposes for human life.

A second question now arises: Granted that it is logically possible that men should always freely choose the good, is it also logically possible that they should be *so constituted* that they always freely choose the good? In other words, is there any logical contradiction in the idea of men being by nature such that they always spontaneously want to do the right thing, so that of their own free desire they life morally flawless lives? . . .

Is it possible to develop an argument that will exclude this as impossible? Can we, for example, draw a distinction, and claim that whilst there is no contradiction in the idea of men being so constituted that they always freely act rightly, there is nevertheless a contradiction in the idea of God so forming them that they can be *guaranteed in advance* always freely to act rightly? At this point the issue moves into that raised by the third in Mackie's progression of questions: Granted that it is logically possible that men should be so constituted that they always freely choose the good, is it also logically possible that God should make them so? Here Mackie's argument is very simple: "If their being of this sort is logically possible, then God's making them of this sort is logically possible."[4]

Mackie's conclusion here seems undeniable. But having accepted it there is a fourth question to be asked. This arises from an important aspect of Christian belief that Mackie (unlike Flew) fails to take into account. According to Christianity, the divine purpose for men is not only that they shall freely act rightly towards one another but that they shall also freely enter into a filial personal relationship with God Himself. There is, in other words, a religious as well as an ethical dimension to this purpose. And therefore, having granted that it would be logically possible for God so to make men that they will always freely act rightly towards each other, we must go on to ask the further questions: Is it logically possible for God so to make men that they will freely respond to Himself in love and trust and faith?

I believe that the answer is no. The grounds for this answer may be presented by means of an analogy with post-hypnotic suggestion, which Flew uses in this connection.[5] A patient can, under hypnosis, be given a series of instructions, which he is to carry out after waking—say, to go at a certain time to a certain library and borrow a certain book—and he may at the same time be told that he will forget having received these instructions. On coming out of the hypnotic trance he will then be obediently unaware of what transpired in it, but will nevertheless at the prescribed time feel an imperious desire to go to the library and borrow the book, a desire that the ordinary resources of the educated intellect will find no difficulty in rationalizing. The patient will thus carry out the hypnotist's commands whilst seeming both to himself and to others to be doing so of his own free will and for his own sufficient reasons. In terms of the definition of a free act as one that is not externally compelled but flows from the character of the agent, the actions of one carrying out post-hypnotic suggestions are free actions and the patient is a free agent in his performance of them. Nevertheless, taking account of the wider situation, including the previous hypnotic trance, we must say that the patient is not free as far as these particular actions are concerned *in relation to the hypnotist*. In relation to the hypnotist he is a kind of puppet or tool. And if the hypnotist's suggestion had been that the patient would agree with him about some controversial matter or, coming closer to an analogy with our relationship with God, trust the hypnotist, or love him, or devotedly serve him, there would be something inauthentic about the resulting trust, love, or service. They would be inauthentic in the sense that to the hypnotist, who knows that he has himself directly planted these personal attitudes by his professional techniques, there would be an all-important difference between the good opinion and trust and friendship of the patient and that of someone else whose mind had not been conditioned by hypnotic suggestion. He would regard and value the two attitudes in quite different ways. His patient's post-hypnotic friendship and trust would represent a purely technical achievement, whereas the friendship and trust of the other would represent a response to his own personal qualities and merits. The difference would be that between genuine and spurious personal attitudes—genuine and spurious, not in respect of their present observed and felt characters but in respect of the ways in which they have come about. For it is of the essential nature of "fiduciary" personal attitudes such as trust, respect, and affection to arise in a free being as an uncompelled response to the personal qualities of others. If trust, love, admiration, respect, affection, are produced by some kind of psychological manipulation which by-passes the conscious responsible centre of the personality, then they are not real trust and love, etc., but something else of an entirely different nature and quality which does not have at all the same value in the contexts of personal life and personal relationship. The authentic fiduciary attitudes are thus such that it is impossible—logically impossible—for them to be produced by miraculous manipulation: "it is logically impossible for God to obtain your love-unforced-by-anything-outside-you and yet himself force it." [6]

For if God had done what Mackie and Flew claim that He ought to have done, namely so fashioned men's natures that they always freely act rightly, He would be in a relationship to His human creatures comparable with that of the hypnotist to his patient. That is to say, He would have pre-selected our responses to our environment, to one another, and to Himself in such a way that although these responses would from our own point of view be free and spontaneous, they would from God's point of view be unfree. He alone would know that our actions and attitudes, whilst flowing from our own nature, have in fact been determined by His initial fashioning of that nature and its environment. So long as we think of God's purpose for man, as Mackie does, exclusively in terms of man's performance in relation to his fellows, as a moral agent within human society, there is no contradiction in the idea of God's so making human beings that they will always freely act rightly. But if we proceed instead from the Christian view that God is seeking man's free response to Himself in faith, trust, and obedience, we see the necessity for our fourth question and for a negative answer to it. It would not be logically possible for God so to make men that they could be guaranteed freely to respond to Himself in genuine trust and love. The nature of these personal attitudes precludes their being caused in such a way. Just as the patient's trust in, and devotion to, the hypnotist would lack for the latter the value of a freely given trust and devotion, so our human worship and obedience to God would lack for Him the value of a freely offered worship and obedience. We should, in relation to God, be mere puppets, precluded from entering into any truly personal relationship with Him.

There might, indeed, be very great value in a universe of created beings who respond to God in a freely given love and trust and worship which He has Himself caused to occur by His initial formation of their nature. But if human analogies entitle us to speak about God at all, we must insist that such a universe could be only a poor second-best to one in which created beings, whose responses to Himself God has not thus "fixed" in advance, come freely to love, trust, and worship Him. And if we attribute the latter and higher aim to God, we must declare to be self-contradictory the idea of God's so creating men that they will inevitably respond positively to him.[7]

To summarize this proposed rebuttal of the Flew–Mackie challenge: God can without contradiction be conceived to have so constituted men that they could be guaranteed always freely to act rightly in relation to one another. But He cannot without contradiction be conceived to have so constituted men that they could be guaranteed freely to respond to Himself in authentic faith and love and worship. The contradiction involved here would be a contradiction between the idea of A loving and devoting him herself to B, and of B valuing this love as a genuine and free response to himself whilst knowing that he has so constructed or manipulated A's mind as to produce it. The imagined hypnosis case reveals this contradiction as regards the relations between two human beings, and by analogy we apply the same logic of personal attitudes to the relation between God and man.

Notes

1. *New Essays in Philosophical Theology,* ed. Antony Flew and Alasdair MacIntyre, London, S.C.M. Press, 1955, p. 152.
2. "Evil and Omnipotence," *Mind,* p. 209.
3. "Theism and Utopia," *Philosophy,* vol. xxxvii, no. 140 (April 1962).
4. J. L. Mackie, "Theism and Utopia," p. 157.
5. Flew, *N.E.,* pp. 161f.
6. John Wisdom, "God and Evil," *Mind,* vol. xliv (Jan. 1935), p. 10. Wisdom's article is an important defence of the position that "It is possible that there is or will be in this world something, say a kingdom of heaven, of so great value that any world without it would be worse than this one and that further the present evil is a logically necessary condition of it." (p. 4.)
7. W. D. Hudson argues along essentially the same lines in "An Attempt To Defend Theism," *Philosophy,* vol. xxxix. no. 147 (January 1964), p. 20. For a different response to the Flew-Mackie challenge, claiming that the notion of beings who are so created that they always freely act rightly is a logical incoherent notion, see Alvin Plantinga, "The Free Will Defence," *Philosophy in America,* ed. by Max Black (London: Allen & Unwin Ltd., 1965).

32

God, Freedom, and Evil

ALVIN PLANTINGA

Was It within God's Power To Create Any Possible World He Pleased?

Is the atheologian right in holding that if God is omnipotent, then he could have actualized or created any possible world He pleased? Not obviously. First, we must ask ourselves whether God is a *necessary* or a *contingent* being. A *necessary* being is one that exists in every possible world—one that would have existed no matter which possible world had been actual; a *contingent* being exists only in some possible worlds. Now if God is not a necessary being (and many, perhaps most, theists think that He is not), then clearly enough there will be many possible worlds He could not have actualized—all those, for example, in which He does not exist. Clearly, God could not have created a world in which He doesn't even exist.

So, if God is a contingent being then there are many possible worlds beyond His power to create. But this is really irrelevant to our present concerns. For perhaps the atheologian can maintain his case if he revises his claim to avoid this difficulty; perhaps he will say something like this: if God is omnipotent, then He could have actualized any of those possible worlds in *which He exists*. So if He exists and is omnipotent, He could have actualized (contrary to the Free Will Defense) any of those possible worlds in which He exists and in which there

From Alvin Plantinga, *God, Freedom, and Evil,* New York, Harper and Row, 1974, pp. 39–57. Reprinted with the permission of Harper & Row and the author.

exist free creatures who do no wrong. He could have actualized worlds containing moral good but no moral evil. Is this correct?

Let's begin with a trivial example. You and Paul have just returned from an Australian hunting expedition: your quarry was the elusive double-wattled cassowary. Paul captured an aardvark, mistaking it for a cassowary. The creature's disarming ways have won it a place in Paul's heart; he is deeply attached to it. Upon your return to the States you offer Paul $500 for his aardvark, only to be rudely turned down. Later you ask yourself, "What would he have done if I'd offered him $700?" Now what is it, exactly, that you are asking? What you're really asking in a way is whether, under a *specific set of conditions,* Paul would have sold it. These conditions include your having offered him $700 rather than $500 for the aardvark, everything else being as much as possible like the conditions that did in fact obtain. Let S' be this set of conditions or state of affairs. S' includes the state of affairs consisting in your offering Paul $700 (instead of the $500 you did offer him); of course it does not include his *accepting* your offer, and it does not include his *rejecting* it; for the rest, the conditions it includes are just like the ones that did obtain in the actual world. So, for example, S' includes Paul's being free to accept the offer and free to refrain; and if in fact the going rate for an aardvark was $650, then S' includes the state of affairs consisting in the going rate's being $650. So we might put your question by asking which of the following conditionals is true:

> (23)   If the state of affairs S' had obtained, Paul would have accepted the offer
> (24)   If the state of affairs S' had obtained, Paul would not have accepted the offer.

It seems clear that at least one of these conditionals is true, but naturally they can't both be; so exactly one is.

Now since S' includes neither Paul's accepting the offer nor his rejecting it, the antecedent of (23) and (24) does not entail the consequent of either. That is,

> (25) S' obtains

does not entail either

(26)   Paul accepts the offer

or

(27)   Paul does not accept the offer.

So there are possible worlds in which both (25) and (26) are true, and other possible worlds in which both (25) and (27) are true.

We are now in a position to grasp an important fact. Either (23) or (24) is in fact true; and either way there are possible worlds God could not have actualized. Suppose, first of all, that (23) is true. Then it was beyond the power of God to create a world in which (1) Paul is free to sell his aardvark and free to refrain, and in which the other states of affairs included in S' obtain, and (2) Paul does not sell. That is, it was beyond His power to create a world in which (25) and (27) are both true. There is at least one possible world like this, but God, despite His omnipotence, could not have brought about its actuality. For let W be such a world. To actualize W, God must bring it about that Paul is free with respect to this action, and that the other states of affairs included in S' obtain. But (23), as we are supposing, is true; so if God had actualized S' and left Paul *free* with respect to this action, he would have sold: in which case W would not have been actual. If, on the other hand, God had *brought it about* that Paul didn't sell or had *caused him* to refrain from selling, then Paul would not have been free with respect to this action; then S' would not have been actual (since S' includes Paul's being free with respect to it), and W would not have been actual since W includes S'.

Of course if it is (24) rather than (23) that is true, then another class of worlds was beyond God's power to actualize—those, namely, in which S' obtains and Paul *sells* his aardvark. These are the worlds in which both (25) and (26) are true. But either (23) or (24) is true. Therefore, there are possible worlds God could not have actualized. If we consider whether or not God could have created a world in which, let's say, both (25) and (26) are true, we see that the answer depends upon a peculiar kind of fact; it depends upon what Paul would have freely chosen to do in a certain situation. So there are any number of possible worlds such that it is partly up to Paul whether God can create them.[1]

That was a past tense example. Perhaps it would be useful to consider a future tense case, since this might seem to correspond more closely to God's situation in choosing a possible world to actualize. At some time t in the near future Maurice will be free with respect to some insignificant action—having freeze-dried oatmeal for breakfast, let's say. That is, at time t Maurice will be free to have oatmeal but also free to take something else—shredded wheat, perhaps. Next, suppose we consider S', a state of affairs that is included in the actual world and includes Maurice's being free with respect to taking oatmeal at time t. That is, S' includes Maurice's being free at time t to take oatmeal and free to reject it. S' does not include Maurice's taking oatmeal, however; nor does it include his rejecting it. For the rest S' is as much as possible like the actual world. In particular there are many conditions that do in fact hold at time t and are *relevant* to his choice—such conditions, for example, as the fact that he hasn't had oatmeal lately, that his wife will be annoyed if he rejects it, and the like; and S' includes each of these conditions. Now God no doubt knows what Maurice will do at time t, if S' obtains; He knows which action Maurice would freely perform if S' were to be actual. That is, God knows that one of the following conditionals is true:

(28) If S' were to obtain, Maurice will freely take the oatmeal

or

(29) If S' were to obtain, Maurice will freely reject it.

We may not know which of these is true, and Maurice himself may not know; but presumably God does.

So either God knows that (28) is true, or else He knows that (29) is. Let's suppose it is (28). Then there is a possible world that God, though omnipotent, cannot create. For consider a possible world W' that shares S' with the actual world (which for ease of reference I'll name "Kronos") and in which Maurice does *not* take oatmeal. (We know there *is* such a world, since S' does not include Maurice's taking the oatmeal.) S' obtains in W' just as it does in Kronos. Indeed, everything in W' is just as it is in Kronos up to time t. But whereas in Kronos Maurice takes oatmeal at time t, in W' he does not. Now W' is a perfectly possible world; but it is not within God's power to create it or bring about its actuality. For to do so He must actualize S'. But (28) is in fact true. So if God actualizes S' (as He must to create W') and leaves Maurice free with respect to the action in question, then he will take the oatmeal; and then, of course, W' will not be actual. If, on the other hand, God causes Maurice to *refrain* from taking the oatmeal, then he is not *free* to take it. That means, once again, that W' is not actual; for in W' Maurice is free to take the oatmeal (even if he doesn't do so). So if (28) is true, then this world W' is one that God can't actualize; it is not within His power to actualize it even though He is omnipotent and it is a possible world.

Of course, if it is (29) that is true, we get a similar result; then too there are possible worlds that God can't actualize. These would be worlds which share S' with Kronos and in which Maurice *does* take oatmeal. But either (28) or (29) *is* true; so either way there is a possible world that God can't create. If we consider a world in which S' obtains and in which Maurice freely chooses oatmeal at time t, we see that whether or not it is within God's power to actualize it depends upon what Maurice would do if he were free in a certain situation. Accordingly, there are any number of possible worlds such that it is partly up to Maurice whether or not God can actualize them. It is, of course, up to God whether or not to create Maurice and also up to God whether or not to make him free with respect to the action of taking oatmeal at time t. (God could, if He chose, cause him to succumb to the dreaded *equine obsession,* a condition shared by some people and most horses, whose victims find it *psychologically impossible* to refuse oats or oat products). But if He creates Maurice and creates him free with respect to this action, then whether or not he actually performs the action is up to Maurice—not God.[2]

Now we can return to the Free Will Defense and the problem of evil. The Free Will Defender, you recall, insists on the possibility that it is not within God's power to create a world containing moral good without creating one containing moral evil. His atheological opponent—Mackie, for example—agrees with Leibniz in insisting that *if* (as the theist holds) God is omnipotent, then it *follows* that He could have created any possible world He pleased. We now see that this contention—call it "Leibniz' Lapse"—is a mistake. The atheologian is right in holding that there are many possible worlds containing moral good but no moral evil; his mistake lies in endorsing Leibniz' Lapse. So one of his premises—that God, if omnipotent, could have actualized just any world He pleased—is false.

Could God Have Created a World Containing Moral Good but No Moral Evil?

Now suppose we recapitulate the logic of the situation. The Free Will Defender claims that the following is possible:

(30)   God is omnipotent, and it was not within His power to create a world containing moral good but no moral evil.

By way of retort the atheologian insists that there are possible worlds containing moral good but no moral evil. He adds that an omnipotent being could have actualized any possible world he chose. So if God is omnipotent, it follows that He could have actualized a world containing moral good but no moral evil; hence (30), contrary to the Free Will Defender's claim, is not possible. What we have seen so far is that his second premise—Leibniz' Lapse—is false.

Of course, this does not settle the issue in the Free Will Defender's favor. Leibniz' Lapse (appropriately enough for a lapse) is false; but this doesn't show that (30) is possible. To show this latter we must demonstrate the possibility that among the worlds God could not have actualized are all the worlds containing moral good but no moral evil. How can we approach this question?

Instead of choosing oatmeal for breakfast or selling an aardvaark, suppose we think about a morally significant action such as taking a bribe. Curley Smith, the mayor, is opposed to the proposed freeway route; it would require destruction of the Old North Church along with some other antiquated and structurally unsound buildings. L. B. Smedes, the director of highways, asks him whether he'd drop his opposition for $1 million. "Of course," he replies. "Would you do it for $2?" asks Smedes. "What do you take me for?" comes the indignant reply. "That's already established," smirks Smedes; "all that remains is to nail down your price.'' Smedes then offers him a bribe of $35,000; unwilling to break with the fine old traditions of Bay State politics, Curley accepts. Smedes then spends a sleepless night wondering whether he could have bought Curley for $20,000.

Now suppose we assume that Curley was free with respect to the action of taking the bribe—free to take it and free to refuse. And suppose, furthermore, that he would have taken it. That is, let us suppose that

(31)   If Smedes had offered Curley a bribe of $20,000, he would have accepted it.

If (31) is true, then there is a state of affairs S' that (1) includes Curley's being offered a bribe of $20,000; (2) does not include either his accepting the bribe or his rejecting it; and (3) is otherwise as much as possible like the actual world. Just to make sure S' includes every relevant circumstance, let us suppose that it is a *maximal world segment*. That is, add to S' any state of affairs compatible with but not included in it, and the result will be an entire possible world. We could think of it roughly like this: S' is included in at least one world W in which Curley takes the bribe and in at least one world W' in which he rejects it. If S' is a maximal world segment, then S' is what remains of W when *Curley's taking the bribe* is deleted; it is also what remains of W' when *Curley's rejecting the bribe* is deleted. More exactly, if S' is a maximal world segment, then every possible state of affairs that includes S', but isn't included by S', is a possible world. So if (31) is true, then there is a maximal world segment S' that (1) includes Curley's being offered a bribe of $20,000; (2) does not include either his accepting the bribe or his rejecting it; (3) is otherwise as much as possible like the actual world—in particular, it includes Curley's being free with respect to the bribe; and (4) is such that if were actual then Curley would have taken the bribe. That is,

(32)   If S' were actual, Curley would have accepted the bribe

is true.

Now, of course, there is at least one possible world W' in which S' is actual and Curley does not take the bribe. But God could not have created W'; to do so, He would have been obliged to actualize S', leaving Curley free with respect to the action of taking the bribe. But under these conditions Curley, as (32) assures us, would have accepted the bribe, so that the world thus created would not have been W'.

Curley, as we see, is not above a bit of Watergating. But there may be worse to come. Of course, there are possible worlds in which he is significantly free (i.e., free with respect to a morally significant action) and never does what is wrong. But the sad truth about Curley may be this. Consider W', any of these worlds: in W' Curley is significantly free, so in W' there are some actions that are morally significant for him and with respect to which he is free. But at least one of these actions—call it A—has the following peculiar property. There is a maximal world segment S' that obtains in W' and is such that (1) S' includes Curley's being free *re* A but neither his performing A nor his refraining from A; (2) S' is otherwise as much as possible like W'; and (3) if S' had been actual, Curley would have gone wrong with respect to A.[3] (Notice that this third condition holds, in fact, in the actual world; it does not hold in that world W'.)

This means, of course, that God could not have actualized W'. For to do so He'd have been obliged to bring it about that S' is actual; but then Curley would go wrong with respect to A. Since in W' he always does what is right, the world thus actualized would not be W'. On the other hand, if God *causes* Curley to go right with respect to A or *brings it about that* he does so, then Curley isn't free with respect to A; and so once more it isn't W' that is actual. Accordingly God cannot create W'. But W' was just any of the worlds in which Curley is significantly free but always does only what is right. It therefore follows that it was not within God's power to create a world in which Curley produces moral good but no moral evil. Every world God can actualize is such that if Curley is significantly free in it, he takes at least one wrong action.

Obviously Curley is in serious trouble. I shall call the malady from which he suffers *transworld depravity*. (I leave as homework the problem of comparing transworld depravity with what Calvinists call "total depravity.") By way of explicit definition:

(33) A person *P* *suffers from transworld depravity* if and only if the following holds: for every world *W* such that *P* is significantly free in *W* and *P* does only what is right in *W*, there is an action *A* and a maximal world segment *S'* such that

(1)   *S'* includes *A*'s being morally significant for *P*

(2)   *S'* includes *P*'s being free with respect to A

(3)   *S'* is included in *W* and includes neither *P*'s performing *A* nor *P*'s refraining from performing A

and

(4)   If *S'* were actual, *P* would go wrong with respect to A'.

(In thinking about this definition, remember that (4) is to be true in fact, in the actual world—not in that world W.)

What is important about the idea of transworld depravity is that if a person suffers from it, then it wasn't within God's power to actualize any world in which that person is significantly free but does no wrong—that is, a world in which he produces moral good but no moral evil.

We have been considering a crucial contention of the Free Will Defender: the contention, namely, that

(30)   God is omnipotent, and it was not within His power to create a world containing moral good but no moral evil.

How is transworld depravity relevant to this? As follows. Obviously it is possible that there be persons who suffer from transworld depravity. More generally, it is possible that *everybody* suffers from it. And if this possibility were actual, then God, though omnipotent, could not have created any of the possible worlds containing just the persons who do in fact exist, and containing moral good but no moral evil. For to do so He'd have to create persons who were significantly free (otherwise there would be no moral good) but suffered from transworld depravity. Such persons go wrong with respect to at least one action in any world God could have actualized and in which they are free with respect to morally significant actions; so the price for creating a world in which they produce moral good is creating one in which they also produce moral evil.

232   OMNIPOTENCE AND THE PROBLEM OF EVIL

Transworld Depravity and Essence

Now we might think this settles the question in favor of the Free Will Defender. But the fact is it doesn't. For suppose all the people that exist in Kronos, the actual world, suffer from transworld depravity; it doesn't follow that God could not have created a world containing moral good without creating one containing moral evil. God could have created *other people*. Instead of creating us, i.e., the people that exist in Kronos, He could have created a world containing people, but not containing any of us—or perhaps a world containing some of us along with some others who do not exist in Kronos. And perhaps if He'd done that, He could have created a world containing moral good but no moral evil.

Perhaps. But then again, perhaps not. Suppose we look into the matter a little further. Let *W* be a world distinct from Kronos that contains a significantly free person *x* who does not exist in Kronos. Let us suppose that this person *x* does only what is right. I can see no reason to doubt that there *are* such worlds; but what reason do we have for supposing that God could have created any of them: How do we know that He can? To investigate this question, we must look into the idea of an *individual nature* or *essence*. I said earlier that the same individual—Socrates, for example—exists in many different possible worlds. In some of these he has properties quite different from those he has in Kronos, the actual world. But some of his properties are ones he has in every world in which he exists; these are his *essential* properties.[4] Among them would be some that are *trivially* essential—such properties as *being unmarried if a bachelor, being either six feet tall or else not six feet tall, being self-identical,* and the like. Another and more interesting kind of essential property can be explained as follows. Socrates has the property of being snubnosed. This property, presumably, is not essential to him; he could have had some other kind of nose. So there are possible worlds in which he is not snubnosed. Let *W'* be any such world. If *W'* had been actual, Socrates would not have been snubnosed; that is to say, Socrates has the property *being nonsnubnosed in W'*. For to say that an object *x* has a property of this sort—the property of having P in W, where P is a property and W is a possible world—is to say simple that *x would have had P if W had been actual*. Properties of this sort are *world-indexed* properties.[5] Socrates has the world-indexed property *being nonsnubnosed in W'*. He' has this property in Kronos, the actual world. On the other hand, in W' Socrates has the property *being snubnosed in Kronos*. For suppose W' had been actual: then, while Socrates would not have been snubnosed, it would have been true that if *Kronos* had been actual, Socrates would have been snubnosed.

It is evident, I take it, that if indeed Socrates *is* snubnosed in Kronos, the actual world, then it is true in every world that Socrates is *snubnosed in Kronos*.[6] So he has the property *being snubnosed in Kronos* in every world in which he exists. This property, therefore, is essential to him; there is no world in which he exists and lacks it. Indeed, it is easy to see, I think, that every world-indexed property he has will be essential to him; and every world-indexed property he *lacks* will be such that its complement is essential to him.

But how many world-indexed properties does he have? Quite a few. We should note that for any world W and property P, there is the world-indexed property *has P in W;* and for any such world-indexed property, either Socrates has it or he has its complement—the property of *not* having P in W. For any world W and property P, either Socrates would have had P, had W been actual, or it's false that Socrates would have had P under that condition. So each world-indexed property P is such that either Socrates has P essentially, or else its complement $\bar{P}$ is essential to him.

Now suppose we define Socrates' *essence* as the set of properties essential to him. His essence is a set of properties, each of which is essential to him; and this set contains all his world-indexed properties, together with some others. But furthermore, it is evident, I think, that no *other* person has all of these properties in this set. Another person might have *some* of the same world-indexed properties as Socrates: he might be *snubnosed in Kronos* for example. But he couldn't have *all* of Socrates' world-indexed properties for then he would just *be* Socrates. So there is no person who shares Socrates' essence with him. But we can say something even stronger: there *couldn't* be any such person. For such a person would just be Socrates and hence not *another* person. The essence of Socrates, therefore, is a set of properties each of which he has essentially. Furthermore, there neither is nor could be another person distinct from Socrates that has all of the properties in this set. And finally, Socrates' essence contains a *complete* set of world-indexed properties—that is, if P is world-indexed, then either P is a member of Socrates' essence or else $\bar{P}$ is.[7]

Returning to Curley, we recall that he suffers from transworld depravity. This fact implies something interesting about Curleyhood, Curley's essence. Take those worlds W such that *is significantly free in W and never does what is wrong in W* are contained in Curley's essence. Each of these worlds has an important property if Curley suffers from transworld depravity; each is such that God could not have created or actualized it. We can see this as follows. Suppose W' is some world such that Curley's essence contains the property *is significantly free in W' but never does what is wrong in W'*. That is, W' is a world in which Curley is significantly free but always does what is right. But, of course, Curley suffers from transworld depravity. This means that there is an action A and a maximal world segment S' such that

(1) S' includes A's being morally significant for Curley

(2) S' includes Curley's being free with respect to A

(3) S' is included in W' but includes neither Curley's performing A nor his refraining from A

and

(4) If S' had been actual, Curley would have gone wrong with respect to A.

But then (by the argument of p. 229) God could not have created or instantiated W'. For to do so he would have had to bring it about that S' obtain; and then Curley would have gone wrong with respect to A. Since in W' he always does what is right, W' would not have been actual. So if Curley suffers from transworld depravity, then Curley's essence has this property: God could not have created any world W such that Curleyhood contains the properties *is significantly free in W* and *always does what is right in W*.

We can use this connection between Curley's transworld depravity and his essence as the basis for a definition of transworld depravity as applied to essences rather than persons. We should note first that if E is a person's essence, then that person is the *instantiation* of E; he is the thing that has (or exemplifies) every property in E. To instantiate an essence, God creates a person who has that essence; and in creating a person He instantiates an essence. Now we can say that

> (34) An essence E *suffers from transworld depravity* if and only if for every world W such that E contains the properties *is significantly free in W* and *always does what is right in W,* there is an action A and a maximal world segment S' such that
>
> (1) S' includes E's being instantiated and E's *instantiation's being free with respect to A* and *A's being morally significant for E's instantiation,*
> (2) S' is included in W but includes neither E's *instantiation's performing A* nor E's *instantiation's refraining from A*

and

> (3) if S' were actual, then the instantiation of E would have gone wrong with respect to A.

By now it is evident, I take it, that if an essence E suffers from transworld depravity, then it was not within God's power to actualize a possible world W such that E contains the properties *is significantly free in W* and *always does what is right in W*. Hence it was not within God's power to create a world in which E is instantiated and in which its instantiation is significantly free but always does what is right.

And the interesting fact here is this: it is possible that every creaturely essence—every essence including the property of being created by God—suffers from transworld depravity. But now suppose this is true. Now God can create a world containing moral good only by creating significantly free persons. And, since every person is the instantiation of an essence, He can create significantly free persons only by instantiating some essences. But if every essence suffers from transworld depravity, then no matter which essences God instantiates, the resulting persons, if free with respect to morally significant actions, would always perform at least some wrong actions. If every essence suffers from transworld depravity, then it was beyond the power of God Himself to create a world containing moral good but no moral evil. He might have been able to create worlds in which moral evil is very considerably outweighed by moral good; but it was not within His power to create worlds containing moral good but no moral evil—and this despite the fact that He is omnipotent. Under these conditions God could have created a world containing no moral evil only by creating one without significantly free persons. But it is possible that every essence suffers from transworld depravity; so it's possible that God could not have created a world containing moral good but no moral evil.

The Free Will Defense Vindicated

Put formally, you remember, the Free Will Defender's project was to show that

(1)   God is omniscient, omnipotent, and wholly good

is consistent with

(3)   There is evil.

What we have just seen is that

(35)   It was not within God's power to create a world containing moral good but no moral evil

is possible and consistent with God's omnipotence and omniscience. But then it is clearly consistent with (1). So we can use it to show that (1) is consistent with (3). For consider

(1)   God is omnipotent, omniscient, and wholly good
(35)   It was not within God's power to create a world containing moral good without creating one containing moral evil

and

(36)   God created a world containing moral good.

These propositions are evidently consistent—i.e., their conjunction is a possible proposition. But taken together they entail

(3)   There is evil.

For (36) says that God created a world containing moral good; this together with (35) entails that He created one containing moral evil.

But if it contains moral evil, then it contains evil. So (1), (35), and (36) are jointly consistent and entail (3); hence (1) is consistent with (3); hence set A is consistent. Remember: to serve in this argument (35) and (36) need not be known to be true, or likely on our evidence, or anything of the sort; they need only be consistent with (1). Since they are, there is no contradiction in set A; so the Free Will Defense appears to be successful.

Is God's Existence Compatible with the Amount of Moral Evil the World Contains?

The world, after all, contains a *great deal* of moral evil; and what we've seen so far is only that God's existence is compatible with *some* moral evil. Perhaps the atheologian can regroup; perhaps he can argue that at any rate God's existence is not consistent with the vast *amount* and *variety* of moral evil the universe actually contains. Of course, there doesn't seem to be any way to measure moral evil—that is, we don't have units like volts or pounds or kilowatts so that we could say "this situation contains exactly 35 turps of moral evil." Still, we can compare situations in terms of evil, and we can often see that one state of affairs contains more moral evil than another. Now perhaps the atheologian could maintain that at any rate God could have created a world containing *less* moral evil than the actual world contains.

But is this really obvious? It is obvious, but, considered by itself it is also irrelevant. God could have created a world with *no* moral evil just by creating no significantly free creatures. A more relevant question is this: was it within God's power to create a world that contained a better mixture of moral good and evil than Kronos—one, let's say, that contained as much moral good but less moral evil? And here the answer is not obvious at all. Possibly this was *not* within God's power, which is all the Free Will Defender needs. We can see this as follows. Of course, there are many possible worlds containing as much moral good as Kronos, but less moral evil. Let *W'* be any such world. If *W'* had been actual, there would have been as much moral good (past, present, and future) as in fact there was, is, and will be; and there would have been less moral evil in all. Now in *W'* a certain set S of

essences is instantiated (that is, there is a set S of essences such that if
W' had been actual, then each member of S would have been instantiated). So to create W' God would have had to create persons who were
the instantiations of these essences. The following, however, is possible. There is an action A, a maximal world segment S' and a member
E of S such that

(a) E contains the properties: *is significantly free with respect to A in*
W' and *goes right with respect to A* in W'

(b) S' is included in W' and includes *E's being instantiated*, but includes neither *E's instantiation's performing A* nor *E's instantiation's
refraining from A*

and

(c)   if S' had been actual, E's instantiation would have gone wrong
with respect to A.

If this possibility is actual, then God could not have actualized W'. For
to do so He'd have had to instantiate E, cause E's instantiation to be
free with respect to A, and bring it about that S' was actual. But then
the instantiation of E would have gone wrong with respect to A, so
that the world thus created would not have been W'; for in W' E's instantiation goes *right* with respect to A.

More generally, it's possible that every world containing as much
moral good as the actual world, but less moral evil, resembles W' in
that God could not have created it. For it is possible that

(37)   For every world W containing as much moral good as Kronos,
but less moral evil, there is at least one essence E, an action A, and a
maximal world segment S' such that

(1) E contains the properties: *is free with respect to A in W* and *goes
right with respect to A* in W

(2) S' is included in W and includes E's being instantiated but includes
neither *E's instantiation's performing A* nor *E's instantiation's refraining from A*

and

(3)   If S' were actual, E's instantiation would have gone wrong with
respect to A.

(37) is possible; if it is *true,* then it wasn't within the power of God to create a world containing as much moral good as this one but less moral evil. So it's possible that this was not within God's power; but if so, then (1) is compatible with the proposition that there is as much moral evil as Kronos does in fact contain. And, of course, what the Free Will Defender claims is not that (37) is *true;* he claims only that it is compatible with the existence of a wholly good, omnipotent God.

The Free Will Defense, then successfully shows that set *A* is consistent. It can also be used to show that

    (1)   God is omnipotent, omniscient, and morally perfect

is consistent with

    (38)   There is as much moral evil as Kronos contains.

For clearly enough (1), (37), and

    (39)   God has created a world containing as much moral good as Kronos contains

are jointly consistent. But (37) tells us that God could not have created a world containing more moral good but less moral evil than Kronos; so these three propositions entail (38). It follows that (1) and (38) are consistent.

Notes

1. For a fuller statement of this argument see Plantinga, *The Nature of Necessity,* chap. 9, secs. 4–6.
2. For a more complete and more exact statement of this argument see Plantinga, *The Nature of Necessity,* chap. 9, secs. 4–6.
3. A person goes wrong with respect to an action if he either wrongfully performs it or wrongfully fails to perform it.
4. For a discussion of essential properties see Plantinga, *The Nature of Necessity,* chaps. 2–4.
5. For more about world-indexed properties see Plantinga, *The Nature of Necessity,* chap. 4, sec. 11.
6. For argument see Alvin Plantinga, ''World and Essence,'' *Philosophical Review* 79 (October 1970): 487 and *The Nature of Necessity,* chap. 4, sec. 11.
7. For more discussion of essences see Plantinga, *The Nature of Necessity,* chap. 5.

33

Modalities in the
Free Will Defence

DOUGLAS WALTON

This paper is a reply to Stephen Davis' "A Defence of the Free Will Defence." [1] With the aid of some elementary modal logic, some of the inner workings of Davis' argument are explored, and the nature of the opposition of the Davis argument to the Mackie thesis [2] is made plainer. It is concluded herein that while Davis argument is interesting and illuminating, it is not conclusive, as Davis appears to think, and that the burden of proof remains on the opponent of the Mackie thesis, i.e., the Free Will Defence defender.

I. The Free Will Defence

The Free Will Defence is a means of reconciling moral or "man-made" evil (as opposed to natural evil such as floods and hurricanes) with the existence of a benevolent and omnipotent deity. Briefly, it runs as follows. It is not God's fault that there is moral evil, but man's because man has Free Will. In creating man, God eschewed the course of creating moral automata, programmed to always do the good, and instead created beings capable of free choice. Unfortunately, men chose to disobey God and occasionally do evil, but the responsibility is theirs, not God's, on the ground that they are free. Now the Mackie-style opponent of the Free Will Defence maintains that it is logically

From *Religious Studies*, vol. 10, no. 3, 1974, pp. 325–31. Reprinted with the permission of *Religious Studies*.

possible that God could have created men who are free but who, as a matter of fact, always do the good. Such a world would be a better one than the existing one, the Mackie argument runs, and hence the existing world manifestly contradicts the hypothesis of an omnipotent, benevolent deity. The Free Will Defence defender, on the contrary, maintains that it would be logically inconsistent that God could create a world in which free men always do the good. If they are programmed to always do the good, they cannot be free, in the required sense. And this latter claim of inconsistency is just the claim that Davis purports to establish.

Davis' strategy, in outline, is as follows. First, Davis purports to prove (*Vide* sec. 2, below) the inconsistency of the pair,

(10) X is ϕ
(13) X can be either ϕ or not-ϕ

Then, by substitution, we have the inconsistency of the pair,

(16) Adam is ϕ.
(17) Adam can be either ϕ or not-ϕ.

And hence we have, in turn, the inconsistency of the pair,

(18) God created Adam such that Adam is ϕ.
(19) God created Adam such that Adam can be either ϕ or not-ϕ.

Finally, reading "one who always chooses the good" for ϕ, we have the inconsistency of the pair,

(20) God created Adam such that Adam is one who always chooses the good.
(21) God created Adam such that Adam can be either one who always chooses the good or one who does not always choose the good.

Since, according to Davis, (21) asserts the element of indeterminacy claimed by the free will theodicist, we may conclude that "God creates Adam such that Adam is free to choose either the good or the evil and such that Adam always chooses the good" is self-contradictory. My strategy in analysing this argument will be to accept the inconsistency of (20) and (21) on the hypothesis that (10) and (13) are inconsistent, and to focus on the arguments for the inconsistency of the latter pair.

II. The Inconsistency Arguments

Davis asks us to consider four propositions

(10) X is ϕ
(11) X is either ϕ or not-ϕ
(12) X can be not-ϕ
(13) X can be either ϕ or not-ϕ

and propounds three arguments concerning the entailment relations that obtain between various pairs of these propositions. Primarily, as we mentioned, Davis wishes to argue that (10) and (13) are inconsistent. This should immediately alert us that there is something non-standard about (13), since if we render (13) according to its surface structure, it is a logical consequence of (10) in the standard Lewis modal systems. (10) entails (11) truth-functionally and (11) entails (13) in virtue of the theorem "p ⊃ Mp." Indeed, the surface structure proposition of (13)

(13a)   M(X is ϕ V ~ (X is ϕ))

is even more obviously a theorem in the standard Lewis systems.[3] The part inside the parentheses is a truth-functional theorem (excluded middle), and in virtue of the Gödel Rule, " $|-a \rightarrow |- La$," prefacing this part by "L," and hence "M" yields a theorem. Thus (13a) is a logical truth and follows from any proposition whatever. For the same reason, (13a) is consistent with any consistent proposition, such as (10). Thus immediately we are alerted that the surface structure representation of (13), namely (13a), is evidently not what Davis has in mind.

III. Argument I

This expectation is confirmed by Davis' first argument for the inconsistency of (10) and (13). According to Davis, (13) is not a simple disjunction like (11), but contains "an element of indetermination" (p. 340).

> That is while (10) states that (it has been determined that) X is ϕ, (13) suggests, at least on some interpretations, that it has not yet been determined whether X will be ϕ or not-ϕ. On (13) the question of whether X is ϕ is still open, but on (10) it is closed.

Davis' assertion that neither alternative in (13) is "determined" suggests that he means (13) to contain the possibility of ϕ as well as the possibility of not-ϕ. But (13a), our surface structure representation of (13), does not imply "M (X is ϕ)"; nor does it imply "M (X is not-ϕ)." This, in turn, suggests that Davis has a different representation of the structure of (13) in mind, one that is not entailed by (13a). And indeed, such a representation of the deep structure of (13) is available, namely,

> (13b) M(X is ϕ)&M(X is not-ϕ)

This proposition implies, but is not implied by (13a), and appears to match Davis' intuitions about the deep structure of (13). Before examining the latter question, however, it may be well to dwell on a seeming incongruity of (13b)—oddly, (13) is an alternation whereas its purported representation, (13b), is a conjunction. How can "either p or q" translate out into "p & q"? This phenomenon does occasionally happen, despite our virtually automatic linkage of "and" with "&" and "or" with "V," and is interestingly indicated by the so-called "Switches Paradox."

To recognize the Switches Paradox, simply observe the disparity between the intuitive invalidity of the following argument

> (S₁) If you throw both switch S and switch T, the motor will start. Therefore, either if you throw switch S the motor will start, or if you throw switch T the motor will start.

and its surface structure representation

> (S₂) $\dfrac{(P \ \& \ Q) \supset R}{(P \supset R) \ V \ (Q \supset R)}$

What this "paradox" shows is that the deep structure of the conclusion is conjunctive, and not alternational as suggested by (S_2). According to the most natural interpretation, the deep structure of the conclusion of (S_1) is best represented as

(C) $(P \supset R)\&(Q \supset R)$

To be convinced, consider the case where S is thrown and the motor does not start. This supposition makes (C) false, but not the conclusion of (S_2). Reflection on the conclusion of (S_1), will show that it is falsified by the supposition under consideration, like (C). Whereas the conclusion of (S_2) is not falsified by the supposition.

What this "paradox" shows is that "or" sometimes expresses conjunction, contrary to our automatic inclination to translate it as "V." Thus despite its surface alternativeness, the deep structure of (13) is the conjunction of possibilia, (13b). Now (13b) is neither a theorem nor the negation of a theorem in the standard Lewis systems, despite its superficial resemblance to the theorem negation, "M (X is ϕ & X is not-ϕ)." The latter is inconsistent, and, as such, implies any proposition you like, including (13b), but (13b) does not entail it. (13b) merely says of a proposition that both it and its negation are possible. This latter assertion, we may standardly presume, is true of the class of contingent propositions, and just that class. This bespeaks well of the felicitousness of (13b) over (13a) as a rendering of the deep structure of (13) since, intuitively, the proposition expressed by (13) is a contingent one, that is, neither a logical truth nor an inconsistency, as reflection on (13) will show.

IV. Argument II

Davis' second argument for the inconsistency of (10) and (13) appears to confirm that (13b), or something like it, matches his inutitions about the deep structure of (13). Davis writes, "(13) maintains the real possibility that either disjunct can be realised," and "(13) is not consistent with the state of affairs where only one of the two possibilities can in fact be realised." So (13b) seems to be the general form of representation that Davis is trying to articulate. On the other hand, (13b) is consistent with (10),[4] and therefore it cannot represent Davis' interpretation of the deep structure of (13). Remember that Davis is arguing for the thesis that (10) and (13) are inconsistent. We have every indication, therefore, that Davis has in mind, in the interpretation of (13), a species of non-standard modality.

This suspicion is quickly confirmed. The salient point of Davis' second argument is that (13) is inconsistent with (10) because (13) asserts that X can be not-ϕ, while X cannot be not-ϕ if X is ϕ. In other words, Davis accepts the axiom.

(A)   X is $\phi \supset \sim M(X$ is not-$\phi)$

According to Davis, (10) and (13) are inconsistent because via (A), (10) implies the falsity of the right conjunct of (13b). This makes it plain that Davis is dealing in non-standard modalities, because (A) is not a theorem of the standard Lewis systems. Indeed, were (A) a theorem, the modal system would violate a basic adequacy condition of the standard alethic modal systems, namely that we must not have "Lp≡p" as a theorem. To have this latter as a theorem would be a violation of the *ab esse ad posse* principle implicit in the standard systems: in any intuitively plausible modal systems, Lp must not be equivalent to any truth-function of p.[5] To see that (A) is tantamount to such a violation we need only observe that "p ⊃ ~M~p" is equivalent to "p ⊃Lp," which, taken together with the standard theorem "Lp ⊃p," generates the offending consequence "p≡Lp." In cleaving to the consistency of (10) and (13), Davis is opting for a non-standard system of modalities. Accordingly, it would be clearer to mark this by recasting the deep structure of (13) on the Davis interpretation as

(13c) $M^*(X$ is $\phi)$&$M^*(X$ is not-$\phi)$

where M^* is recognised as a deviant type of possibility wherein

(Ac)   X is $\phi \supset \sim M^* \sim (X$ is $\phi)$

holds. Now (Ac), though regarded as deviant for the reasons mentioned above, is a thesis not without a history—it has often been associated with fatalism.[6]

V. Argument III

We have now given an explicit derivation of Davis' claim that (10) is
inconsistent with (13). From (10) and (Ac), we can derive "~M* (X
is not-ϕ)." This latter expression is the negation of the right conjunct
of (13c). Hence (10) is inconsistent with (13c), and if (13c) is a representation of the deep structure of (13), then (10) is inconsistent with
(13). This clear and consistent view of the matter is clouded by Davis'
third argument that (Ac) is an extension of the Law of Non-Contradiction.

> [the claim] that X cannot be not- ϕ if X is ϕ, amounts to a claim that
> (10) and (12) are inconsistent. This claim appears to me to be a simple
> extension of the Law of Non-Contradiction, an extension which would
> read something like "A thing cannot be other than what it is."

The various principles that Davis seems to have in mind here, such as
"~M(p&~p)," a version of Excluded Middle, "(X)(X=X)," a Law
of Identity, are quite logically distinct from (Ac), and are no conceivable use (by themselves) in establishing the inconsistency of (10) and
(13). The expression "X cannot be not-ϕ if X is ϕ" is, however, extremely ambiguous—it may suggest some version of Excluded Middle
or some Law of Identity, it may suggest (Ac), or it may suggest something similar to (Ac) with the modal operator shifted to the left of the
parentheses.

(Ad)~M* (X is $\phi \supset$ X is notϕ)

Truth-functionally, (Ad) reduces to "~M* (X is not- ϕ)" or, more
simply, "L* (X is ϕ)." Now I presume that this is not meant to be the
mediating principle whereby (10) is shown to be inconsistent with (13)
since "L* (X is ϕ)" is itself inconsistent with (13c) without even having to assume (10) at all. Thus I take it that (Ad) is an unfortunate
confusion of (Ac) with other standard principles such as Excluded
Middle that really have no place in the discussion at all. On the other
hand, perhaps (Ad) is an oblique way of rephrasing (Ac) since in a
system with (Ac), containing the theorem "L*p$\equiv$p," it might not be
too surprising to find L*p as a theorem. However this may be, I will
take it that (Ac) is the important mediating factor in establishing the

MODALITIES IN THE FREE WILL DEFENCE247

inconsistency of (10) and (13) and that the introduction of the Law of Non-Contradiction is a *feu follet* introduced by the unfortunate ambiguity in the scope of the modal operator made explicit in the contrast between (Ac) and (Ad).

VI. Burden of Proof

Davis' proof for the inconsistency of (10) and (13), consists essentially in the acceptance of a deviant alethic modal logic containing the theorem "L*p≡p." In such a logic, truth and necessity are co-extensive and interdefinable—all true sentences are necessarily true, no truths are contingent. Mackie's thesis, we will remember, is in direct opposition to such a scheme. According to Mackie, it is logically possible for Adam to always choose the good without doing so of necessity. For Davis, on the contrary, if Adam does X then it is necessarily true that Adam does X. On our analysis, the opposition clearly pivots on the acceptance of (Ac). Davis accepts (Ac) whereas Mackie's inclinations would appear to be opposed to the acceptance of (Ac). Essentially, Mackie accepts standard alethic modal logic and Davis opts for the deviant M* type of system.

Davis' defence of the Free Will Defence thus rests on the acceptance of (Ac) and therefore is considerably less compelling than he appears to think. The Mackie claim that it is logically consistent that God create men who always [*de facto*] choose the good appears to stand relatively undamaged. Of course Davis is accurate in his conclusion that it is logically impossible that God create men such that it can be guaranteed that they will always freely choose the good, in so far as there is logical tension between free action and action that is "guaranteed." But the Mackie thesis does not require that it be consistent with free action that men do the good of necessity, or that they are guaranteed to do the good, or that they do the good in all possible worlds, or that they must always do the good, or whatever modal idiom is preferred. The Mackie thesis only requires that it be consistent with free action that, as a matter of fact, not necessity, men always do the good. Davis rebuts the Mackie thesis by identifying what men do with what they must do.

On balance, it seems to me that the burden of proof rests on the Free Will Defence defender to argue against the more solidly entrenched opposition posed by the *prima facie* plausible Mackie thesis. It is best left to the reader to decide whether Davis' argument for the inconsistency of (10) and (13) is the best defence of the Free Will Defence. In its defence it can be said that it is an interesting, subtle, and consistent (albeit non-standard) approach, once its Leibnizian modal underpinnings are exposed. Davis' clear-headed, deliberate, rational explorations of the modalities of divine action throw considerable new light on this classical problem.

Notes

1. Stephen T. Davis, "A Defense of the Free Will Defence," *Religious Studies,* Vol. 8, No. 4, December 1972, 335–44. The Editors regret that considerations of space precluded the inclusion of Professor Davis's article in this collection.
2. J. L. Mackie, "Evil and Omnipotence." See Selection 1.
3. For an account of the "standard Lewis system," T, S4 and S5, see G. E. Hughes and M. J. Cresswell, *An Introduction to Modal Logic* (London, Methuen, 1968), chapters 2 and 3. System T (due to Robert Feys) is the basic system of which S4 and S5 are extensions. T was proved equivalent to the System M of von Wright by Sobocinski in 1953. The essentials of System T are quite simple (for our purposes).

   System T

   Ax. 1: $Lp \supset p$ [Axiom of Necessity]

   Ax. 2: $L(p \supset q) \supset (Lp \supset Lq)$

   Rule 1: If α is a theorem, $L\,\alpha$ is a theorem [Gödel Rule of Necessitation]

   Definition: $Mp = df \sim L \sim p$

   Also note that System T is an extension of PC: all truth-functional rules and theorems are assumed to hold.
4. '$\sim(p \dashv 3 \sim(Mp \& M \sim p))$' is not a theorem in the standard Lewis systems.
5. *Vide* Hughes and Cresswell (*op. cit.*), p. 28.
6. For some systems of this type see Robert Feys, *Modal Logics* (edited with some complements by Joseph Dopp, E. Nauwelaerts, Louvain, Belgium, 1965), p. 133 f.

34

The Mystery of Omnipotence Is Too Deep for Human Reason

CHARLES HARTSHORNE

I should like to sum up the religious meaning of neoclassical theism by considering the oldest known discussion of the "problem of evil," the Book of Job. "Does Job serve God for naught?" was the initial question in that sublime book. It is too often overlooked that the implied answer was affirmative. The voice from the whirlwind promises Job nothing and threatens him with nothing. It merely calls his attention, somewhat humorously, to the grandeur and mystery of a cosmos in which man is but an item. Job seems finally to understand, not that his demands have an answer too deep for his comprehension, but that individual demands are not in order. We serve God, or we settle for a less rational aim, and if we do the former it should be because we want to have the right or reason-satisfying aim now, not because some less rational aim, like eventual personal advantage, will thereby be accomplished. There is no appropriate reward for serving God; simply there is nothing else (able to withstand criticism) for a conscious being to live for.

The voice from the whirlwind does not explicitly say that Job or his comforters were in error concerning divine justice. The voice says nothing about justice. It deals rather with the mystery of cosmic power. Job's mistake was in supposing that he knew what is meant by

From Charles Hartshorne, *A Natural Theology for Our Time,* La Salle, Ill., Open Court, 1967, pp. 116–20. Reprinted with the permission of The Open Court Publishing Company. Copyright © 1967 by The Open Court Publishing Company.

unsurpassable or divine power. No man has ever created a star, an element of nature, or an animal; nor has he ever governed a cosmos. How then, in the mouth of such a being, could words like "create" or "govern," applied to the cosmic situation, have any clear sense?

The shallow view of the divine rebuke to Job is that he is brought to admit that the relation between God's power and his goodness, or perhaps the goodness itself, is beyond human grasp. This interpretation supposes that at least we know what divine power is, and only its use by divine justice is too deep for us. However, is not this idea of divine power already, just in itself, quite as mysterious as that of divine justice? The mystery is in both terms and not simply in one, or simply in the relation between the one and the other. If we really knew what it would be like to create or rule cosmically, we should also know what it would be like to do so wisely or righteously, and vice versa. But can we know either?

A careless objection to the message from the whirlwind is that Job is overawed by a mere show of force, that he grovels before brute power. But the sublime thing about this ancient document is that there is not a hint or suggestion that the power is to be taken as a threat. Job is not warned to take care lest the power be used against him; and he is not invited to consider how it might be used to reward him should he submit and confess his mistake. The almost unbelievable nobility of this old writer shows in the dignity with which Job's disinterestedness is respected. He is not scared or bribed into humility, he is simply shown his actual cognitive situation. And what is that situation? That he has been brought up on a theory of all-mightiness whose meaning no one understands. What is the use of trying to derive consequences from a concept that one does not possess? There was no clearly understood notion of God's power to give rise to a problem of evil, of why God "does" this or "does" that. What does it mean to say, "God does something"? To accept such language as clear, but find a puzzle in the divine motive, *why* God does things, is, as Berdyaev said, once for all, to treat as a mystery a problem which one has "already overrationalized." The puzzle begins one step earlier. Human "power" we know something about, but what sort of analogy enables us to speak of "divine power"? Until we have this analogy straight, there is no clearly defined problem of evil.

Traditional theism and traditional atheism are alike in this, that they overestimated the claims of "omnipotence" to constitute a well-defined premise from which conclusions are deducible. God's power or influence must of course be worshipful, unsurpassably great; but to identify this unsurpassability of power with its sheer monopoly, a control by which all concrete details of existence are determined, leaving the creatures with nothing to determine for themselves, no genuine options of their own, is to burden the divine worshipfulness with a logical paradox of our own making. The monopoly theory is at best no more than a theory. To worship God need not be to accept the theory. But really, it is less than a theory, for no one knows what it means.

Bibliography

(Not including material in this volume)

Omnipotence

Bonifacio, A. F. "On Capacity Limiting Statements." *Mind* LXXIV (1965), 87–88.

Cargile, J. "On Omnipotence." *Noûs* I (1967), 201–5.

Cowan, J. L. "The Paradox of Omnipotence Revisited." *Canadian Journal of Philosophy* III (1974), 435–45.

D'Arcy, C. F. "The Theory of a Limited Deity." *Proceedings of the Aristotelian Society* XVIII (1917–18), 158–84.

Dummett, Michael. "Bringing About the Past." *Philosophical Review* 73 1964), 338–59.

Duns Scotus. "Can it be demonstrated by natural and necessary reason that God is omnipotent?" *God and Creatures: The Quodlibetal Questions.* F. Alluntis and A. B. Wolter, ed. & trans. Princeton, N.J.: Princeton University Press, 1975 (Qu. VII).

Flew, Antony. "Compatibilism, Free Will and God." *Philosophy* 48 (1973), 231–44.

Geach, P. T. "Omnipotence." *Philosophy* 48 (1973), 7–20.

Geach, P. T. "An Irrelevance of Omnipotence." *Philosophy* 48 (1973), 327–33.

Gellman, Jerome. "Omnipotence and Impeccability." *The New Scholasticism* LI (1977), 21–37.

Gendin, Sidney. "Omnidoing." *Sophia* 6 (1967), 17–22.

Grave, S. A. "On Evil and Omnipotence." *Mind* LXV (1956), 259–62.

Keene, G. B. "A Simpler Solution to the Paradox of Omnipotence." *Mind* LXIX (1960), 74–75.

Keene, G. B. "Capacity Limiting Statements." *Mind* LXX (1961), 251–52.

Mackie, J. L. "Theism and Utopia." *Philosophy* 37 (1962), 153–58.

Mayo, Bernard. "Mr. Keene on Omnipotence." *Mind* LXX (1961), 249–50.

Olding, A. "Finite and Infinite Gods." *Sophia* 6 (1967), 3–7.

Pike, Nelson. "Omnipotence and God's Ability to Sin." *American Philosophical Quarterly* 6 (1969), 208–16.

Plantinga, Alvin. "The Free Will Defence." *Philosophy in America.* Max Black, ed. Ithaca, N.Y.: Cornell University Press, 1965.

Ramsey, I. T. "The Paradox of Omnipotence." *Mind* LXV (1956), 263–66.

Schiller, F. C. S. "Omnipotence." *Proceedings of the Aristotelian Society* XVIII (1917–18), 247–70.

Swinburne, Richard. "Omnipotence." *American Philosophical Quarterly* 10 (1973), 231–37.

Thorburn, W. M. "Omnipotence and Personality." *Mind* XXIX (1920), 159–85.

Wainwright, William J. "Freedom and Omnipotence." *Noûs* II (1968), 293–301.

Walton, Douglas. "Time and Modality in the *Can* of Opportunity." *Action Theory.* Myles Brand and Douglas Walton, eds. Dordrecht: Reidel, 1976, pp. 271–87.

Omniscience

Adams, M. McC. "Is the Existence of God a 'Hard' Fact?" *Philosophical Review* 76 (1967), 492–503.

Boethius. *The Consolation of Philosophy,* Pt. V.

Casteñeda, H-N. "Omniscience and Indexical Reference." *Journal of Philosophy* LXIV (1967), 203–10.

Edwards, Jonathan. *The Freedom of the Will.* Indianapolis, Ind., and New York: Bobbs-Merrill, 1969 (esp. Part II).

Kretzman, Norman. "Omniscience and Immutability." *Journal of Philosophy* LXIII (1966), 409–21.

Ockham, William of. *Predestination: God's Foreknowledge and Future Contingents.* N. Kretzmann & M. McC. Adams, eds. New York: Appleton-Century-Crofts, 1969.

Pike, Nelson. *God and Timelessness.* New York: Schocken Books, 1970 (esp. Chap. 4).

Pike, Nelson. "Of God and Freedom: A Rejoinder." *Philosophical Review* 75 (1966), 369–79.

Prior, A. N. "The Formalities of Omniscience." *Philosophy* 47 (1962), 114–29.

Saunders, J. T. "Of God and Freedom." *Philosophical Review* 75 (1966), 219–25.

Thomas Aquinas, St. *Summa Theologica,* Ia, qus. 14–15, 25. *Summa Contra Gentes,* qus. 65–68.

Urban, L. "Was Luther a Thoroughgoing Determinist?" *The Journal of Theological Studies* XXII (1971), 113–39.

Valla, Lorenzo. "Dialogue on Free Will." *The Renaissance Philosophy of Man.* E. Cassirer, P. D. Kristeller, & J. H. Randall, Jr., eds. Chicago, Ill.: University of Chicago Press, 1948.

The Problem of Evil

Aiken, H. D. "God and Evil: A Study of Some Relations between Faith and Morals." *Ethics* XLVIII (1958), 77–97.

Ducasse, C. J. *The Philosophic Scrutiny of Religion.* New York: The Ronald Press, 1953 (esp. Chap. 16).

Farrer, Austin. *Love Almighty and Ills Unlimited.* Garden City, N.Y.: Doubleday, 1961.

Ferre, Nels. *Evil and the Christian Faith.* New York: Harper and Row, 1947.

Leibniz, G. W. *Theodicy.* New Haven, Ct.: Yale University Press, 1952.

McCloskey, H. J. "The Problem of Evil." *The Journal of Bible and Religion* XXX (1962), 187–97.

McTaggart, John. *Some Dogmas of Religion.* London: Edward Arnold, Ltd., 1906.

Mill, John Stuart. *Nature and Utility of Religion.* G. Nakhnikian, ed. New York: The Liberal Arts Press, 1958.

Pike, Nelson. *God and Evil.* Englewood Cliffs, N.J.: Prentice-Hall, 1964.

Wisdom, John. "God and Evil." *Mind* XLIV (1935), 1–20.

Index